Life Cycle
and Other New Poems
2006 – 2016

Collected Poems volumes 31–34

First published by O-Books, 2016
O-Books is an imprint of John Hunt Publishing Ltd., Laurel House, Station Approach,
Alresford, Hants, SO24 9JH, UK
office1@jhpbooks.net
www.johnhuntpublishing.com

For distributor details and how to order please visit the 'Ordering' section on our website.

Text copyright: Nicholas Hagger 2016

ISBN: 978 1 84694 580 9
978 1 78099 727 8 (ebook)
Library of Congress Control Number: 2016946103

A CIP catalogue record for this book is available from the British Library.

Design: Stuart Davies

Printed in the USA by Edwards Brothers Malloy

We operate a distinctive and ethical publishing philosophy in all areas of
our business, from our global network of authors to production and
worldwide distribution.

Life Cycle
and Other New Poems
2006 – 2016

Collected Poems volumes 31–34

Nicholas Hagger

BOOKS

Winchester, UK
Washington, USA

Also by Nicholas Hagger

The Fire and the Stones
Selected Poems
The Universe and the Light
A White Radiance
A Mystic Way
Awakening to the Light
A Spade Fresh with Mud
The Warlords
Overlord
A Smell of Leaves and Summer
The Tragedy of Prince Tudor
The One and the Many
Wheeling Bats and a Harvest Moon
The Warm Glow of the Monastery Courtyard
The Syndicate
The Secret History of the West
The Light of Civilization
Classical Odes
Overlord, one-volume edition
Collected Poems 1958 – 2005
Collected Verse Plays
Collected Stories
The Secret Founding of America
The Last Tourist in Iran
The Rise and Fall of Civilizations
The New Philosophy of Universalism
The Libyan Revolution
Armageddon
The World Government
The Secret American Dream
A New Philosophy of Literature
A View of Epping Forest
My Double Life 1: This Dark Wood

The front cover shows the Ferris wheel in the Rotes Rathaus Christmas market near Alexanderplatz, Berlin. The cabins suggest episodes in a cyclic life and also poems in a collection.

A corner-mark ⌐ at the beginning of a line denotes that there is a break in the text – a gap – before that line. This gap has been obscured because it falls at the end of a page. (See p.177.)

CONTENTS

Indexes:

Preface

My *Collected Poems* 1958–2005 contained 30 volumes of my poems, 1,478 poems spanning 47 years. *Life Cycle and Other New Poems*, 2006–2016, contains volumes 31–34, a further 210 poems (if the 11 poems in 'India: Revisiting the British Raj' are counted separately). None of these new poems appeared in my most recent selection, *Selected Poems: Quest for the One* (2015). These new poems include four of the 318 poems in *Classical Odes* (see below), and if these are discounted they bring my total tally of poems (excluding my two poetic epics *Overlord* and *Armageddon* and my five verse plays) to just over 2,000: to be exact, 2,002 (1,478 + 318 + 206).

By and large these new poems are in event order within each volume (the order in which events happened). They are therefore not always in chronological order (the order in which poems were written), as can be seen from the index on pp.351–359 (poems within each volume). The dates on which all the poems in all four volumes were written are listed in the index on pp.361–370. Each poem in the text ends with the date (or dates) on which it was written and notes (if any).

Readers of my works will know that I derive my poetic inspiration from the 17th-century Metaphysical poets and have sought to unite the later Augustan and Romantic traditions. They will also know that in the 1960s some of my poems (such as 'The Silence') were in the Modernist tradition, and that following my visit to Ezra Pound in Rapallo on 16 July 1970 I returned to Wordsworthian and Tennysonian principles and narrative. I asked Pound if compression – which he had used in *The Cantos* – was really a good method for a long poetic epic, and unconvinced by his answer moved away from compression to the narrative blank verse of Tennyson's *Idylls of the King* in my two poetic epics, *Overlord* and *Armageddon*. In many of my poems that focus on Nature, including those in volume 32, *In Harmony with the Universe*, I am aware of following Wordsworth's principles. I have consciously sought to continue the poetic tradition of Wordsworth and Tennyson, but also the classical tradition of ancient Greece and Rome: many of my poems (for example those in *The Gates of Hell*) were rooted in the works of Catullus, Ovid and Virgil. In my poetic works I have sought to reconcile the classical and Romantic traditions.

As readers of my works will know, my poems reflect the fundamental theme of world literature, which I identified in *A New Philosophy of Literature* as having metaphysical and secular aspects that are in conflict: a quest for metaphysical Reality (the One); and condemnation of social follies and vices in relation to an implied virtue. My Universalist approach reconciles and unites these two very different aspects.

Volume 31, *Life Cycle*, presents a poem with a title I first glimpsed in 1962 when, sitting with my eyes closed in the air above Ur, Iraq, I received the words 'life cycle', which seemed to come from the beyond. It is a reflection on the pattern in our lives. Volume 32, *In Harmony with the Universe*, conveys the vision of oneness with Nature to which the quest leads. (It includes some poems omitted from *Collected Poems*.) Volume 33, *An Unsung Laureate*, focuses on public events within the British nation-state and on international political themes that include the contemporary history of the UK and the EU and their dealings with Russia and the Middle East. The first four poems appeared in *Classical Odes* (2006) and are reproduced here as they anchor the volume's political theme: development from a nationalist to a supranationalist outlook. I condemn follies and vices in 'Zeus's Emperor', which is a sequel to 'Zeus's Ass' (a poem in volume 29 in my *Collected Poems*). Volume 34, *Adventures in Paradise*, reflects the questing of my travels to remote places thought of as Paradise and ends with the greatest adventure that awaits us all: death.

I would like to say a little more about the European thread in volume 33. My poetic works have mirrored the state of European civilization: the horror of ruined Europe at the end of the Second World War (*Overlord*), the declining Europe of the 1960s ('Old Man in a Circle', 1967) and the resurgent European Union after the Lisbon Treaty of 2009 (*The Dream of Europa*). In my study of civilizations I saw the European nation-states passing into a resurgent conglomerate, the European Union, that subsumes them just as the Soviet Union subsumed the regions of the Russian Federation. I attempted to catch the dismay at the passing of an era of nation-states and hopes for the new regional union in the odes in *Classical Odes*, which are represented by the first four poems of volume 33. Over the years I have tried to catch the feelings of nation-staters opposed to a European superpower – feelings that can be found in supporters of Brexit, of a British departure from the EU – and the feelings of pro-Europeans who support the EU and in many cases a coming World State (*The Dream of Europa*). Having worked as a British intelligence agent for my nation-state and having then journeyed through to an international, supranationalist perspective, I have been well-placed to hold a mirror up to both sides and harmonise them within volume 33.

In my poems and my prose works I have often used "algebraic thinking" which reconciles opposites. I have seen the universe as a dialectic of opposites reconciled within a synthesis: $+A + -A = 0$. Volume 33 presents both sides of the dialectic – $+A$ (supporters of nation-states and Brexit) + $-A$ (supporters of regional and international conglomerates, of the EU and a World State) – and attempts to reconcile them within the whole that includes them.

Volume 33 contains two poems on Iraq. I am still amazed that at 22 I intuitively knew I should find my way to Iraq and lecture at the University of Baghdad, and that Iraq would somehow be central to the world's problems in the late 20th and early 21st centuries. Since I was in Iraq Saddam used mustard gas to kill 5,000 Kurds at Halabja, and his Sunni successor in Iraq, IS (or Daesh), has used mustard gas in Marea, north of Aleppo, on at least four occasions after April 2015 – Saddam's unaccounted-for stock which our weapons inspectors could not find? My second poetic epic *Armageddon* told how (according to the ex-1st Executive Chairman of the UN Monitoring, Verification and Inspection Commission, Hans Blix, in 2004) bin Laden acquired 20 nuclear suitcase bombs the size of laptops and targeted 10 American cities, and there is concern that these were not retrieved when bin Laden was killed and may have found their way into the hands of IS. I sometimes feel I was shown the Middle East early as I would have to write about it in later years. Sometimes there seems to be something Providential about the Way I chose, or which chose me.

Volumes 1–30 traced this Way, along which the soul is awakened, undergoes purgation and illumination, is transformed and progresses to a unitive vision in which it instinctively perceives the universe as a unity, all contradictions reconciled. Volumes 31–34 contemplate the pattern in our lives, the soul's harmony with the universe, the conflicts within Western society, and truths and echoes of Paradise that can be gleaned from the inspiring cultures of remote civilizations reached by adventurous journeys.

Volumes 31–34 are a natural progression from volumes 1–30. One day a new *Collected Poems* including all 34 completed volumes may confirm this progression and end with a 35th volume of poems in the narrative tradition of Shakespeare's *Sonnets* and Wordsworth's *Prelude*, to which I intend to devote my last years.

12–13, 26–27 January, 11, 13 February, 23 March, 1, 4, 14 April 2016

LIFE CYCLE
2014

Life Cycle

"At the start of the mid-year break [in Baghdad], on 18 January 1962, we flew to Basra. In the air above Ur, sitting with my eyes closed, I received the words 'Life Cycle' and scribbled down headings for a work on a whole life and its cycle."

Nicholas Hagger, *My Double Life 1: This Dark Wood*, p.142

I. Garden

I sit in my garden in autumn sun
Above a dozen curved, perfumed rose-beds
Whose flagstone paths present a Union flag –
That still holds in our dwindling, fractured time –
Around a fountain plashing to a bowl
And gaze past oaks and fields to the dark wood
That inspired my view of my double life
On this rim of the crater round seven hills,
And muse upon the ages of my life
And on the stages all lives pass through from   10
Their hatching and larvae to winged flight.
In the arbour near a camellia bush
I look beyond the pool at buttercups
Like those that filled my childhood fields and muse
On my twelve seven-year ages that grew me
And the twelve cycles that propel all growth:
Twelve cycles like medieval labours.

II. Reflection: Twelve Seven-Year Ages

Birth, infancy and childhood spring and strain.
Species, once born from womb or hatched from eggs,

1

Transmogrify into their final form.   20
Animals' life cycles metamorphose
Through three or four stages and life cycles:
Fish, mammals, reptiles and birds are born from
Mothers or hatch from eggs, are young, then grow
Into adults; amphibians like frogs,
Which hatch from spawn into wriggling tadpoles,
And newts metamorphose from gills to lungs,
Breathe under water and then air on land;
From eggs insects become wormy larvae,
Inactive pupae, then adults that fly;   30
Dragonflies, grasshoppers and cockroaches
Pass from eggs into nymphs and then grow wings
In three stages, not four; spiders have three;
Reptilian snakes hatch from eggs as snakelets;
Birds hatch from eggs to chicks, fish and brown bats
Are born as pups as are all great white sharks.
Transforming paths of metamorphosis
Take species from three to seventy years.
Humans waul and grow towards adulthood
Through families and schools, strict pedagogues.   40
I bang my high-chair tray, map on the wall
Of Europe showing front lines in the war,
At peace as my mother moves like a giant.
I sit among buttercups and acorns
In a gold field and bask in gold sunshine
In harmony with the blue universe,
Under the dome of the One-sheltering sky.
But at night I cower within my bed
As the sky fills with droning doodle-bugs
And my father sits and reassures me   50
And then limps off from childhood polio,
And I shudder at transitoriness
Beneath the enduring, sheltering heavens.
My forebears dug, pruned trees or vines, sowed seed
Under Aries, the ram, in the night sky,

Symbol of Amon-Ra shown with ram's horns,
At the start of the zodiacal year,
The Great Year whose labours begin in March,
And cycle of existence, spirit's birth.
Amid my memories of lopping lime-trees   60
And forking beds and making piles of weeds
To prepare for growing and sprouting seeds,
The Wheel of Life shows One revolves many.
The Wheel of Life shows One becomes many.

Youth, school-days. First in short trousers, then long,
A child of the socialist Welfare State,
I grew away from Nature under rules,
Nightly homework and organised ball games.
I caught tadpoles in the Strawberry Hill pond.
I studied newts and spotted butterflies,   70
And alone in a dark garden I gazed
In wonder at a night sky full of stars
And felt I was one with the universe.
But school work closed round me, I ceased to see.
Textbooks intruded on the mystery.
I munched meals at the high nursery table
In my family, worked and went to bed
And now my path was through my school's classrooms
And playing-fields, and not the universe.
I had three sisters who did not survive   80
Post-war infancy, and I lamented
The transitory, fleeting lives we have
Beneath the sunshine and the cloudless blue
And the faint breeze from an eternal source.
My ancestors planted, picked flowers, hunted
And I recall the zodiacal bull
As I hoed in the garden of my soul.

Adolescence brought me my destiny.
Nature still warmed me like a summer's day.

I relive long grass below the first tee   90
And clacking grasshoppers and warm sunshine
And again blend into the universe
And live above the buzzing of the bees.
I see Eden sitting beside Churchill,
Stand up for our Empire, speak on Suez
And watch bemused as he withdraws our troops.
And sitting on a seat on lower field
On a spring day at school, at seventeen,
I read *The Faber Book of English Verse*
And know I will one day be a poet.   100
A month on I bend by Horace's spring
And scoop its limpid water in cupped hands
And know that I will pen odes of my own.
I was in harmony with a great power
I glimpsed in moments, as when at college
One early March morning, a cloudless sky
Torn between two guides like heavenly twins,
I took my father's letter to the lake,
Walked through an arch and sat on a stone seat
And read that I could change to Literature,   110
Griffins and sphinxes round me on the stone,
Fabulous imaginary creatures.
I had escaped the Law and, rising, stood
Beside the lake, my shadow before me,
And gazed at the reflection of the sun,
The bending trees and sky, and blended in
With what I saw. And now the universe
Was one, including me, and I the breeze
Within the surface of the sunlit lake
And knew a oneness behind all I saw   120
That pulsed through me and rippled through the leaves.
I am transported to that sunny lake's
Weeping willows and relive that morning
That changed my course and shaped who I am now.
A shield with martlets and a spiral stair

Up to the library, I worked all night
And now my path veered from legal cases
To great works by past writers and poets,
Away from lawyers' fees to deft phrases,
Quests for the One and skewering vices.   130
But back whence the letter came, a sadness:
A brother diagnosed diabetic,
Syringing twice daily and weighing food.
The future beckoned but the transience
Of our home life weighed heavily on me
Amid my studies of my ancestors'
Hawking and dallying in courtly love.

Early manhood. A lover and husband,
I sweltered in the Baghdad desert heat.
Above Iraq, flying high over Ur,   140
Sitting eyes closed I received 'Life Cycle'
And wrote it down, not sure of what it meant.
In years to come I probed the life cycle
Of civilizations, and then of all
The flowering, creeping, prowling, flying forms
Of Nature's ordered scheme, all births and deaths,
And now, fifty-two years on, I apply
These words to the progression of all lives.
I grew to my full size and fatherhood
And learned how my father had cared for me.   150
I lived in a Japanese bungalow
With bamboo round my study window-panes
And sat among Zen seekers with closed eyes
And peeped for Light near sawing cicadas
And glimpsed a shaft amid my early drafts
And saw the oneness in raked, swirling stones.
I walked in horseshoe valleys by the sea,
Pinned snakes in forked sticks beneath swooping shrikes
And found a whelk shell on the empty beach.
In China, talking with a sick student   160

I spied the Cultural Revolution
Which was too startling to be believed,
And in Saigon I heard guns thump at night.
And back in my forest I saw a pond
Blend sky and mud into a universe
That blazed with dazzling harmony in sun.
My family gave me a new meaning
And I was on a path of fulfilment
Between our walks, my work, my study desk.
But I thought back with sorrow to the months   170
When my father was ill in heart and brain
And told me "This is the end" and then died
And I mourned the frailty of fragile
Closeness that seems as if it will endure
But fades away, leaving just memories.
I was a smart young man among roses
And my praised faith in art procured my pain.
All round me as I burrowed like a crab
I saw barefooted peasants cutting rice
And thought of the hay harvest on home farms   180
And all the mowing and shearing of sheep
Our medieval ancestors once did.

Adulthood, and a secret grieving time.
In desert heat I met my controller
And was driven down Tripoli's waterfront
And debriefed under palms and crescent moon,
And in harm's way I lost my family,
Watched them fly off to safety and new life,
Leaving me alone near the Sahara
Where between a great sweep of sand and sky   190
I saw a lone Tuareg stand in oneness
With Nature and sizzled with harmony.
Amid the bougainvillaea and palm trees
I loved the silver light of evening sea.
Like Orpheus I went to the netherworld

And, looking back, lost my Eurydice.
And back among London's surveillance squads
When streets become a nightmare of footfalls,
Fighting in the Cold War for Africa,
I opened to the Light which flooded in   200
And filled me with purgation's energy.
My fingers glowed from influxes of Fire
And I was on a path of inner growth
That would lead to projects I had in me
Like seeds hidden under a spruce cone's scales.
But I was still forlorn as I had lost
A marriage that seemed strong but, swept away,
Now seemed transitory, an illusion.
Now on Cold-War business, followed by groups,
I strutted and prowled the streets like a lion,   210
My mind on reaping and the wheat harvest
But having to flail facts for my masters.

Manhood, and new marriage and family
And new responsibility as I
Marshal, organise and administrate
As Head of Department in a large school
And move into a large Victorian house,
A former vicarage where at bedtime
I tuck up two young boys and read stories
And make a snowman in our walled garden.   220
I gaze at the red Virginia creeper
Cascading down a wall, and a pear-tree,
And feel a peace among these garden fronds.
And my path leads through my new family,
Through leafy works and Light, and more visions.
I am settled and fertile, but lament
The transitoriness of this great house
Which will be sold to a well-known actor.
We will leave its permanent solidness.
In Virgo I dream of my ancestors   230

Who threshed the grain in fields and lived quiet lives
Close to the seasons and twilit fireside.

Early middle age and financial growth
As I take over my old school and stand
By the old oak-tree amid buttercups
Where I lay in the sun among acorns.
I mow the fields in decreasing circles,
Pass harvest mice swinging in grass and chug
Past prehistoric plants beyond railings,
At one with my cradle ringed round with trees,   240
Oaklands! ever dear, a benign nanny,
Who trained me as a child and nurtures me
Now I am her curator and her guide.
I am in harmony with her hawthorns
And with the breeze that swishes through the leaves,
And also with the sea that washes in
Round the small harbour where we holiday,
Which I look down on from our seaside house
And across to the Black Head promontory.
I built a house by the blue acacia   250
Cedar, a stone's throw from the Wren door I
Installed by where the Nature table stood
When as a boy I watched newts paw the glass
Of the aquarium filled with pondweed
And now my path will lead through schools and words
For I will have leisure to write my work
And block Communist imperial designs.
But I mourn the passing of my mother
From heart attacks and strokes, and her transience.
She seemed so permanent but now she's gone.   260
In Libra I recall my ancestors
Who hunted and harvested and trod grapes
As I read *Peter Rabbit* to my boys.

Middle age and further financial growth.

I found a school and gaze at a holm-oak
Planted (it is said) by the Virgin Queen.
I wander in the walled garden and cross
The stream among old trees and in the Hall
Find the room where Churchill came to succeed
Lord Liell as MP, and his wartime room   270
Where he slept nearby wounded officers
In the now requisitioned stately home.
I drive up its lane each morning, and write
My books under Oaklands' blue acacia
Cedar, pour Light into their moulds like bowls
In harmony with all that warm summer
When the Berlin Wall fell and East joined West,
My path now running schools and writing books,
The first two of which were launched in London
By three 'elder statesmen' who were so warm   280
And seemed enduring but were transient.
Two died and one grew old, all receded.
I found the pattern of world history:
All civilizations pass through stages
Which individuals battle or bring in:
One man, like Churchill, cannot on his own
Rescue an empire whose loss he laments;
One man, like Lenin, brings a new stage in.
History has a pattern of progression.
Alongside my forest, in Scorpio,   290
I got words in my head down on paper,
I grew my businesses where ancestors
Ploughed fields and sowed their seeds for next year's crop.

Late middle age and new maturer works.
I travel round Europe and stand before
Hitler's home and recall the flying bombs
That terrorised my childhood and made me
Aware of imminent death in the nights.
I retell the story of Churchill's war

And pen poems and stories, and 'think' books,   300
And revive a historic Tudor Hall
Moated and unchanged amid time's cruel winds.
I stand under roosting peacocks and walk
Round the knot-and-herb garden with actors.
I was rooted in seven centuries
Of bricks and beams, nooks and crannies that leaked
Memories of America's founding.
My path took me past faces of the dead
Who spoke to me as if they were alive.
It seemed I would live there until I died   310
But, a third school crowding, it proved transient –
Hall, actors, history and their visitors –
And now is just a memory like gone mist.
Now I think of the archer with his bow
And of my ancestors' hunt for acorns
They scooped into held aprons for their pigs,
And sigh for Tudor dreams that are no more.

Early old age, and now at this great house
I toil long hours and collect all my works,
Bent near a screen, bundles in plastic box,   320
Sifting, sorting, preserving a life's work.
9/11, Afghanistan, Iraq –
I stood up to fundamental Islam.
I write on terror and world government,
Retired from schools which a strapping son runs,
And dandle my new grandson on my knee
Aware how transient is his infancy.
With a banking crisis looming, alert, I sell
Properties by the sea and Essex farms,
Bought as investments, to fund new building.   330
They seemed so enduring, were transient.
I have come to rest within my forest
Which nurtured my boyhood, whose tossing trees
Measure unseen wind like the inspired breeze

That wafts words to my head and down cramped hand.
I wander to my pool to feed my carp
And muse at the lily rooted in mud
That glows above the pictured trees and cloud
And as I fling handfuls of feed that float
I feel in harmony with fish and sun   340
And the long line of trees that sweeps the sky
And reflect I'm near the end of my life.
My path now leads backwards through my old works
And then forward with offerings I've found.
I recall the goat now firmly tethered
And how my ancestors killed pigs and baked
For a feast at this time of the Great Year.
I live with memories on a forest heath.

Old age and forty books all round my head
And I have not slowed down or got ill, yet.   350
But I'm slower, don't dash around as much
Though still go to the gym every Friday,
Don't drink, eat vegetables and bowls of fruit.
In my garden hang a dozen bird-feeds
Where comes the woodpecker, nuthatch, goldfinch
And flit a host of blue tits and small birds
Watched from beneath by magpies and jackdaws
Waiting to peck dropped seeds, while on the lawn
Green woodpeckers hunt worms and tap on trunks
And ten green parakeets flash between trees.   360
I sit and watch their toings and froings
As the sun climbs and sundial's shadow creeps,
My shadow still before me in cold sun,
In harmony with flittings and swoopings
Against the blue sky and the red sunset
As the blood sun sinks and black bats cavort.
And in this Paradise in which I toil
A flow of projects overbrims my mind
And plashes into my fountain's still bowl

Amid the roses in Union-flag beds.   370
All round secularism challenges
As does the Arab civilization.
My grandchildren are wide-eyed as they play,
Hunting for conkers to put in pockets,
As sun shines, rain squalls, winds gust round the oak
Before the field that shields this house from gales.
I stand and watch them absorbed in the now.
My path is onward as I make an end,
Go through my papers, label them in piles
And prise remaining works out of my skull.   380
For forty years my wife has kept my house
And now after two new hips and a knee
She is less mobile, and I have to face
The transience of the long walks that she made
In four continents, as when, clambering
Over boulders, we found albatrosses.
Water gushes down into my fish-pool.
Thinking of the water-pourer who poured
Two too truthful views of my double life,
I recall how my ancestors carried   390
Wood for their fires, hunted and then feasted
Towards the end of their Great Year and life.

The final seven-year cycle is ahead:
Advanced old age and attendant complaints.
I see myself sitting in a wheelchair
Beside the twelve beds of the rose garden
Whose paths describe a Union flag, and then,
Rug on my knees, a nurse not far behind
Under the apple-trees, and looking down
Beyond the arbour to field and meadow   400
Where rabbits scamper and a lone fox prowls
And glimpsing Death the Reaper with sickle
And knowing I still have time left before
He reaches where I sit in harmony

With the twilit universe and swallows
That skim the waves of grass and sweeping bats,
In last serenity and contentment,
In quiet happiness after struggle.
Back in my study I sit at my desk
And see in alcoves – Rodin's 'Thinker', busts   410
Of Milton, Homer – and the human skull
I bought at a school's closing-down auction,
A *memento mori*, a reminder
Of the fate that awaits when I am done,
When my work's finished, when I've reached an end.
I calmly face approaching death and bless
The essence of a well-led, rounded life
That has sought wisdom and understanding,
Good knowledge of life and humanity,
Transcendence of my experiences   420
And the elegiac tone of my youth.
Time that has creased my face wastes my body
But my soul, my universal being
Beneath my ego, follows timelessness.
I know with Einstein, time's an illusion:
The past and future are like north and south,
Everything's happened simultaneously
And so the future already exists
And the universe can supply all needs,
Obeys commands and sends 'future' events   430
From 'south' rather than 'north', gives what we want.
The eternal world wears the cladding of time,
And so my death has already happened.
My path leads onwards to this peaceful skull
And, in my memories, which slowly flick
Across my mind like moving screensavers,
Photos drawn from scanned-in places I've been,
I am aware of transitoriness,
The transience of all the images
Of my life, of all I saw, thought and did,   440

Which I reflected in my mirroring
Of our Age and left behind to a new
Generation, the distilled truth I found,
Evidence for my quest and life's follies,
My probing of its vices and my work
In letters, philosophy and history.
I reconcile time's transitoriness
And the eternal, ringing infinite.
+A + −A = zero,
Time + the eternal = the One.   450
I think of my fish and in Pisces smile
At my ancestors sitting by their fire,
Their caught fish being cooked and heart twanging,
Wood cut, ditches cleared and new-born lambs fed,
Warming their hands beside the leaping hearth
And warming their souls at their Great Year's end.
I am in harmony with the great One
In the face of coming death and stillness.

III. Meaning: A Completed Life
A life cycle in twelve seven-year ages
Between birth and death and showing striving,   460
Transforming and achievement and wisdom
Among ripe apples on the orchard boughs.
I knew the Light and found the infinite
Which enfolds our universe like a sea
Round an island. I found the rise and fall
Of civilizations, called for one world.
My voice cried in the wilderness, in vain?
I found a life cycle of forty-two
Episodes in my double life, within
The seven-year cycles that are also found   470
In body cells and hair, all forms of growth.
I found the growth of the poetic mind
And saw the self of time die back within
The universal being as a seed

Dies back to bring forth a caterpillar
And, after chrysalis, a butterfly.
I died back from ego to unity,
Peace, happiness and joy and I found out
That the universe supplied all my needs.
I opened to the universe's power   480
And effortlessly words flowed through my brain
Which I transcribed on pages as memoirs
And left behind to strengthen future souls.
I searched and found, my life ran to an end
Like the timed gushing through my fish-pool pipe.
The end of our search is the infinite.

I grew through ages and found harmony
With Nature and the One in twelve places
And found a path as I transformed my self.
I hatched and emerged from my chrysalis   490
And flew like a glorious swallow-tail.
I found a path that led to this great House
And mourned the transience of each cycle.
I loved the sun, the rain and the rainbow.
I found the eternal in harmony
With the universe and the infinite,
I found its permanence and reconciled
All opposites, and from zodiac signs found
The months of the medieval Great Year.
Sitting in a garden like Paradise   500
I breathe in harmony with unseen breeze
And know I was here to find, and I found.
Fifty-two years on from words above Ur
I have put flesh on the words I received.
My life cycle had a pleasing outcome.
Life cycles propel growth and progress lives
And shh! whisper it just to those who know,
One life cycle does not merely reveal
The phases of a human life's pattern,

It gives it meaning as we find our paths   510
And progress through time to our end and goal.
It is our universal destiny.

Sitting in my garden I sense ahead....
Out there, somewhere in the future, I hear....
No words or syllables, just heaving breaths
As each breath struggles into words and fades
Into the silence beneath each brief sound
And slowly sound merges into silence
As words become indistinct syllables
And syllables are heard as indrawn breaths   520
And inhalation and exhalation
Slow down and grow more faint and are at one
With the underlying silence so sounds
And silence pass into eternity

And shallow fainter breaths pass into
                              death.
*30 August–2 September, 27–28 October, 14–15 December 2014; 31 July, 17 August
2015; 13–14 February, 23 March 2016*

As the epigraph indicates, Nicholas Hagger received the words 'Life Cycle' in
the air above Ur while flying from Baghdad to Basra, Iraq, on 18 January 1962.
A life-cycle human pattern with twelve seven-year cycles reflects the renewal
cycles of body cells and hair every seven years. It complements, without contra-
dicting, the life cycle of 42 episodes outlined in *My Double Life 1: This Dark Wood*
and *My Double Life 2: A Rainbow over the Hills*. The Great Year of medieval
labours – the Labours of the Months, twelve scenes of rural activities linked to
signs of the zodiac – began in March and ended in February.
176–177. The Elizabethan portrait miniature by Nicholas Hilliard 'Young Man
Among Roses', c.1587, thought to be of Robert Devereux, 2nd Earl of Essex,
leaning against a tree among white roses, has a legend in gold letters '*Dat poenas
laudata fides*' ('My praised faith procures my pain').
III, heading, 'Completed', 'having all its parts, entire', 'finished', 'made whole
or perfect', 'ended'. (*Concise Oxford Dictionary*.)

513–525 This passage was inspired by Holst's *The Planets*. The final movement of 'Neptune' (composed in 1915) tails off at the end, suggesting death.

32

IN HARMONY WITH THE UNIVERSE
2009–2016

In Harmony with the Universe

I

I sit on a stone seat with two sphinxes
And griffins each end by the stone arch, see
Near the lake where I sat fifty-one years
Back and read a letter releasing me
From Law for Literature, and just as then,
The weeping willows and chestnuts, the sun
Mirrored in the lake blend with the blue sky
And I sense the harmony of the One.

I watch the Harbour-master's House in storm,
Rain lashing my cheeks. It snuggles on high   10
Ground as ferocious seas break on the pier
And fountain up under a thunderous sky.
I pulse the energy of sea and wind
And contrast our domestic huddling still
So peaceful under the cliff – storm and calm,
Elemental forces round Charlestown's hill.

Behind the storm and calm I see the One
In moonlit night when branches drip stars raw
That gleam and twinkle in the frosty air
Round a black hole in our galaxy's core,   20
And I am at one with the black sea flecked
With a streak of moonlight and a sky lit
By a round moon hanging low like a lamp –
All creation in one system's orbit.

And in the Forest over hills the wind

19

Swooshing through tossing trees is balanced by
The gentle breeze in summer sunshine when
All is still like lilies on mirrored sky.
And I have loved the sparkling on the waves
As sun, sky, sea exult in harmony 30
And flash out jumping light as if rain were
Pelting and splashing a thunderstorm's glee.

II

Experiences of harmony instruct,
But elsewhere in the world, outside our law,
The order of the stars and hatching grubs
Co-exists with chaotic forces, war.
Missiles kill children in a Gaza street,
In Syria homeless families squat;
And a school is invaded by masked men,
A hundred and thirty-two children shot. 40

Dreadful things are done for dubious causes.
Think of the Blitz and Dresden's fire-red sky.
When trains pull into Auschwitz platform
Grim men select those who should live or die.
Lines of condemned walk to chambers and soon
The crematorium door is open wide.
So a race is suppressed with ruthlessness,
Systemic and inhuman genocide.

Order in the Levant under ISIL?
A dozen masked men walk with Syrian bound 50
Pilots, take knives held out in a basin,
Stand behind, make prisoners kneel on the ground,
With one hand gently push lined heads to sand,
With the other slit each lined throat and saw;
Synchronised beheading and hand movements
On docile men who do not twitch a jaw.

Harmony in the universe is hidden
By men who have fanatical beliefs
And are intolerant of opponents;
By men's brutal coldness to others' griefs.   60
In every discipline men question soul
And materialist atheism rules.
Yet atheists, who see a dung-hill earth,
Are more humane than cruel Islamic fools.

III

And so I stand apart from all beliefs
And see seven billion souls as absolute,
Deserving of respect, freedom from war,
Disease, famine and poverty, and hoot
The nation-states' fanatical zealots
Who disable in advance and pre-empt,   70
Who scorn life and subordinate prisoners
To a stale ideology's contempt.

I follow one principle that is true:
Plus A plus minus A equals zero.
Storm, calm; evil, good; ego-centred faith,
Altruism; chaos, order; rot, flow;
Are reconciled and co-exist within
The fundamental unifying One
That restores harmony and shines when men
Behold the ordering cosmos like a sun.   80

There is a fundamental truth and law
In the secret universe's ether
That reconciles all opposites, and so
Hunter, hunted; eater, eaten; lover,
Loved – all are in a greater harmony
Than their conflicting appetites suggest,
Just as day, night; life, death seem in conflict
But harmonise Nature's forces' contest.

21

And so I'll seek out lakes and seas and skies
And pay attention to all crawling things   90
Which are creatures like me in the system's
Birth, breeding and decay – all flying wings –
That fills all Nature with conflict and love
And organisms that love and disperse.
I'll look out for all species and live in
Smiling harmony with the universe.
13–14, 16 February, 3 April 2015

1. Nicholas Hagger sat on the stone seat at Worcester College, Oxford on 21 June 2010.

The Ghadames Spring: Bubbles

The spring! The spring! Clear, warm, smelling of ponds,
Green fir-weed, frogs, white warm bubbles wobbling
Up, it is as old as the Great Pyramid. Conduits
Carry it to Roman baths, the fields. Squabbling

Tuareg pass, mouths covered. This is their oasis.
Here after the long haul across the Red
Stony Desert, here under the roofs the veiled
Women keep to in this City of the Dead

Whose ground floor is underground and down tunnels,
And, like nightingales, sing news from at night,   10
Here sit at the foot of these six polished steps
That shine with the ripples of reflected light,

And, toes in the warm water, stare at small eels,
And dragonflies that hover against the wind
And hang still, look at those wobbling bubbles,
Look how they come, warm, from the soft, thin-skinned

Saharan goodness! They float, white clusters
Of saline images on this rippled glass
Until, plop, an urchin in a red *fez* drops
A taunting stone, bare feet on dusty grass.   20

Well-sides of sandstone blocks, two white arches,
Tuareg with muffled mouths passing the wall
As if words were dirty. See how the scum floats
To the edge, leaving the centre clear to the ball

Of yellow fire that is the source of this
Source, that gave light to this place when a snorting horse
Gashed the sand with stamping hoof. This is the end
Of the desert quest and self-stripping, this mystic source.
1970; revised 9 January 2016

This poem was written following Nicholas Hagger's visit to Ghadames and the Ain el Faras spring in February 1970. It was omitted from *The Gates of Hell* as its tone did not fit, but is well suited to the present volume's theme of harmony with the universe. *The Gates of Hell*, volume 7 in *Collected Poems*, included another poem on Ghadames, 'Ghadames Spring (Poems like Bubbles)'.
27. There is a local legend that the well was created by a horse gashing the desert sand with a hoof.

Daisies

Sit at the foot of this tree;
Now in the April sun
A thousand white daisies
Strain towards the One.

Sit and feel their existence
As they tremble in the breeze,
Sit in their timeless being
While the birds sing in the trees.

We are busy with time,
We hurry towards and away;
Sit and thrill to the One
On this Paradisal day.
12 April 1975

Crystals

The April sun sparkles
Like crystals in the sun.
These crystals on my palms
Glisten from the One.

Last night in the moonlight
Tiny stones in the frost
Sparkled like crystals
Or stars that had got lost.

The sparkling stones outside,
This sparkling sea and skin,
Rejoice in the one Being
That shines out from within.
9 April 1990

See Nicholas Hagger, *Diaries*, 9 April 1990: "The sea out of my window is sparkling. It is a one: an image of Being, not existence. Seeing the crystals I am at peace."

Nightingale

As I stood near the red-hot pokers
Breathless on my garden stroll,
From the trees in the cliff-top field
A trilling thrilled my soul.

I listened in the still evening,
Gnats round a moon like a gong,
In the stillness of the twilight
To a thrilling nightingale's song.

It sang and then fell silent,
And then it trilled again,
Filling the creeping sea-mist,
Pure as an artist's pain.

I tiptoed from the pokers,
My head a trembling fire,
And the whispering of the wavelets
Was like wind round a frosty spire.
27 May 1990

See Nicholas Hagger, *Diaries*, 27 May 1990: "Wrote 'The Nightingale' and 'A Crystal'; a magically still evening with an orange sunset and a twilight part clear, part overtaken by a creeping sea-mist. Stood breathless."

Fragment: Question

And have you, when you are lost in a fog,
Visibility almost nil, alone,
Known you were in a quantum vacuum
Which stretches from your nose to farthest star,
Gives out all germs of living and still things,
Takes them back in the process of decay
And's filled with waves and voices from afar?
2 February 1992; 16 December 2014

Further Undated Unused Fragments for *Overlord*

1.

Once more, o you woods and fields of Essex,
Once more I return to your open arms.
Buttercups of Oaklands, to whose crannies
I have returned, back to my beginning,
That I might tell a most important tale.
Here I sat that year when flying bombs fell
And the heart of Europe was torn in two.

2.

As Mount's Bay fishermen winch in crab-pots
From shimmering waves where muffled church bells toll,
And raise weed from old spires where salt wind blows
Its tides through Lyonesse, and veins all shells,
Raise crab-pots where drowned church bells toll old prayers....

3.

Six-spot burnets settle on cliff ragwort
Near where Michael appeared to fishermen.

4.

Solitary the keeper in Smeaton's lighthouse
Pounded by billows, who climbs granite steps
To shine out from a tower a beam of fire.

5.

Nuzzling bees gather the honey of Light.

6.

A dappled sky like silver mackerel's skin.

7.

As wave after wave pours in wind to shore
So cascaded the advancing Russian ranks....

8.

A shower of stars leaks through the sky's dark roof,
A billion stars leak through and fall as dew.

9.

So walk with Beauty to a field of wheat,
Lie on your back and watch the dancing gnats
While a dog sniffs the hedge, and be the heat!

10.

See an eternal image briefly caught,
A fleeting image of an eternal sort.

11.

Foxgloves, herbs and purple rhododendrons
Crowd round this house which endures on its own.

12.

Each walks
In silence, breathes in Light, breathes out decay.

13.

Breathe in meaning and purpose quiet met,
And walk to the long room, bright eyes alert.

14.

All are sent to weave one tuft in the Whole,
Revere the latent thread of Light in all
Without emotion. Lives are a spiral:
Situations return, tugged in to fall,
We are hooked in at a higher level.
In one life-span, yearning can transform. Know
This maze of books and thought can be broken.
Carpets teach freedom and release it so.

15.

As fishermen put down forty crab-pots
And mark them with a float and then return
One day later and winch up pot by pot
And take out huge crabs, and sift and throw out
The small, the white, the soft, and keep the rest –
So artists put down pots for new ideas
And take what the ocean gives them each day
And smile a 'thank you' at the crawling chests.

16.

See angels in a ring like skydivers
Before their parachutes lift them away,
Some on the side of reform, others on
The side of revolution. See Michael....

17.

Does God sanction revolutions as well
As reforms? Or are they the Devil's work?

18.

Angels feed
On the honey of Light in Beauty's hives.

19.

Go down the steps that lead to Charlestown's beach,
Halfway enter the tunnel on your left,
Hear your echo and the stillness beneath,
Then go on down to the shingle and sea.

20.

As a sunned body climbs from Charlestown beach,
Enters the tunnel, hears its own echo,
Then emerges to quay, inner harbour
And shops, so three worlds that have been unseen
Surround all on the beach, although unknown.

21.

From the tunnel at high tide, see the bridge
Go down so the inner harbour is joined
To outer sea, lets a ship in, then goes
Back up with seaweed from the deep trailing.

22.

Just as when the wind blows white petals fall,
So the pure spirits floated to the ground.

23.

Europe is now the guardian of the Light
And so has its origins in Egypt.

24.

I fed ducks on a brown pond that lapped light
And leapt with golden leapings in which ducks
Were dim dark shapes in dazzling floodlights.

25.

Where dragonflies flit and where acorns fall,
And beechnuts lie near gold water lilies.

26.

And chugging off Dunwich on the North Sea
Stop your motor and listen to the waves
And hear the tolling of a hundred bells
From the submerged churches of Sigebert's town
And know as your nose dips, they toll for you.

27.

Remember when Rommel was on the run
And the rain came and our tanks were bogged down?
Recall how we beat him to Tripoli,
Staked our supply lines on a ten-day win,
How we did it in eight days, two to spare?

28.

And after El Alamein we dug graves
And created seven thousand crosses.
Slowly, inexorably, the sand blew
Across the empty battlefield, tearing
The paint off rusting tanks, filling dug-outs,
Banking around land-mines and lost lanyards,
Obliterating tyre tracks and footprints
Till there were only rows of white crosses.
A Bedouin camel passed ungathered mines.

29.

As a worshipper of a folded rose
Peels back petals, inhales the sweet essence,
So he smelt the soft satin folds....

30.

As when a Tantrist sits with his Sakti
And his sticky essence mixes with hers
And his skin glows in a smooth sheen, and now
His aura brightens to a rippling health
And burns like a candle for flitting souls
To see, fly to and feel round, like beetles
Round a lantern in a Pacific night....

31.

As when at a meeting two paper chains
Snap and drift down on a strict Head who stares
Stonily while her staff smirk and titter,
And resumes the debate with high disdain,
So did the angel's irreverent descent
Set the throng asmirking behind their wings.

32.

As a tree puts out buds to every wind
Which flower and fruit and branch, so his young soul

Budded language, and grew to leafy thought.

33.

As in a Raphael God sits at the top
And Christ below with all enlightened men
Who have attained a place in their Heaven,
And underneath the dove of the Spirit
Descends to an altar and men who seek
And turn in different directions to catch
Spiritual Light and grasp that all is one;
So God pulsed Light from the great throne of Fate
And men below milled in a basking crowd.

34.

As a lopped tree puts out new sprigs in spring
Which grow to branches and put out more twigs,
So the idea pushed into a branched form
Filled with green sap that would soon snap bone-dry
And dissolve back into the formless sea.

35.

As a child, given finger puppets, makes
A puppet show of chairs and rug and stool
And, crouching, has dog belabouring mouse
And cat and talks in squeaky high-pitched tones,
So God's great fingers filled the empty clothes
Of Satan's rebel angels, knocked their heads,
And bowed them low when their master appeared.

36.

Like a whirling corona of white clouds,
Each like a swimmer in a rolling sea,
Wings gleaming in its billows, some trillions
Of angels ducked and surfaced in the waves,
And threw a ring around the dazzling sun.

37.

As a palm grows and loses its first fronds....

38.

Rise with Horus, and between his steel wings
Look down on matter which condensed to cloud.
Europe's below, a snowscape with snowhills
And white snow as far as the eye can see,
And who can doubt Europe's a unity?
Paris, Berlin, Brussels, Amsterdam, Prague,
Vienna, Budapest – and London, snow.
It will melt but we'll enjoy winter first.

39.

The woods are charmed, in Copped Hall's gallery
A Midsummer Night's Dream was first performed
As Southampton's mother married Heneage.
Cupid's flower Oberon asked Puck to find
Is woodland pansy: 'love-in-idleness'.

40.

As when pickets line up against police
And a car takes a miner back to work
A roar goes up, a surge, a hail of bricks
Long after the car has passed, the police
Are driven back, one has blood down his face,
A coach is burnt out near a fallen pole....

41.

Like hens in a battery, putting their
Combed heads through bars, the prisoners on the train
Shook heads from side to side as they drew out.

42.

A cluster of poems like coloured balloons.

43.

As sheep stand in a green field that is seen
From a motorway, so stand....

44.

As grey clouds drift across a blue sky and
Show golden white clouds in winter sunshine
High up, so....

45.

As trees look blank in a winter sunset
So stood the devils....

46.

As horses nuzzle on a hillside and
Glint in golden sunshine, so the distant
Souls gleamed in the golden ethereal light.

47.

                                        Satan's
Troops made smoke to veil the Light, but in vain....

48.

As a mist gathers on a tossing sea
And all things creep and hide, so did a mist
Fill Heaven, and taken by surprise Angels
Crept home and waited, not realising
Satan's troops made smoke to conceal the Light.

49.

Men, women and children were forced to dig
Their own graves and lie face down in their earth
And all were shot in the back of their heads,
The bullets spurting blood and spattering brains....

50.

Like a rainbow with many hues, an arch
Of many-splendoured prismatic colour
That was so insubstantial he could walk
Through it....

51.

As a rainbow hangs on a misty sun
And rain gathers, bringing a squall, beating
On the window-panes of slum-dwellers who
Huddle from the lowering storm clouds, and stop
And look with wonder at its beauty, so....

52.

As when a host at a summer buffet
In a garden lies back on a sun-couch
In shade and voices his wife invited
Become more remote and he falls asleep
At his own party, then wakes with a start
To a different topic of conversation,
So....

53.

Just as an anaesthetised patient comes
Round in Recovery to hear a nurse
Say "You've made it" and, disorientated,
Wonders what artefact he has just made,
So, befuddled by....

54.

Just as a patient returned to his ward
Looks down at two heavily bandaged legs
And feels waves of pain spread from his ankles
And greedily gulps down two painkillers,
So....

55.

Just as a patient convalescing in
A hospital basks in well-being as
The papers, pills, meals come at intervals
And nurses who take his temperature and
Blood pressure give injections, plump pillows,
Lies on his tilting bed with a remote
That controls height and the angle of tilt,
And one that calls nurse and controls the light,
Radio and television, and through all
Feels he is in a hotel rather than
A hospital where some men are dying,
So....

56.

If we live correctly, positively,
The Devil is redundant, otiose,
For his purlieu is what is negative
And correct living bypasses his hedge
And does not trespass across his snared field.

57.

On death the spirit of man emerges
Into a new form like a butterfly
Clothed with subtle stuff, a spiritual
Body, and thinks faster than we do with
Our sluggish brains and lower vibrations.

58.

And looking at the skull he wondered how
The Light shone into it; far simpler to
Believe there is no Light and mind is brain.

59.

Hell a disused, deep iron-ore mine shaft

60.

Men take on bodies with tubes through which chewn
Food passes and exits so that their minds
Can make a statement and improve the earth,
Leave it a better place for their presence
Before they depart, their bodies decayed.

61.

They got nowhere near the highest Heaven,
Just to the entrance to its lowest ring.

62.

Just as the German army could not cope
With the huge numbers of Russians taken
Prisoner, so now the Allies could not cope
With the massive numbers of gaunt German
Prisoners of war from the German collapse.
Like the Russians the Germans were herded
Into rolled barbed wire and were left to graze
For food like cattle on the dusty ground.
1994–1996

'Further' in title. The first batch, 'Undated Unused Fragments for *Overlord*', is in
volume 28 of *Collected Poems*.

Unused Draft for *Overlord*

The German atomic bomb program was
In the hands of Heisenberg, who had found
The uncertainty principle; he was
A major scientist who had remained
In Germany to work for Hitler when
He could have lived in the US. He had
Met Bohr in Copenhagen, and 'let slip'
(Under the guise of discussing moral

Issues) Hitler's atomic bomb program.
He had signalled to Bohr that Germany
Could not and would not build an atom bomb,
And hoped the Americans would desist.
Bohr had been angry. Heisenberg was in
A program of military research
And said he knew he would make atom bombs
While *he* was in an occupied country.
With sticks Heisenberg had drawn a box which
Was a reactor, not a bomb; Bohr, then,
Did not know that reactors could produce
A fissionable material, plutonium.
Heisenberg had told the Nazis a bomb
The size of a pineapple could destroy
London, but, when asked by Franck, he had said
There was no prospect of an atom bomb
Before the end of the war. That next June
Himmler spoke of "powerful new explosives",
And Hitler told Marshal Antonescu
That the atomic bomb "had advanced to
The experimental stage" and had "such
Colossal force that all human life is
Destroyed within three or four kilometres".
Yet a report said Heisenberg delayed
"The work as much as possible". And now
He moved to Hechingen. In Leipzig his
Personal and scientific papers
Were destroyed in fire-bombing, as Max Planck's
Were in Berlin. He moved to Hechingen,
Where Adolf Reichwein asked if he would join
A conspiracy against Hitler. He
Correctly surmised the conspirators
Would be caught and punished, and so declined.
Soon after the Americans threatened
To destroy Dresden with an atom bomb
Unless the Germans surrendered before

The end of August. Göring's aide asked, "Do
The Americans really have the bomb?"
Heisenberg did not think so, and again
Maintained the Germans could not make the bomb
Before the end of the war.
1994

This passage on how Heisenberg slowed down Hitler's atomic bomb program
originally came after *Overlord* book 1, line 2333, but was omitted.

Quarry

I sit above the stone quarry
Where Greek prisoners of war hewed out
Great blocks of limestone for temples
And challenged Syracusan doubt.

I see chisel marks where they scraped,
Scratched, cut, gouged, hewed under duress.
Each block was dragged and hoist with rope,
And then examined for whiteness.

The prisoners spent their lives hewing
Till, tortured with aches, pains and falls,
Their being gave out and they left
A life of blocks in others' walls.

I have a quarry in my mind
In which a prisoner toils to hew
Stanzas that must be ever white –
And's quarry to guards who pursue.
6.50 a.m., 19 July 2000; revised 16 December 2014

'Quarry', noun, 'a place from which stone may be extracted'; 'the object of
pursuit by hunters'. (*Concise Oxford Dictionary*.)

Terrorist

(For Christopher Ricks)

The due day's come and no news is grave news:
You must befriend the Thug with hooded head.
O eyes, ears, feet. You'll no more share your views,
With exact words shape form, gleam rhyme, guide tread.
My undertakings will now be unchecked,
Checked by undertakers, Death's dreadful mob.
He kidnaps, strews, leaves a life's order wrecked,
Greats' texts unread, and a fifty-year sob:
"You opened their lifetime's works and my eyes,
And trained my ear to hear the whispering deep,
And like a compass northed my feet, star-bright.
When the vile Terrorist steals your last sighs
May you pass painless on to dreamless sleep
And be surprised by everlasting Light."
15 September 2007

Two in One

(For Nadia and Ian)

Each separate in blood and bone,
A bride and groom smile out at guests
Through mirth and music, wine and jests,
Yet like two shells in a split stone

Their two like halves make up a whole,
A non-duality's begun:
Apart yet joined, mysterious one,
Two hearts in bodies, in one soul.
10 July 2008

Six-spot Burnets

Above the Needles, scan
A Cold-War site and, free,
See where test rockets on gantries
Were fired above the sea.

Now long grass has engulfed
Abandoned Batteries,
And six-spot burnets flutter through
The tall yellow daisies.
23 July 2008; 28 February 2015

House Martins

House martins swoop and dart
Round ancient harbour walls,
Swerve, veer and dive, back-forth,
As if the place enthrals,

As if each flit were joy
As they zip past my head,
Exulting in their play,
Alive with verve, not dead.
21 August 2008

House Martins in the Eaves

House martins in the eaves
Make a temporary home,
Chatter in the mornings
And dart and swoop and roam.

I have made my abode

Under these Forest eaves
And dictate each morning,
And swoop through words and leaves.
21 August 2008; 28 February 2015

8. 'Leaves', pages in a book.

Undated Unused Fragments for *Armageddon*

1.

As a schoolboy makes blots and smudges, so....

2.

As Snowdon hangs in mist in autumn Wales
And a cloud covers its towering peak, so....

3.

As a castle stands on a watery loch,
Abandoned now but once the centre of....

4.

As when a man walking between a light
And the moon sees two shadows, one before
And one behind, so....

5.

The tree was already rotten. I gave
It a good shake and rotting apples fell.

6.

As an astronaut, stepping onto the moon,
Said "One small step for man" – he meant "a" man –
"And one giant leap for mankind", and became
A recluse because, in awe of seeing
The earth as a small ball, he knew we had

To unite into a world government,
So....

7.

Just as three kings sit at Abu Simbel,
A rising tide having drowned them, so three....

8.

I look through my manuscript and alight
On passages like a butterfly, then
Flutter on and settle on another
Head of a flower, and bask in the warm sun.

9.

Just as a thunderstorm's lightning sweeps up,
A daddy-long-legs dancing through a room....

10.

As penguins in the Antarctic gather
And thousands huddle in South Georgia
And scarcely move as visitors walk through,
So....

11.

Just as a patient, wheeled into the room
Outside the theatre, has a drip fixed in
The back of his hand and then has a jab
And feels the numbness spreading to his legs
And tries to count to ten and reaches four
When a great wave spreads up his body and
He knows no more until he half-wakes in
Recovery, drowsily asks if he's
Had his operation and's reassured,
So....

2008–2009

A Breathless Calm

A breathless calm, sky pinks
And prinks glassed sea this dusk.
The skied sea like a rose
Smells of satin and musk.

A breathless calm, light fades.
I crane to see my words.
The whole sea is now pink.
I roost like the cliff birds.
31 May 2010; 16 December 2014

Gigs, Insects

On a calm sea this May evening
Two gigs glide past, their earnest crews
Each row six oars, and leave behind
Curved trails of wake in greens and blues.

They crawl like small insects towards
The headland's tiny harbour, flee.
Now I still see the curved traces
Of young strivings on a smooth sea.
31 May 2010; 16 December 2014

Daisies, Mower

How tall the daisies stand
Smiling up at the sun
Amid the buttercups,
Laughing and full of fun.

How straight the mower's lines

As he roars to and fro.
How green the new-mown mound,
No trace of daisies' glow.

3 June 2010

At Great Milton Manor House: On Life and Death

Manor and church, body's and spirit's call:
The senses stimulated through a meal –
Taste, smell, touch, sight and hearing all challenged
With perfect flavour, incense, tactile feel,
Look and harmony – and the Dormer tomb
Summons all to face their end like a yew.
Taste and tomb, what unites body and soul.
An immortal eye sees through to what's true.

I wander back to the *Manoir* and pass
Lavender beds and manor house's minds,   10
And reach the Tea House of the wind and moon,
Where the *Lotus Sutra*'s dewy path winds
Through Paradise – blending Buddhist, Shinto
And Taoist images – and mental space.
All pilgrims journey through their interior,
The Tea garden requires a pilgrim's pace.

Here wander slowly over stepping-stones,
A path that slows and takes to views, pay heed
And at the Tea-House door shake off the dust
Of the world and in English oak, thatched reed   20
With bulrush ridge, split hazel rods, and lime-
Plastered walls, feel the serene peace, its power,
With transcendent detachment glimpse the One,
The *yugen* or the consciousness's flower.

In refined poverty, rusticity,

Ponder the pavilion's Japanese name,
Fugetsu-An, 'wind and moon', sounds 'forgets':
Pavilion of deep love of Nature. Aim
Here to forget the everyday world's cares,
Be absorbed in Nature's beauty, no strife,   30
At one with the One, and know that spirit
Will survive death and have eternal life.

In Japanese Tea House forget this life
By a 'stone torch-basket', a stone lantern
That holds a light like an enlightened soul
And shines illumination from its 'urn',
And then wander to the stew pond where fish
For Friday meals were fed, then caught and cooked
So the nuns could keep body and spirit
Together to pray while their lit souls looked.   40

Next morning I encounter Raymond Blanc
On crutches, open-necked shirt, shake his hand,
Hear how he fell down stairs and broke his leg
In four places, and his foot as well, and
I say I understand the winding path
Of stepping-stones from the world to a place
Where the soul is lit like a candle flame
And shines with infinite, eternal grace.

I see an image of myself in him:
He has two hundred and thirty staff, I   50
Two hundred and forty. He has diners,
I parents, who pay fees so staff get by.
He has to be excellent in the service
He provides as do I. He has to please.
I see his smiling face and sense my own.
I too sought in Japan's gardens. I freeze.

In sun by an armillary-sphere sundial

Designed by 'Ptolemy the Greek' I sway
To read a hexameter in Latin:
'*Eternum tibi semper adesse*   60
Puta', 'Remember thou art ever on
The brink of Eternity'. One fall down
Stairs, failed breath, creeping shadow, and I'd be
Like Dormer in a tomb, in shrouding gown.

O armillary sphere, much-looped sundial
With VII to VI, Roman-numeral hours,
And a sunlit shadow on a curved band,
You tell the hours of senses amid flowers,
Scents, tastes and sighs in tactile rustling wind,
But also foretell winter's coming chill;   70
And beyond that, in the seeds of today,
The flowers of all tomorrows and spring's thrill.

The infinite surrounds and permeates
Our universe of souls and scented flowers.
The eternal surrounds and permeates
A looped sundial that tells the passing hours:
Beauty in scents and tastes and thrilling sense.
Nothingness presses into form, and death
Is a return to Nothingness, the Void,
That's fountain-source of all, the Light – and breath.   80
18–19 July 2010

The Japanese Garden was created by the chef Raymond Blanc after a visit to
Japan in 1991. Nicholas Hagger stayed there on 18 and 19 July 2010. The Tea
House's Japanese name, *Fugetsu-An*, means 'Wind and Moon', suggesting
'pavilion of deep love of Nature'. The '*yugen*' ('flower') in Eastern thought is the
experience of the Light. 'Armillary sphere', 'a representation of the celestial
globe constructed from metal rings, and showing the equator, the tropics etc.'.
(*Concise Oxford Dictionary*.) The Dormer tomb is in nearby St Mary's church,
Great Milton. This poem reflects Nicholas Hagger's view that a poem is a
meditation or contemplative reflection on life and death.

Storm

All night the wind lashed rain in constant gusts
And roared in the chimney, while pounding waves
Flung layers of white surf up the dark beach.
The windows shook before its force and raves.
30 October 2010; revised 17 December 2014

See Nicholas Hagger, *Diaries*, 30 October 2010: "A storm blew outside – wind and sea."

Dripping Stars at Midnight

Crab-pots and dripping stars.
I walked along the quay,
A thousand stars splashed down
Like raindrops from a tree.

I turned and saw the Plough
Caught in a crab-pot net.
A universe aflow,
Night sky all dripping wet.

Crab-pots and dripping stars,
A universe aweep,
And mine a poor sole eye
And all the world asleep.
31 October 2010; 16 December 2014

Leaves Falling 1

Leaves falling on green grass,
Nature has shed and strewn.
The grass is strewn with gold,

A treasure trove at noon.
4 November 2010

Skimming Stones

I bend and skim a stone
Across the glassy lake.
It touches twenty times
Between each gliding break.

So does an ancient soul
Touch Being, leave, move on
To touch again, reborn,
Twenty times each aeon?
12 November 2010; 17 December 2014

Concorde

(For Ben)

I fold my sheet into a paper dart,
To me it's Concorde gleaming in the sun.
It rises, nose first, takes off with a roar,
It hurtles faster than the speed of sound.
A big bang shakes the windows of my room –
But no, it is the front door being banged.
24 November 2010

Oak

I gaze at the oak-tree's
Wintry structure, grey-brown,
Leaves now shed, sinewy,

With trunk, branches and crown.

It mirrors my own work:
A universal spine,
Thick *genres* branching off,
Boughs and twigs that entwine.

O wonderful oak-tree
So still in winter sun,
May I be as serene
As I gaze at the One.
Connaught House, 11 December 2010; 17 December 2014

A Wish for my Granddaughter

I

I walk through corridors and peer through glass
At wards where babies sleep in shallow cots
And at the end find my new granddaughter
Lying with screwn-up eyes in slumber's knots,
Brown hair and tiny fingers, toes and nails.
She peeps from under a hospital shawl.
I bend and marvel at new-arrived life,
A shallow rapid breathing, peaceful sprawl.

My grandson sits on the radiator
With his father by the open window.   10
I recall how an hour after his birth,
I held him, how he took my black biro
From my shirt's breast pocket in his tiny
Fingers as if to say, 'I'm going to write.'
My wife sits by the new baby's mother,
Who beams, her labour done, the future bright.

A nurse comes by and fiddles with the shawl,

Checks notes, asks if all's well, opens a pack.
And then a hefty sister bustles in,
An African, and stops, taken aback,   20
And says, "Only partners are allowed here
On the first day." My son explains his son
Had only just left school and was meeting
His sister for the first time, truths well-spun.

She stares us out and lets out a big sigh
Like an order to vanish without trace.
She turns on heel and goes, and we now leave,
Our breach of the rule firmly put in place.
We wave and are lost in the corridors
And pace and turn and, back in the car park,   30
I survey all the cars of visitors
With more right than ourselves as it grows dark.

II

And now I think of the society
You have been born into, my granddaughter:
A land divided between rich and poor
With social-service cuts, young minds a blur,
Rising unemployment and drunkenness.
So many youths escape into a dream.
Some streets have knots of idle yobs at noon,
It's best to cross the road if there's a scream.   40

I sit before my screen and dream of days
When the family spoke round the table
And we ran freely out into the dusk
For a game of cricket before nightfall.
My grandchildren will spend years round a screen
And in the cashless society they
Will inherit, will pay great swathes of tax.
And where will be our love of our today?

I sit before two hundred scanned photos
Of my grandparents and a different life, 50
Of a large house with lawns and greenhouses
Behind a hedge, children, husband and wife
In deck-chairs in the garden, side by side,
Or holding tennis-rackets, having fun,
A settled life. My mother stands near flowers
And I sit on a rug in friendly sun.

I think of the new baby and our world
Of cameras, snoops and what is too costly,
Of deficits and debts that dog one's work,
The vapid smiles of each celebrity. 60
And I feel sad for what she will find out.
Will she learn betrayal like splintered glass?
Like my grandson who in our car recounts
How the music master turned on his class.

III

Out there's a world that ranks by achievement
And awards prizes like an uncouth shout
You'll be urged to compete for, and ignores
All who don't play its game by opting out.
I think of Marvell and Voltaire, who both
Held that one should not seek to win the bays, 70
But feed off one's garden, be real among
The plants and shrubs of the early spring days.

The garden is a joy, o little girl.
Don't chase rainbows beyond the hedge, chase words.
Forget the world's praise or denigration,
Produce your work between feeding the birds
And, watching carp rise in the shaded pool,
Chasing a heron, watching a fox slink,
Be in Nature's rhythm of four seasons
And grow a lily where your waters think. 80

Tell of newts in your early school stories,
Of frogspawn and hovering dragonflies,
Of clover on the grass, yellow cinquefoil,
White stitchwort, purple vetch and sunny skies,
Walk under apple trees to rockery blooms,
Visit lavender amid humming bees,
Look out for painted lady butterflies
And smile at the robin that hops to please.

The world you will live in is passing strange.
Technology's advancing all the time   90
And yet terrorists menace, nowhere's safe.
Some things were better in my youthful prime.
You'll live with a smartphone, be more informed
Yet distil less knowledge when, calm, you gaze.
O little girl, may you rediscover
The simple things and love of garden days.
10 February 2011; 26, 28, 31 July 2015

Snails

On my seaside lawn
In the drizzling dark
Under the street light
Twenty snails inch and lark,

Shells jauntily on
Slug-backs as I pass,
Their two horned eyes peer
As they sip the wet grass.

O snails who congregate
In dark to break your fast,
Why don't you fear my tread
As I pick my way past?

28 May 2011; 17 December 2014

Grace

(For Ingrid Kirk's poesy book)

"I made a posie, while the day ran by."
George Herbert

Orphaned at just fifteen,
She honed her skills each day,
Carved herself as mother
And many-skilled PA.
A Grace by a fountain
That brims near Apollo's stair,
She pours truth into books
With plashing, loving care.
27 June 2011

Bone

I have a bone jutting out from my hand.
It's a knobble alongside my wrist bone.
I can't recall a knock, it does not hurt.

So that's what happens when you grow too old.
The skeleton breaks up and bones jut out,
Push through the skin into weird knobbly rounds.

I look at my hand bone near my right wrist
And am sad that the years have peeled away
And let my structure through by this light sea.
21 July 2011

Near Teignmouth

A grey sea, rocks and cliffs,
A misty, cloudy sky,
Green seaweed on the sand
And gulls that stand or fly.

No sign of alien man
Who lives in blocks of stone
And leaves this wetland sand
To the sky and wind's moan.
5 August 2011; 17 December 2014

Splashes of Light

A thousand lights splash on
The sea in the sunshine,
A thundershower of light
That dazzles up my spine.

Each splash a dazzling white
As force bombards the sea
And flurries of wind send
Small icebergs scudding free.

O sparkling sea and wind,
Splashed light and ice that stun,
You are both wiped away
As a cloud blocks the sun.

I grasp that what I saw
Beneath me, though a joy,
Was but an illusion
Like magic to a boy.

Now I gaze at a sea
That's wrinkled under cloud
But I know Nature leaps
When sun removes this shroud.

Down here is in shadow,
A dark that sometimes lifts
When a world of light shines
Its dazzling on what drifts.

The storm of light has passed,
The world's again rain-grey.
The wrinkled sea is still,
The One has had its say.

8 August 2011; 17 December 2014

Bronze Age

North Teign river rises
Among ancient Bronze-Age
Stone cairns and settlements,
And winds past tors to rage

In a foaming torrent
Into the modern town.
So history's rushing flow
Pours relentlessly down

From a forgotten past
To our machine-run time
That's heedless of its source
And of its inner climb.

20 August 2011; 17 December 2014

River, Headlong

How fast the river flows,
Rushing through stones, an urge
Headlong in movement's flux,
Relentless, restless surge.

And where did my life go
Rushing headlong, doing?
Where was there time to be,
Still as a stone, musing?

I sit, still as a stone,
As the torrent froths by.
All lives rush to their end,
Both man's and moth's – oh, why?
20 August 2011; 17 December 2014

Sky

In the water garden
Small brown trout rise for flies,
A ripple on the sky
Each time an insect dies.

Above, between the trees,
A buzzard soars, its wings
Outspread, and, lord of sky,
It hunts for crawling things.

I sit not far from where
Bronze-Age farmers once chose
To build hut circles, cairns,
Settlements and stone rows.

They too must have seen trout,
Watched ripples swallow flies
And seen the buzzard soar,
In awe of the One's skies.
20 August 2011; 17 December 2014

Fragment: Rain

It rains in my heart
Like the fine rain
That mists the tranquil bay.
I have work to do
And must wait, must wait.
I cannot brook delay.
2 September 2011; 17 December 2014

The Wheel of Creation

I

I gaze up at the red Great Laxey Wheel
Which turns seventy-two feet above the glen
And draws water from the underground mine,
Spews it into the main adit so then
It runs into the river that pours by.
It turns ceaselessly with a measured thump,
Circular motion converted by crank
To horizontal motion that drives pump,
Rod and plunger up the valley to bring
Water from flooded mine to gush and sing.   10

The turning Wheel under Snaefell's high peak,
The largest water-wheel in the world, red,
Draws water from three hundred and forty-
Seven fathoms down beneath a river bed.

Each downward stroke forces pooled water up
Pipes to the next level until it's found
The Adit Level, tunnel with daylight
One end, where it drains away above ground.
I gaze at its waters that tumble down
Across boulders beneath its straining frown.   20

The mine was first probed in seventeen ninety.
This Wheel has turned since eighteen fifty-four,
Once pumped two hundred and fifty gallons
Of water a minute from metal ore
One thousand five hundred feet below ground.
I walk between a tinkling river filled
From the glen's hill slopes and the brambled fern
And pumped-out floodings of the mine, now milled,
And head for the black hole in the green dell
And peer in the groined, wood-framed square tunnel.   30

Above and either side's uneven rock.
The floor has puddles several yards in girth.
I leave the daylight and peer past wall lights
To where the first shaft drops into the earth.
Here miners came, looking for lead and zinc,
Copper and tin (that, mixed, made bronze) in Stone-
Age times when bronze heralded a new age.
Here miners braved twenty tunnels alone
At descending levels, in dark not dry,
The last as low as Mount Snaefell is high.   40

In the Carboniferous age from three
Hundred and twenty million years ago
Strange movements in the earth's tectonic plates
Fractured its cracking crust and surface dough.
Fluids with dissolved minerals thrust up which
Cooled and crystallised to veined lodes of ores.
Down in twenty-two miles of deep tunnels

Men chipped out lead and zinc from massive stores
To be crushed, cleaned and sorted for shipping,
Risked flooding to bring out ores sun-gleaming.   50

II

I know a mine where images still gleam,
That's flooded by environment's seeping
And is pumped out as a poetic flow
By a rod fixed to a Great Wheel turning
Each day with measured pace, the poet's work.
Ceaselessly turning, poets pump a flow
Of energetic verse and, within, mine
Images of truth from a dark below;
And when a torrent of inspired words stalls,
Chip images from minds' dark cavern walls.   60

I stand and gaze at the stream by the Wheel
And know poets' daily endeavouring
That repetitively turns on round and round
Pumps out a flow from their own darkest spring
That mixes with environment's seepings
And leaves the tunnels of the mind like night
So that a creeping soul can hold a lamp
To forms that glitter when brought up to light
Like precious stones of very scarce supply,
Know that creation pumps the mind's mine dry.   70

The true poet's Wheel turns each day to gush
Environmental seepage from raw truth
And fluids with dissolved minerals from deeps
That contain bits of the earth's remote youth.
Work, flow and image are integrated
In process, like wheel, water, mineraling.
I see creation as the three-legged
Sun-symbol of the Isle of Man's Norse king
That's by the Wheel. It blends with much churning

Hard graft, energy and truth, craft turning.   80

I muse that the Manx kingdom's royal arms',
The three-legs', motto proclaims – "*Quocunque
Jeceris stabit*", "whichever way you
Throw it, it will stand" – the Manx self-rule's way
Which is stable and cannot be flung down.
It is true of the Norse king Cuaran
Who had a wide, tenth-century dominion,
Whose three legs were Norway, Dublin and Man,
And of Man's three thirteenth-century kings who
Ruled Gaelic Scotland's Hebrideans too.   90

It is also true of Creation's power
Whose Wheel turns ceaselessly and three legs run
Clockwise in the sun's course, repeatedly.
It always stands, turning with legged sun.
Its Wheel grinds through hard work, and pumps a flow
Of verse that contains nuggets of truth's wit
That is hidden in darkest depths and yet
Glints out on Mount Snaefell's towering summit:
The running One will height, breadth, depth unite,
In work, flow, image, through three-legged Light.   100
2–4 September 2011

Nicholas Hagger visited the Great Laxey Wheel in the Isle of Man on 1
September 2011.
28. 'Milled', 'frothed like a mill-race'.
29. 'Dell', 'small wooded hollow or valley'.
30. 'Groin', 'an edge formed by intersecting vaults, an arch supporting a vault'.
'Groined', 'built with groins'.
32. 'Girth', 'the distance around a thing'.
40. The lowest level was 302 fathoms, 1,800 feet. Mount Snaefell is 2,036 feet
high.
44. 'Crust', 'the hard outer part of a loaf of bread'; 'the outer portion of the
earth'. 'Dough', 'a thick mixture of flour and liquid for baking into bread,

pastry'.

46. 'Lode', 'a vein of metal ore'.

59. 'Stalls', 'stops because of an inadequate supply of fuel'.

86. 'Cuaran', the Three Legs emblem is on the coins of the 10th-century Norse king Olaf (also spelt Anlaf) Cuaran.

Fragment: Gold

How gold the fields after cut corn
And the round harvest sheaves, cornstalks
Bundled and tied after reaping
That wait in rows to be scooped up
And be turned into loaves of bread,
In the rain round Aylesbury's fields.

18 September 2011; 17 December 2014

Sunlight

I look at an image on a screen,
I'm writing a poem sitting on rocks.
I close up on the poem I was writing
But sunlight obscures the words, the sunlight shocks.

I go closer, but pixels blur.
It's like looking at a Dead Sea Scroll.
I sat on rocks in sun twenty years ago
But my poem's faded like an old parchment roll.

I look ahead to a time when I
Will be a fossil within such rocks
And my work's indecipherable parchment
And I shiver, for now the sunlight mocks.

19 September 2011; 17 December 2014

Robin

I walk to fields in mist
But by the open gate
A robin holds a worm.
I stop and gaze, and wait.

O robin, I must not
Tread where you tamely stand
And frighten you to drop
The worm you think so grand.

I turn and walk ten yards
To the next gap, then twist,
And still my robin holds
His worm in morning mist.
20 November 2011; 17 December 2014

Fragment, Where are my Friends

Where are my friends, and where my family?
I do not know if they're still living now….
Undated, ?2012

The beginning of a poem about a solitary. Nicholas Hagger reports: "These two lines seemed to come from the beyond."

Magpie in Snow

A bird taps my window.
Why are you fretting, bird?
The feeder's full of seed.
Why so urgent? I heard.

I draw the curtain – snow!
On every tree, so still.
A grey-white sky bodes more.
Magpie tracks on the sill.

I go out in the snow.
It's seven inches deep.
A statue wears a crown,
A fox's tracks are steep.

I look back at my house.
Snow hangs from the roof, bright.
Shrubs bow beneath its weight,
Branches are all half-white.

Round feeders on my tree
Tits peck for nuts and feed.
A magpie prowls for crumbs,
It cannot extract seed.

Magpie, I now know you,
When you tapped my window,
Said, "White's covered the ground,
Please feed me in this snow."
5 February, 7 May 2012

Song Thrush Piping

I sit in morning sun
And hear the clear piping
Of a song thrush: four calls,
A trilling, throstling.

Three calls and then a fourth
In the clear morning air.

It seems a joyful tune,
And reminds us of where

Like a cornucopia,
Three hidden worlds behind
The one that I can see
Gush forms like song. We're blind:

"Out of the One was born,"
Its piping herald sings,
"Non-Being, then Being
From which Existence springs.

"All Existence has poured
From the One's teeming gush
So love all living things,
Love the One's bounteous rush."

Four worlds meet in the now
And I, all ears, see one.
And I am glad my thrush
Calls me to love the sun.
29 March, 27 April, 7 May 2012; 28 February 2015

Ladybird

Ladybird who has lived
In my window cracks' heat,
Now you have flown and sit
By my hand while I eat.

Your red wings with black spots
And white head markings blend.
Have you come to see me,
Are you now my new friend?

Ladybird, I've carried you
To the leaf-box I keep
On my stone balcony,
Make your home there and sleep.
29 March 2012; 17 December 2014

Owl

Whoo–who–who, the owl hoots
From the darkening trees.
Night falls on the garden.
Owl swoops on a vole it sees.

Whoo–who? The barn owl asks,
Who are you, human who
Sits in your lit window.
Your paper won't feed you.

Who are you? the owl asks.
What are you doing there?
You stare at strange paper
While I hunt for my fare.

Who are you? the owl asks.
Humans must know their route.
I know mine, who I am.
I feed my brood and hoot.
29 March 2012; 17 December 2014

Honey-bees

The honey-bees nuzzle
The cowslip bells and tongue
Nectar to make honey,

Pollen to feed their young.

Back in their hive they make
A honeycomb so their queen
Can lay eggs in each cell.
All know what each must glean.

O keep away the mite
That takes food from their lips
And makes them all fall ill
And fall down like rain drips.

The honey-bees nuzzle
Primroses in the sun
To feed their colony
And work the ordered One.
29 March 2012; 17 December 2014

8. 'Glean', 'collect or scrape together'. (*Concise Oxford Dictionary*.)

Spruce Cone

I pick up a spruce cone
And trace its spiral swirls.
One way I count thirteen,
The next twenty-one twirls.

The Fibonacci plan
Packs seeds under hard veils,
Makes best use of the space,
Protects seeds with hard scales

Until the right time comes
To release winged seed
To find its way to soil

And grow and thrust and feed.
1 April 2012; 28 February 2015

Song Thrush Dead

The apple blossom hangs
Like snow this Eastertide.
But look, beneath it lie
Two large birds on their side.

Oh no, they're song thrushes
Amid feathers, grey down.
Their eyes are dry, their claws
Are spread and stuck out. Frown.

What killed you, song thrushes?
A sparrowhawk? Fox springs?
A tiding of magpies?
What stopped your piped tidings?

I dig a hole and lift
You on my spade, drop you
In the earth so you lie
Side by side as you flew.

I listen to birdsong
Near the branch you sang on,
But your clear piping, one-
Two-three-four, trill, has gone.

One day I will be found
Lying still near this lawn
And my clear piping call
Will no more trill each dawn.
1 April, 7 May 2012; 28 February 2015

Skull

A many-coloured skull,
Painted red, green and blue.
Vacuous and vapid,
And overpriced? Not true.

We pretty up ourselves
Although we are but skulls.
The celebrity life
Ignores death's frequent culls.

The artist is saying
Our way of life's a fraud.
We paint our skulls' faces
And ignore Death's sharp sword.
5 April 2012; 28 February 2015

Damien Hirst's exhibition at the Tate Modern, which opened on 4 April 2012, included a skull daubed with paint.

Gulls

Green cliffs with chalk-white walls,
The sea's not far away.
We drive to a seafront hotel,
Drink tea and watch the spray.

And I gaze at the pier
As the green waves roll in
And at the hindward-hovering gulls
That rest on wind. We grin.

Then I think of the time
We walked the promenade

Before our stiffening limbs consigned
Us to this window, barred.
27 April 2012; 1 March 2015

Tea was in the window of the Langham Hotel, Eastbourne, which overlooked
the sea, the pier and Beachy Head, on 26 April 2012.

Smile

Snow on the upper crags,
Across the valley slate
And Snowdon's browny peak.
Peek at the pass, oh wait.

The mountains rise and plunge,
Sheep cling round plunging stones.
The valley sides smile green
And I smile through my bones.
6 May 2012; 1 March 2015

Sun and Snow

The river Dee glints sun
And froths the five-arched bridge.
Sheep graze on sloping hills
Beyond the distant ridge.

By ivied walls the frown
Of a black horizon.
I wince as a text pings:
"It's snowing on Snowdon."
6 May 2012; 1 March 2015

Written outside the Grouse Inn at Carrog, Wales.

Time 1

Time is like a cottage
Its frothing river flicked,
Whose roof has fallen in
And is now derelict.
6 May 2012

Time 2

A priory, then a manor house;
A thirteenth-century dining-room.
I sit near the log-fire in peace.
Here Time is boss as in a tomb.

But out in the walled garden, by
A Tudor sundial much wind-blown
And gouged yet still intact, I know
Time's blocked by monuments of stone.
7 May 2012; 1 March 2015

Written after afternoon tea at Madeley Court Hotel, Shropshire.

Smiling Buttercups

A lawn of buttercups,
A meadow in the sun.
Each yellow flower smiles
And basks in the warm One.

But now the gardener
Is back from holiday.
He mows through the meadow,
Trailing neat lines each way.

And now there's a green lawn
And upside-down stalks where
A thousand buttercups
Smiled out in sunny air.
6 June 2012

Wind: Change

Winds beat my window, in the chimney roar.
White surf froths round the rocks outside, waves leap
Round the dark cliff where, rain-lashed, grey gulls soar,
Hover and plummet, peering at the deep.
Spray blows inland like smoke, the sea waps and
Dances in harbour walls and to the force
That flings surf to cavort with Gull Island.
All is in flux, a changing, thrusting source.
Wind, sea and tide obey a hidden law
And somewhere in their energetic fume
Is a calm stillness, silent Nothing's store,
From which this battering, dashing, flung spume
Emerged to dynamic movement and still
Rules all this gusting with a changeless will.
7, 10 June 2012

Buddleia: From Nothing to Form

Spring. The gardener cuts back
The buddleia to its stumps.
Alas, for butterflies
Can't feed on low-down clumps.

Summer. From living shoots
Mauve flowers wave in the breeze.
Hooray, for butterflies

Can sip nectar at ease.

From nothing – lumpy stumps –
A force has burst to form,
Creation's miracle,
From rain and sun and storm.
7 August 2012; 14 December 2015

Olympian

He crosses the line with arms raised,
Wins the gold medal and a bouquet –
Applewood, rosewood, mint – and smiles
At what his performance can say:

Six hours a day, six days a week
In cold and fog, in wind and rain,
An amateur's will to succeed,
Training through dawns and gruelling pain.

I too have toiled seven days a week
And like an Olympian have strived
To push myself to higher things
So I can smile at what has thrived.
7 August 2012; 15 December 2015

Sea, Sky: Whole View

On television the pitch is huge,
How close the players' warm-up stint.
But in the stadium, how small
The pitch and distant all the men who sprint.

I sit before the choppy waves

And take in where the sea meets sky,
And am content with a whole view
That distances each headland and gull's cry.

7 August 2012; 15 December 2015

Mist over the Sea

A mist over the sea,
Rain slants at my window.
White surf foams towards shore,
All's murk and mist like snow.

17 August 2012

Downpour

I stare at the grey sea
Beneath my open sash
And see it showered with sun
And smile and jump and splash.

And now the still sea sulks
Like a stretch of grey sand.
Now it winks and twinkles
With blobs of rain. On land,

I screw my eyes and thrill
At sea dancing with light
That pours in a downpour
And splashes, dazzling, bright.

22 August 2012; 1 March 2015

Storm II

Wind roaring in the chimney,
Rain lashing on the panes.
Spray drifting in like blown smoke.
Waves and troughs surge, tide strains.

A storm's blanketed this port
Under a misty cloud.
And where, o where's the sun gone?
The sky is like a shroud.
24 August 2012

Squirrel

Squirrel, go away.
Don't eat the birds' seed.
Go away, go away.
Let the nice birds feed.

Squirrel, go away,
Don't you glare at me.
Go away, go away.
Let the nice birds be.
22 September 2012

Squirrel's Reply

Human, I need the seed
To bury now winds blow
So I can dig it up
And feed during the snow.

Grumpy, leave me alone.

Please do not shout at me.
Don't clap your hands and shoo.
Be quiet and let me be.
26 September 2012

Drowned

The rains have drowned green Lincolnshire,
The rivers have burst their banks,
Lush pastures pant beneath dark lakes
And still it rains as the train clacks and clanks.

As the train thunders through this waste
Bearing folk who've not gazed
Out of the steamed windows, I feel
For the green land that's yearning to be grazed.
23 December 2012; 3 March 2015

At Beverley Minster

I join four hundred 'pilgrims' on a train
Chartered for a carol concert at one
Of the four medieval pilgrimage
Shrines, Beverley minster, whose stone towers stun.
Today the pilgrims are tourists, they play
Cards on the train and take part in a quiz.
Their light-hearted banter recalls the tales
Chaucer's pilgrims told, words brimming like fizz.

I sit in the nave and identify
Early English and Decorated styles,   10
And Perpendicular, squint at seventy
Stone carvings holding above the North aisle's
Pillars lutes, bagpipes, horns and tambourines.

Some hold instruments that are now unknown.
I sense the oneness of the styled marble
Amid the harmony of towering stone.

The choir sings medieval anthems, I
Muse on kings and barons, castles and knights,
Ploughing, reaping, painted halls and chambers,
Coats of arms, feasts, hunting and falcons' flights,   20
Tournaments, Black Death, armour and gardens,
Roses, merrymaking, monks of that time.
The congregation sings carols, the packed
Minster has come to life as voices climb.

I go down to the high altar and find
The Percy canopy that Hotspur knew,
Elaborately decorated in stone,
And carved misericords in choir-stalls, view
The thirteenth-century stained glass in the east
Window in the retrochoir where in awe   30
Pilgrims have knelt for a millennium.
I sense a history that's borne peace and war.

I climb the winding stair up to the roof,
Watch the treadwheel raise a round boss, in dread
Look down a hundred feet at the altar.
Through this hole long oak trusses were hoisted
To build the roof of sloping great timbers.
I walk through to a dingy space and see
A clear-glass rose-window and, dazzled, peer
Down at the world, the town of Beverley.   40

I climb perpendicular steps and walk
Along the gantry, cross the minster, frown
And leave eternity. A winding stair
Leads back to time. Now I walk through the town
To where, under awnings in drizzle, lurks

The market which has no Christmassy stalls.
I walk back to the train and the 'pilgrims'
Resume their cards and boisterous, raucous calls.

The pilgrims' quiz-master, in red nightcap
And twinkling bobble, swigs from his hip-flask   50
And calls the answers to the quiz he set.
Dinner is served. I sip red wine and bask.
We four hundred have begun to grow old
And I bow to all who so gamely climb
The winding stair to new knowledge and look
With angels' eyes down on the world of time.

Among those growing old are many who
Are content to pass time with quizzes, cards.
A few still seek new insight on the past,
The universe and their lives as life guards.   60
Wisdom is where one can survey the earth
From a great height and with perspective's glow –
If one consents to climb the winding stair –
Bask in truth by a dazzling rose-window.
24 December 2012

Nicholas Hagger visited Beverley Minster in East Riding, Yorkshire, on 22 December 2012. The spiral staircase was built c.1220.

Marble

See the marble-scraper
Press marble flecks and scour
And polish on a wheel
To make a perfect flower

With delicate petals
On the side of a cup

That will not scratch, will last
For two aeons and up.

So a poet presses
His words onto a bowl
And polishes each line
To outlast every soul.
27 February 2013

Pirates: Question Mark

Black-out and razor wire
Round low points of our ship.
We steam through pirate seas.
In dark I bite my lip.

I sit on the rear deck.
The wake eddies and goes.
A question mark of stars:
Will pirates, when I doze…?

Night on the Arabian Sea.
I watch like a look-out,
Sure that no pirate will
Clamber aboard and shout,

And storm the captain's bridge,
Nonchalant as a prank,
Point a musket at us
And make us walk the plank.
8 March 2013

Looking Down: Not Bestriding

I look down from my plane:
Two ringed palm trees in sea.
Dubai's development
From a *quasi*-colony.

I look again: round black
Discs in the Saudi sand.
Oil once ours Churchill sold
For a million Yanks to land.

I look once more to find
Larnaca's killing street
Where Colonel Grivas forced
British troops to retreat.

I look down one more time:
The Izmir-to-Troy road.
I look for where the Greeks
Held firm and so bestrode.
13 March 2013

7. Churchill signed away British oil interests in Saudi Arabia to Roosevelt to
bring 1 million American troops into the war.

The Seven Hills of Loughton

Like Rome, Loughton is built on seven hills
And has its own Quirinal, Esquiline,
Capitoline, Viminal and Caelian
Districts, and Aventine and Palatine,

In each of which at first small settlements
Were bonded into one community

And covered with houses. But the seven hills
Of my new Rome stand out for all to see.
3 April 2013

Savage

I am an undiscovered region in
A remote continent's jungle, musing
I live like a loin-clothed savage, unseen
By overflying prying eyes filming.

I live as unknown as a primitive
Native who worships the sun with tribal pomp.
My hieroglyphs will be a mystery
If Europeans penetrate this swamp.

But I am happy scratching on my own,
Recording my tribe as they walk through trees
And contacting the woodland numinous
Civilised men recoil from like disease.
3 April 2013

Sun

I flew to the One, following the flight
Of Plotinus, yet I did not really soar.
I opened up my soul behind closed eyes
And basked in its white rays that fill each pore.

But, in harmony, I also sunbathed
And soaked in the rays of the summer sun.
Like Icarus, who flew too near its warmth,
I spent too long in its heat and was undone.

I loved the sun too much (the physical
Copy of the invisible white Light)
And had three carcinomas cut from my back
And now must sit in shade and avoid what's bright.

I was too long in the sun that scorches wings
But I can still bask in the One's white rays.
I am still in harmony with Nature
And still warm to the sun's blaze as I gaze.
Idea: 2 May 2013. Written: 15 December 2015

Taking Wing

A still, calm silver sea.
A panting of a wave,
A clear sky in the dusk.
My thoughts are of my grave.

Endings: evenings, old age.
I must take wing and fly
Like a gull back to roost
Within the headland's sky.
25 May 2013

One's Reflection

Smiling, gentle waves
On the sand that lulls,
Rocks in bladderwrack,
Flocks of screaming gulls.

Children in the pool,
A moored yacht nearby
Reflects in the still

That reflects the sky.
7 August 2013

Unaware

The sea's a-sparkle,
A thousand splashes bright,
A girl with surfboard
Amid the sparkling light.

On harbour walls squat
People, unaware they
Are in light shower
That splashes round their day.
8 August 2013

Moonlight

Moonlight on the water,
Half-moon in sky, on quay,
And white surf waves come thundering in
And all is sky and sea.

Moonlight behind squint eyes,
Full moon in my night sky
And all is calm within the din
And in each breathless sigh.
23 October 2013

Rain Hisses

Rain hisses on my panes,
A boisterous storm at sea.

A wild wind whistles round
As if it's after me.

Wind rattles at the glass,
It blows, abates, then roars
And lashes on my panes
And rattles all my doors.
18 December 2013

Sea Bird

The rain streams down my panes,
A lashing sea-thrust rain.
It blows in stormy gusts
And moans and howls its pain.

A sea bird on the wind
Sweeps down on surf and soars,
A white fish in its beak,
Pleased squalls have filled its jaws.
18 December 2013; 1 March 2015

The Old in the Cold

Who will feed me with crumbs
Like a robin in snow
Perched in a patched-roofed bird table,
Waiting in wintry woe?

How will I eat and keep
Warm under my patched roof
Where I shelter from snow and wait
For my next meal, aloof?
24 December 2013; 3 March 2015

Ruby

We found you a ruby
In an antique gold ring
To mark your engagement,
In a much-loved diamond setting,

In a little shop near
Gloucester Road's underground,
Late Victorian, now hard
To tug over your finger's round.

I have had it widened
With five pieces of gold
For our ruby wedding.
Here's one more ruby ring to hold.

A ruby when we sailed
You can now wear again,
And now one more ruby
As we have crossed the tossing Main.

We all get worn and frayed
But love has a constant range
Like north on a compass.
Between rubies there is no change.

2 March 2014; 7 March 2015

Discovery of Inflation: At One with the First Cause

Remote on our earth, on just one of five
Hundred billion stars in our Milky Way,
One of five hundred billion galaxies,
South Pole observers have confirmed infla-

-tion: photons pulled and squeezed by peaks and troughs
Of gravity waves in the vacuum
Of the cosmos aligned packets of light
In certain directions, creation's thrum.

A change in light's polarisation caused
By gravitational waves from the first
Hundred million billion billion billionth
Of a second after the Big Bang burst.

The echoes of creation pulse and hiss
Order, the fingerprint of God the mage,
From 10 divided by 35 noughts
Seconds into the universe's age.

In mind at the South Pole I am at one
With the first second of creation, see
"The 5 sigma at point 2" that confirms
The Big Bang and inflation and takes me

To the first moment when the universe
Was just an atom and went whoosh in size
To a ping-pong ball in a split second
(A moment I've just seen behind my eyes),

Then ninety-three billion light-years across
Containing half a trillion galaxies
And as many stars as the grains of sand
That can be found on all the earth's beaches.

Ripples in space-time from the first second
Fourteen billion years back have spread as laws
Through the universe and into my eyes –
So I can be at one with the first cause.
18 March 2014; 5–7 March 2015

In March 2014 researchers at the South Pole observatory confirmed the existence of inflation from the evidence of packets of light, which behaved in ways that they would not have behaved had they crossed space. Lines 6 and 10 assume the existence of the gravitational waves Einstein predicted in 1915 though their discovery was not announced until February 2016.

Spring

Spring has sprung out today,
Called "Bo" to make me jump.
Blossom and daffodils
Startle in gold sunshine and bump.

Spring sprang out suddenly
After its winter sleep,
Surprised us with her dress
Of daffodils and grazing sheep.
23 March 2014; 2 March 2015

Fading

I walked up to the gate.
The daffodils looked down,
Their heads looked at the ground,
Were burdened with a frown.

And the cherry blossom
Shed petals like snowflakes.
Don't fall off yet, blossom.
We like white the wind shakes.

O daffodils, blossom,
I know it's hard to bloom
But lift your heads and smile,

Don't wilt and fade in gloom.
30 March 2014; 2 March 2015

White Hawthorn Blossom

The daffodils bask in the April sun,
White puffs of cloud drift in the azure light,
The grass is green and buds are flecked with spring,
And o the hawthorn blossom is snow-white.

Near where two rabbits lollop by the hedge
A dozen bushes are decked out in may.
In sweltering sunshine their heady white
Calls me to leave my work and seize the day.
1 April 2014; 3 March 2015

8. 'Seize the day', *'carpe diem'*, Horace's *Odes* (1.11), 23BC.

The Wind's Whistling

The wind's whistling tonight,
Above the rolling waves.
The wind's strident tonight
And urgent as it raves.

The wind rises to screech
And indignantly jeers,
And there is a tumult
That moves the sea to tears.
7 April 2014

Discord: Humans who Drop

Below my window by the rolling waves
A car reverses, picnic is displayed.
Two children sit beneath the open boot
And eat sandwiches, kick off shoes in rain.

Crusts of bread strew the pristine tarmac slope
That I paid for so residents can turn.
They gather up their shoes and shake out crumbs.
Four children inside, the car noses out.

Two herring-gulls peck at the crusts of bread,
Scornfully dip yellow beaks, spear up crumbs.
Cleaned up, the tarmac gleams pristine in rain.
The gulls look out for new humans who drop.
13 April 2014

The Mild Wind's Blow

I sit in the garden,
Rooks cawing from treetops.
As I sip milkless tea
Trundling time brakes and stops.

I'll soon be seventy-five
And soon begin to know
A different stopping peace
But now – the mild wind's blow.
17–18 April 2014; 3 March 2015

Written in the grounds of Le Manoir aux Quat'Saisons.

A Blackbird's Clear Piping

I sit in the walled garden
Under a cloudless sky
In early morning sun,
Watch a buzzard drift by.

All round my head birdsong,
The rooks' distant cawing,
And arched apple blossom
And a blackbird's clear piping.
18 April 2014

A Family Like Vases

I sit by Tudor stables in the sun,
Sip coffee with my family, home-made.
Nine of us laugh at youthful memories,
Then lunch in a courtyard round a sunshade.

I hear a great-nephew's diabetic.
That's three – what gene in our mother's side's blood
Has come out in this poor eight-year-old boy?
I shake my head and pull a face and thud.

Our contact is over, our memories
Of our old childhood home that unite us   10
And brought us from four counties to sit here
And find common ground in what we discuss.

I wander round the eighteenth-century house.
The dressing-room walls show a family
Of Etruscan vases Adam designed,
All similar but different, like each tree.

We are like vases, all individuals
Though similar in style and in a set.
A few have loops that vary from the rest
And mark us with a diabetic threat.   20

O Etruscan vases, why have you marked
Out three of us with loops and lifelong strife?
Why does your beautiful Roman design
Contain kinks which will damage some for life?
4 July 2014; 4 March 2015

Written following a family meeting at Osterley Park, Middlesex.
11. Four counties: Bedfordshire, Essex, Kent and Surrey.

Song Thrush

One – two – three – four sings the song thrush
From the oak by the field.
One – two – three – four, or was it five
Churs the tuneful master-singer pipes, to which I yield.

Clear piping, then chi-chur, chi-chur.
All's metric in June sun.
The shadows lengthen, no birds sing
Save for the thrilling trilling of the song, still not done.

Dusk, the song thrush's song is stilled,
Bats flit above the lawn.
But in my head I can still hear
The measured piping and refrain that's left me forlorn.
15 July, 16 December 2014

Mouse

I turn on the loft light.
The trap. A mouse twitches, lies still.
It's huge, has a long tail.
Is it a rat? I fill

My dustpan with its shudders
And carry it out to the fence,
Tip it into the forest
To die in a bush that's dense.

O mouse, you ate the cheese
From several traps and left your shout,
Your droppings, in my loft
But then your luck ran out.
1 October 2014; 3 March 2015

Time, in Tiers

The sea gently curls foam in four surfed tiers.
I watch, hypnotised by each surging dune,
And think how time curls in its quartered years
And see decades wash in to a lagoon.

My life's days gently surge towards their end,
Each day, week, month surfs in with calm progress
And foams and froths into a standing pool
And I glimpse beyond time my timelessness.
27 October 2014; 3 March 2015

Parakeets

Two green parakeets hang on the feeder

Outside my window. I approach, they see
And fly off, a fluttering of bright green,
And sit in the oak leaves, assessing me.

Now they return, emboldened, and peck at
A block of feed, and twist and turn and clown,
But when I look they catch my eye and flee.
They only feel safe when my eyes are down.

And now they've gone, but I know they'll be back
When they feel hungry, knowing food is there.
They feel secure in my garden for they
Feel looked after although fearing my stare.
?7 November, 16 December 2014

Poppies

The poppy fields are red as blood
But bear addictive opium seeds,
So are set on fire by soldiers
In Afghanistan as bad weeds.

Yet poppies round the London Tower
For brave soldiers of the Great War,
One for each who laid down his life,
Are good, and leave all feeling raw.

O poppy, both evil and good,
Your blood-splashed petals bear beauties,
Your black seeds scowl uglinesses.
You blend the soul's two contraries.
19–20 November, 16 December 2014

Green Woodpecker

The green woodpecker's pecking in the grass.
His red head moves in rhythm as he pecks.
He raises his long pointed beak, then down
He drills in the autumn grass, and then checks.

What is he looking for? A worm? A grub?
Has each thrust found a mouthful? I compare
His ceaseless pecking to an optimist
Who's always looking, to see what is there.
November, 16 December 2014

Brilliant Stars, Snapped Gravity

A night of brilliant stars.
I walk to the harbour wall
And peer at a thousand lights,
See the Plough curl and fall.

Cassiopeia has gone,
Its W's broken free.
I see Orion's belt
And the twins of Gemini.

I sit on the wall and gaze
Up the tree the stars hang on,
And flit! a shooting star
From right to left, now gone.

And flit, another flares,
Trails and's gone like a gust.
A Geminid meteor
Shower, burning comet's dust.

And now I feel giddy
From peering with craned neck.
I feel gravity wobble
As on a small sloop's deck.

I feel gravity snap
And I plunge headlong, face
Up into a crowd of stars,
Hurtle out into space.

Gravity loosens its hold
On my ankles and my doom.
I turn and stride back home
And shelter in my room.

Out there vast galaxies.
I bend at my desk and sigh.
My roof will keep me safe
From falling up into the sky.
15–16 December 2014

The experience Nicholas Hagger describes happened on Charlestown's harbour
wall on 13 December 2014.

Founder's Song

Onward, ever onward,
Aspiring to each height,
No dark can hold us back
As we stride into light.

We work hard and play hard
And polish our talent,
Buff up skills and burnish,
Shine out each achievement.

We seek out what is new,
We delve and find the truth,
We think things out and choose.
Our reward's composed youth.

Body, mind, soul, spirit
One as we strive and share,
Following our founder
And in our founder's care.
16 December 2014

Blue Tit Chirping

Good-o, there are nuts
In the feeder today.
Let's skip through the air
And peck in the tray.

Good-o, there are nuts,
We'll soon be well-fed.
It's wintry out there
But we're contented.
10 February, 19 March 2015

Hooting Owl

Half past ten and an owl's hooting.
It's in the copse beyond our fence.
Who-hoo-who-hoo, it hoots and hunts,
Familiar sound in dark that's dense.

Once its hoot meant impending death.
It hunts from the copse for mice and voles.
Who-hoo-who-hoo, the hooting owl

Reassures me, petrifies moles.
8 March 2015

The owl was a tawny owl.

Daffodils, Sunlight

The daffodils poke through
The black iron railings,
Bending to the sunlight
From their bank's shade which clings.

All along the railings
Daffodils' heads poke out
Seeking for the sunlight
That will nourish their sprout.

And here under this tree
Twelve stunted daffodils
Whose bowls have not opened,
Stuck in a gloom that stills.
3 April 2015

Full Moon

Full moon above the harbour,
Pale stars, the waves adance,
A wide shimmering causeway
Across the sea to France.

I wander through the moonlight,
Stand on the harbour wall,
And now the causeway's missing.
It's behind Gull Rock's sprawl.

I look out at the black sea
And at the full moon's eye
That watches human follies,
An incredulous spy.
3–4 April 2015

Sheep

Through my bedroom window
A dozen sheep, heads down,
Crop the grass on the hill
Heedless of the sea's frown.

In my bedroom window
I rhyme my words, head down,
And crop my written lines
Heedless of the sea's frown.

The wrinkled waves resound
As they beat to the shore
But the sheep crop their grass
And I my rhythmic score.

O sheep, with backs to sea,
Heedless of drowning waves,
You and I are at one
With harmonies and graves.
5–6 April 2015

Horses

I gaze across the hedge
At my neighbour's meadow.
A dozen horses crop

The grass in late sun's glow.

O horses, so distant
Who feed in the fresh air,
You have all that you need,
For you there's no despair.
5–6 April 2015

Dancing Light

Easter and bright sunshine
And on each curling wave
Splashes of dancing light
The sea mirrors in rave.

The sea smiles and dances
For joy in the bright light
And flashes a message
To human souls: be bright.
6 April 2015

Rainbow

When I am gone
You'll find me in a wood far from the crowd
As I appear and shine with sunlight smile
And then fade behind cloud.

When I am gone
You'll find me in the rainbow in the sky
As I appear and catch your attention
And then fade with a sigh.
7 April 2015

Blackbird

The light is fading and head down
I set out words on paper, 'sing'.
A breeze wafts through my pushed window.
I stop, for a blackbird's piping.

It sings so cheerfully nearby,
Somewhere in the twilit oak's bark
And then stops in mid-trill. Silence.
My dusk fades into early dark.
16 May 2015

Ridging Waves

The white crests rise with ridging waves
And fade as their waves dip.
My cabin window climbs to sky
And drops to troughs as ridges slip.

The rising, falling waves are in
An endless excitement
And my ship rocks and rolls and dips
Unbowed by foam's endless dissent.
26 May 2015

Blushing Sky

The round orange sun sinks
Beneath the darkening sea.
It glows an orange fire
And streaks the sky with glee.

And now the sun's rim drops,

The wrinkled waves dark-clad,
A twilit gull flies off,
The blushing sky is sad.
26 May 2015

Helsingor

Now Helsingor Castle looms up
Where Hamlet's father stalked
Along towers and battlements.
I gaze where Hamlet walked.

Did Shakespeare know this remote place
Or write it from hearsay?
I sit above the tossing waves
Lost in another day.

A cormorant flaps past below.
Are you Prince Hamlet's soul?
My heart is in the green turrets
On the now square-walled mole.
27 May 2015

Crown Prince's Palace

I stand by the palace.
A flag and sentries show
The Crown Prince of Denmark's
In residence. All know.

The Hamlet of our times,
Does he peep down and see
The tours' size and measure
His popularity?

27 May 2015

Vikings

A cold dark Viking sea,
This is where my forebears
Set sail for North Europe
To settle free from cares.

They all missed their lord's hearth
And sailed for "Land ahoy!",
Dreaming of green pastures
We descendants enjoy.

If they all had to loot,
Pillage, plunder and burn
To bed in their presence,
Then that's not our concern.

28 May 2015

Ghost

In the cruise lounge two violinists play,
Bowing faster and faster with great glee,
Then one scherzos into purest birdsong
And I'm aware you're sitting next to me.

You're smiling in approval that at last
I'm applauding what your violin has done,
The instrument you played, taught and lived by,
Which I did not follow, though your first son.

Now in the cabin my wife's foot spray smells
Of the oil you rubbed on my infant brow

And chest, singing with me "Camphor-camphor-
Camphorated" as I hear you sing now.
7 June 2015

At the Van Gogh Museum: Obscurity

I enter the Van Gogh Museum and walk
Past several self-portraits – he was too poor
To afford models, so he used himself –
And peasants and farm scenes he held in awe,
Japanese paintings, then, after Gauguin
And he quarrelled and he cut off his ear,
The asylum garden and near the end
Wheatfield with crows, death's thunderclouds are near.

I pause at one of eight hundred letters
He wrote to his younger brother Theo,   10
Who for the last ten years of Vincent's life
Sent money in return for paintings though
He did not like, and so did not sell, them.
Vincent shot himself at thirty-seven. After
Six months Theo died, and his wife had him
Exhumed and buried next to his brother.

Theo's wife Jo had eight hundred paintings,
All unframed – on backs of canvases, some.
She paid to have them framed and, her husband
Having kept Vincent out of their income,   20
She sent his works to the exhibitions
And encouraged her son to demand – begging –
A gallery to house his uncle's work.
And so this museum came into being.

I recall the artist Gwen Broad, who came
To my christening as a world war loomed. She

102

Came here just after this museum opened
And was deeply impressed and wrote to me:
"This genius – often in mental care –
Died poor, not recognised, without a friend.   30
Now there's a gallery." She was urging,
'Stick at it, art can come good in the end.'

I see her words as an appeal to me
To keep writing despite obscurity.
I glimpse myself in Van Gogh's long struggle.
I too keep going as a solitary
And am in contact with the One, a power
And energy that comes in like a dream,
I too have self-portraits and recognise
His lonely dedication to his theme.   40

In ten years Van Gogh produced nearly nine
Hundred paintings and eleven hundred drawings.
I have amassed some two thousand poems
And twelve hundred short stories like paintings.
Like him, I'm driven by an energy
That's from the One and shows the One to be
In images in obscure books that may
Too grace a museum I will never see.
7, 11 June 2015

38. 'Come in like a dream.' Van Gogh wrote in Arles in 1888 (*The Letters of Van Gogh*, 687/4:284): "The painting comes to me as if in a dream."

Long-legged Fly

Save your energy, long-
Legged fly dancing low,
Then up my window-pane
With endless to and fro.

103

Stop all your exploring.
You can't get in, so cease.
It's best to fold your wings,
Be still and sense the peace.

I too dance to and fro,
Too little still, don't rest
As I perform my tasks
And dance while on my quest.

26 June 2015

House Martins Darting

A hot day and a flock
Are hurtling to and fro,
Swooping up to the sky,
Flying past my window,

Joyfully twittering "Hi,
We're back from overseas.
We're here in your garden.
We love your lawns and trees."

Forked tails in a big V,
They swoop and dip and veer,
Close in and break apart,
White undersides – come here!

I sit outside, they dart
To and fro round my head
And swoop from every side
To say, "Glad you aren't dead."

They wheel by me, missing
By inches, from north, south,

East, west and as I duck
Whizz past my nose and mouth.
29 June 2015

House Martins and Carnival

The village carnival.
Beauty queens, dressed-up style.
Twelve dancing old ladies.
Cars pull floats, watchers smile.

And in the harbour, see
The house martins swooping,
Loving the atmosphere,
Flitting, hurtling, darting.
30 July 2015

Storm, Surge

A roaring wind, blown spume,
A mist of spray like smoke.
My spattered window-panes
Rattle as lashes soak.

The wind gusts round the house,
Surf tiers tear in on sand.
All Nature's an urgent
Surge from boiled sea to land.
5 August 2015

Force

High tide, the rippling waves

Shimmer with flecks of light
In the dazzling sunshine.
Each crest flashes out white.

I see the energy
In green waves dance, disperse
And sense a tidal force
Surge through the universe.
7 August 2015

Shooting Star

A late-night walk by sea.
The dog days, specks of light.
Sit on the harbour wall,
Gaze up at starry night.

A pale bird flits and's gone
Into the star-ripe tree.
It was a shooting star.
Will fruit crash down on me?
7 August 2015

Meteorite

A Perseid shower tonight.
I sit in my garden and gaze
Beneath Cassiopeia
For a meteorite's blaze.

Then whoosh! a bright rocket
Trails sparks across the sky,
Then burns out in the dark –
But not in my inner eye.

12 August 2015

Heron

The heron's in the tree
Waiting to spear our fish.
Go away, heron, go.
Our carp are *not* your dish.

The heron rises up,
Reluctantly beats wings;
Long neck and beak pass by
With insolent flappings.

18 August 2015

Spider

A spider's spun a web
From my open casement.
It's bulbous, I shudder
At its poisonous scent.

I shut the window fast
And lock it with a key.
O spider, you're outside,
You cannot poison me.

21 August 2015

Bat

An orange, yellow, green and blue sunset.
The fields and trees are quietening to sleep.
A bat flits and darts through the evening net.

The light has nearly gone and I can see
The dark silhouettes of the slumbering trees
But still the bat darts to and fro in glee.
21 August 2015

Moth

A moth on my window.
I try to let it out.
It flies up to a light
And flits about, about.

O moth, you dance to light
As I do in my way.
You are welcome to share
My room this fading day.
21 August 2015

Stag

O stag with great antlers,
You've munched most of our pinks
And the low green apples
Above where the dew winks.

And on the lawns and paths
Droppings from your six does
As they roamed our garden
For heather and each rose.

I saw you towards dawn,
Antlers in beam-crossed light,
Now in mind disembowel –
Gralloch – you for last night.

24 August, 19 September 2015

Carp, Goldfish

Don't be so greedy, carp.
You've got your green fish food.
The red's for the goldfish.
They gulp air, don't be rude.

Don't gobble down the red
Pellets the goldfish miss,
Don't push aside goldfish.
Carp, be polite, don't diss.
2 September 2015

8. 'Diss', street word for 'disrespect'.

Box-Leaf Caterpillars

Hungry caterpillars
In our crenellated
Box hedge that was once green.
Most's now withered and dead.

Box-leaf caterpillars,
A well-camouflaged green,
Only feed on box leaves.
The hedge is best not seen.

How wonderful Nature
Allocates territory
To each different species
So food goes round amply.

10

Thousands of round green eggs
On leaves within the hedge,
New-hatched caterpillars
Will munch towards the edge.

I love all living things,
Eggs, caterpillars, moths,
And also fresh box leaves –
And probe for green egg-froths,   20

From stems pick a hundred
Still caterpillars, lulled.
Nature's good in balance.
Infestings must be culled.

I pick caterpillars
Off leaf-clumps as they chew,
Then spray from underneath
So new box shoots push through.
2 September 2015

20. 'Froth', 'a collection of small bubbles in liquid' (*Concise Oxford Dictionary*),
i.e. the eggs are like small bubbles.

Red Moon

In the pre-dawn night sky
The moon has turned blood-red,
Huge at its perigee,
Eclipsed by earth with dread.

Ancients thought a blood moon
Heralded the world's end,
An evil omen whose
Blood foretold doom. My friend,

As it's closest to earth
It's a sixth bigger, it   10
Is a third brighter now –
There's no need to be frit.

The blood-red supermoon
Scattered with earth's sunlight
Won't happen again till
I'm ninety-four. Night night.
27–28 September 2015

The blood-red supermoon was visible between 3 and 4.30am on 28 September 2015.
3. 'Perigee', 'the point in a celestial body's orbit where it is nearest the earth'.
12. 'Frit', Yorkshire dialect for 'frightened'.

Blue Tit

A tiny blue tit pecks
On nuts by my window
And peers its thanks at me
From tonsured head aglow.

Oh no, my blue tit lies
On its back with claws up.
Did a sparrowhawk swoop,
Dash you like a buttercup?

O blue tit, what happened?
You lie and look so bleak.
You flew at a window.
Look, there's blood on your beak.

I love the peeking birds
And feel sad at their end.

O life, that gives and takes,
Your opposites offend.

1 October 2015

Snowfields

I glide above snowfields,
A bleak landscape of ice
With hills, an Antarctic
That's pure as paradise.

A wilderness of cloud,
Uninhabited waste.
As I fly through my mind
I bask in snow, wind-chased.

4, 27 October 2015

'Snowfield', 'a permanent wide expanse of snow in mountainous or polar regions'. (*Concise Oxford Dictionary*.) The snowfields are cloud seen from a plane.

Bay in Sun

Phaleron sea in sun:
The sweep of the great bay,
Across the satin swell
Attica falls away

And I lurch back to when
The Persian fleet appeared
And threatened peaceful Greece
With ruin as it neared.

7, 27 October 2015

The Persian fleet appeared in September 480BC.

Planetary Trio

A late-night walk, the wind
Tears hair, sprays me with brine.
Look east, across the sea
Three stars in a curved line:

Venus, Mars, Jupiter
(The brightest of the three)
Cross paths, and will next time
Turn out too late for me?
25, 27 October 2015

The planetary trio – three planets orbiting at different speeds and slowing down at their farthest points from the sun – took place in October 2015. The next time would be in 2021.

Wind Whistles, Force

Wind whistles round the roof and lashes spray,
The angry sea roars surging crests, froths-foams.
The beach beneath my window boils white surf
And wind now spatters rain on huddled homes.

Outside a gusty roaring round my house.
A great force buffets the glass near my skull,
A power that lashes wind and whips up sea
Makes all cower save for one lone wind-blown gull.
26–27 October 2015

Golden Rose

Queue at the bag-drop gate
And scan your boarding card,
Tag your bag with a twist,
Now security guard.

Take the driverless train
Whose doors open and close.
So much automation
But look, a golden rose.

27 October 2015

Scudding Stars

A full moon and moonlight
On windy harbour wall.
And, my shadow beside me,
I gaze where bright stars fall.

White clouds scud to the east,
In between the stars rest –
Oh no, the stars are moving,
They're scudding to the west.

Order has broken down,
Stars zip through clouds and zoom.
I quickly rise and hurry
Back to my secure room.

27 October 2015

In Gerard's *Herball*: Snake's-Head Fritillary

In my library I pick up a fat book,

Gerard's *The Herball or Generall Historie*
Of Plantes, second edition, which appeared
(I read inside) in 1633.
It has an engraved title-page that shows
Bearded Gerard and Dioscorides,
Theophrastus, Ceres and Pomona,
Each named above their heads or below knees.
I used it to identify each plant
In Tudor Otley Hall's grounds that enchant.   10

An article in *Country Life*. The rare
First edition has four unnamed herbalist
Bearded figures on plinths, who Griffiths sees
As Gerard, Dodoens (Flemish botanist),
Lord Burghley and a fourth: Shakespeare. Gerard
Designed gardens at Cecil House and bleak
Theobalds for Burghley, who, it is claimed,
Employed Shakespeare to find Latin and Greek
Snippets on plants and write verse for him, though
He had "small Latin and less Greek" – not so?   20

Lord Burghley, having hastened Mary, Queen
Of Scots' beheading and much-satirised
By writers, fought back by plucking Shakespeare
From obscurity to do what he devised
And asked him to urge Southampton to wed
His own granddaughter Elizabeth – this
Is why Shakespeare addressed seventeen sonnets
To the Earl, and *Venus and Adonis*,
And later wrote *A Midsummer Night's Dream*
When her marriage to Derby made Burghley beam.   30

If the fourth man is Shakespeare, then his true
Likeness at thirty-three has been revealed.
I forget the Cobbe and Chandos portraits
And gaze at his laurelled, bearded head, keeled

Curling moustache and hybrid of *toga*
And *paludamentum* (or cape), to impress
With an immense bow on his left shoulder –
Elizabethan take on Roman dress –
And compare his look and swaggering thrust
With ten-years-on Droeshout face and church bust.   40

Poets were nicknamed from their best-known works,
Shakespeare was 'Adon' to Edwards' insight.
This man's left hand holds maize, corn of the cob –
Adonis being god of corn. His right
Holds snake's-head fritillary, a purple flower
Which grew from Adonis' blood and is billed
In Gerard as the checkered daffodil.
I think of a meadow near Otley filled
With snake's-head fritillaries one week each year.
Links with Adonis hint this is Shakespeare.   50

But there's also the rebus on the plinth:
4E, it seems to say, and below OR,
And underneath W. The 4E
(It's claimed) is *'quatere'*, 'to shake' – there's more
For *'quateor'* is Renaissance spelling
For *'quatior'*, 'I am shaken'; 'or', 'gold',
Hints the gold family coat of arms (it's claimed).
A vertical line hints a sphere, we're told.
The code is 'Shakespeare', W – William.
The rebus hints Shakespeare's a cryptogram.   60

But the rebus may be a printer's mark.
The engraving's "imprinted at London
By John Norton", and 4E can be read
As N and with OR as NOR for Norton
And W as John's uncle William.
A garden's shown like Theobalds' design
In which, it's claimed, the Queen walks with Gerard

Above a Tudor rose and eglantine
(Her emblem). Two gardeners hoe, unaware.
If the Queen was walking, would they not stare?   70

The greatest literary discovery
In four hundred years? Cracked Tudor code and spin?
A copy of *The Herball* has W S
S S WS in a margin
Beside the fourth man in an ancient hand.
Is the fourth man William Shakespeare, or just
Dioscorides, symbol of herbal
Pharmacy, laurelled like Asclepius, trussed
God of medicine, Apollo's son? I peer.
We may never know, all hope it's Shakespeare.   80
28, 31 October, 1 November 2015

Mark Griffiths, writing in *Country Life*, 31 May 2015, claimed that the fourth man in the engraving in the first edition of Gerard's *The Herball or Generall Historie of Plantes* (late 1597 or early 1598) is William Shakespeare and contains an illustration of how he looked at the age of 33. This view was supported by Edward Wilson, the former Garden Master at Worcester College, Oxford (where the Shakespeare scholar Jonathan Bate is Provost). The first edition was for sale at 25 shillings and 7 pence. The second edition appeared in 1633 and had a different engraving.

12. 'Herbalist', 'a dealer in medicinal herbs; a person skilled in herbs, especially an early botanical writer'. (*Oxford Concise Dictionary.*)

20. "Small Latin and less Greek". Ben Jonson's 'Ode to Shakespeare' in the First Folio, 1623.

28. Shakespeare dedicated *Venus and Adonis* to the Earl of Southampton in 1594. The 'god-father' of his 'invention' was, on Griffiths' view, Burghley.

34. 'Keel', botanical, 'a prow-shaped pair of petals in a corolla'. (*Concise Oxford Dictionary.*)

40. The Droeshout portrait appears in the First Folio.

42. Thomas Edwards referred to Shakespeare as 'Adon' in 1594.

45–47. Snake's-head fritillary, see Shakespeare, *Venus and Adonis*, 1168: "A purple flow'r sprung up, check'red with white." The *Fritillaria meleagris*.

48. 'Meadow'. The meadow was at Framsden in Suffolk, and hundreds of purple mottled bells drooped down: 300,000 in all, according to *The Times*. (See Nicholas Hagger, *My Double Life 2: A Rainbow over the Hills*, p.554.)
51. 'Rebus', 'enigmatic representation of a word (especially a name) by pictures, suggesting its parts'; 'heraldry: a device suggesting the name of its bearer'. (*Concise Oxford Dictionary*.)
60. 'Cryptogram', 'a text within a cipher'. (*Concise Oxford Dictionary*.)

Sea Lights

From the windy harbour wall see
The distant pulsing light
Of Eddystone lighthouse,
Six pulses, then a long seventh, watch-out white.

And all along the horizon
A dozen yellow flares
As ships on tossing waves
Send messages they're there and kind bewares.
28–29 October 2015

Mist

A mist behind the tree,
I cannot see the field,
The trees beyond do not exist,
Everything is concealed.

A mist hides my future.
It's not seen, though I stare.
But just as there's a field, and trees,
Is it already there?
1 November 2015

At Connaught House: Weather-vane

I round the bend: the red-brick L-shaped house
With windows where wisteria clusters fall
And climbing rose, and near the porch a palm,
And blue clematis tumbling down a wall.
I look at the gold-numbered annexe block
And lo! above it is the weather-vane.
Above the arrow, winged Pegasus
Heads for heaven with Bellerophon, who'd slain

The fierce chimera that ravaged the land,
The fire-breathing beast with a lion's head,   10
A goat's horns in the middle of its back
And a dragon's behind that inspired dread
And had laid waste Caria, and Lycia,
His kingdom, by taming the winged horse.
He slew the monster and then tried to fly
To heaven, win immortality by force.

I wander to the knot-garden and squeeze
Through lavender and smell its scented stir
And gaze at the central knotted box hedge
And the four arrows of wall germander   20
At each corner, and see the One pour out
Into Nature, civilizations, curb
Sixteen brick beds and mirror Creation
In which the soul's scented like a mauve herb.

Amid the lavender I grasp the gods
Unseated Bellerophon indignantly
As an overreacher cast down and killed
As he aspired to immortality.
He rode with his immortal soul and slew
The chimera, the secular ego   30
That ravaged the land to a wilderness

And, transformed into spirit, shone, aglow.

I wander down steps into the orchard.
Rosy apples hang on each bough in sight:
Each tree full of ripeness, red-green poems.
I now perceive the winged horse's flight
As seeking poetic inspiration.
Bellerophon's soul and pennant, eyes fired,
Flew towards heaven as if towards the moon
To capture a symbol and be inspired.   40

I live among woodpeckers and rabbits,
Where jackdaws pick and herons glide to rest
Near the fish-pool, and among parakeets
That hang from bird-feeders by bills. Their guest,
I watch squirrels frolic and foxes prowl,
Buzzards circle and kestrels soar and stress,
And at twilight bats flit and dip and wheel
As I stand in the lavender, breathless.

By the fishpond where carp laze in the sun
I see Bellerophon as a transformed   50
Self who dominated his King's ego,
His lion's roar, goat-like sensual urge – warmed –
And his dragon's behind that terrifies.
I see him rise and transcend his mind's split,
I see him vanquish all his distractions
And ride to heaven as an unveiled spirit.

I gaze into the pool where the sun shines
From heaven among lilies rooted in mud.
Not here the materialist chimera
That tyrannised the land and sapped the blood.   60
Among fish I float, a yellow lily
In heavenly sun, uniting light and roots,
Both air and water, a bowl of the soul

That's immortal and yet basks among newts.
2, 4, 10–11 November 2015

46. 'Stress', 'subject [verb] to stress'. (*Concise Oxford Dictionary.*)

Leaves Falling 2

The oak leaves have turned golden,
The lawn is strewn with leaves.
I watch as leaves flutter down.
A gust, leaves falling peeves.

The trees behind are russet.
Migrating birds appear,
Fly to and fro and gather.
Leaves falling, autumn's here.
3 November 2015

Leaves Flutter

Leaves flutter yellow from their trees
Like soldiers from bombed towns.
A tribute to our armed forces.
I watch the stares and frowns.

Red holly berries splash like blood
Down seventy prickly years.
A rock singer whispers, giggles.
Widows in black shed tears.

Windfall apples still rot on grass.
Rock singer sings his head,
Then waves and raises thumbs as it's
About him, not the dead.

The meadows' flowers have all withered.
O rock singer, has-been,
If you sang at the Cenotaph
Would you still strut and preen?
10–11 November 2015

Return to Suffolk

A stop for Eggs Benedict at Marks Tey,
Then I am driven to Suffolk, not knowing
My destination, for I am three score
And ten, the allotted span of living
According to the *Bible*, and we're on
A surprise mystery tour for my birthday.
Through narrow lanes we reach Hintlesham Hall
Where we sometimes ate when we were this way.

I greet it like a familiar friend,
Smile at its Tudor chimneys and Georgian   10
Seventeen-twenties *façade*. From our room
I look down at a tree and lawned garden,
Go down for tea outside the oldest wall.
Our children appear with our two grandsons
And five yellow chicks edge between our feet,
Mouths open, starving. We feed them from buns.

And sitting in the ancient drawing-room
I open presents: a fossilised shred
Or slice of a pine-cone, and desert glass
Made by a meteorite that collided   20
With Libyan sand – cold tektite – twenty-seven
Million years ago, beauty burnt from waste.
In the last thirty-five years my inner
Sand's been transformed to glass beauty, now traced.

We dine round a round table and all chat.
We then sip red wine in the library.
A cake is brought through, I blow a candle.
We slice the inscription, 'Happy Birthday'.
Drowsed from the air, we sleep and next morning
We breakfast and then sit in warm sunshine.   30
I learn two chicks died in the night: Nature
Is no respecter of birthdays like mine.

We drive to royal Sutton Hoo and walk
Among the burial mounds and stand before
The ship burial of King Rædwald, Anglo-
Saxon warlord whose power came from an oar.
We dine that night on crab and smoked salmon,
Sip white Sauvignon, and the atmosphere
I bask in is of a peaceful family
That echoes the Georgian Age: family cheer.   40

Next day we walk to the herb garden – see
A barley field nearby – and stand and yarn,
Then leave and drive to leafy Otley Hall
Where it's Open Day, park near my old barn
And wander through grounds I once supervised
To the moated Tudor Hall I restored
And stand again under the ancient beams
That were mine, back in a past I left, awed.

Like disguised Odysseus, I have returned
To my hall unrecognised and in gloom   50
Decline to buy the guidebook that I wrote,
Climb stairs to peep into my old bedroom.
As I walk back through the overgrown grounds
I pass my peacock, and then a grass maze
Based on my first poetic work's cover.
My identity's still here, where I gaze.

I take my leave of Suffolk, more aware
Its open fields and hedges, its sunrise,
Its flatness and its crops around Otley,
Its night silence, windswept trees and large skies   60
Called but could not keep me from my forest.
I've moved back to my boyhood haunts and thrills
But still warm to East Anglia's Tudor halls
Though a poet of Essex woods and hills.
12, 14–15 November 2015

Nicholas Hagger returned to Suffolk from 22 to 24 May 2009 to celebrate his 70th birthday, and revisited Otley Hall.
54. The grass maze was a maze mown in grass that replicated the cover of Nicholas Hagger's *Selected Poems: A Metaphysical's Way of Fire* (1991), which in turn was taken from the floor of Chartres Cathedral.

Birds and Beasts: The Lament of Orpheus

We were together in the One
Till you were taken from me. Spurned
I went down to your Underworld
And led you back. You turned, returned.

And now I charm all birds and beasts
With my lyre and my plaintive song
While you, a shade in your Underworld,
Ponder a choice that's been lifelong.
25 November, 12 December 2015

Snake
(Orpheus to Eurydice and Hades)

I recall an adder under my bin,
And the snakes I caught in a forked stick held in my hand.

I wonder, that snake bite that took you away
To the gods of the Underworld, did they have it planned?

I knew that my music had charmed the gods
And I was allowed down to Hades, wearing black,
And to bring you up to the land of the living,
But I doubted you would follow and looked back,

And, worshipping Apollo, I was torn
To pieces by the Maenads in my crags.
Did the gods snatch you back when I rescued you?
My dismembered head still sings, but surmise nags.

Idea: 25 November. Written: 12, 15 December 2015

Ferris Wheel: Life Cycle

A Ferris wheel with cabins.
I soar a hundred feet.
Below, the Christmas market,
The skating-rink. I greet

The past like rooftops. Behind,
The Park Inn I can't see,
The tower, and church – the future.
Back down to reality.

So I was born and rose to
Manhood and then declined.
Now I sense my life cycle,
Blind to a future behind.

6, 12 December 2015

The Ferris wheel was in the Rotes Rathaus Christmas market near
Alexanderplatz, Berlin, and the ride on it took place on 6 December 2015. It is
shown on the front cover.

Muntjac

A muntjac's standing in the field,
More like a pig than a deer.
It's black and squat and hungry.
Go away, muntjac, you're too near

Our fence, our heathers and roses.
Go off and eat elsewhere.
Don't steal the plants from our garden.
Go away, muntjac, you're too near.
8, 12 December 2015

Stars, Waves

No moon, knees pressing sea wall,
I peer up at the Plough.
I could reach a dozen stars
And shake them from their bough.

The streetlight behind throws my
Giant waist-up shadow down
The dark beach and across waves
Under whose curls I drown.
13–14 December 2015

Rain

Rain lashes on the panes, wind howls.
I walk against the storm
Bent under a tugged umbrella
Towards the waves and warm.

Back home my shoes and trousers dry

On radiators' heat,
And in my dressing-gown I peer
At spume blown up the street.
14 December 2015

Sea Surges

Sea surges in ridges towards the shore,
I count seven rows of foam, white froth between.

My mind surges in ridges to complete
This layered statement that can now be seen

To be the foam of seven disciplines:
Seven ridges with one meaning that is green.

Like sea and mind a poem is just one,
A seven-ridged unity that is serene.
14 December 2015

The seven disciplines are: mysticism, literature, philosophy and science, history, comparative religion, international politics and statecraft, and world culture.

Vein

I am like a leaky garden hose,
A vein sprays blood under my skin
And pools rings of oozing crimson.
My mind takes old age in.

I leak from my worn-out body.
In vain my flesh rules its long reign.
Like a monarch whose kingdom's strained

I take in my breached vein.
14–15 December 2015

Pied Wagtail

I put my head outside the door,
The wind tore through my hair.
A dapper pied wagtail strutted
And dabbed its tail with flare.

The wind whistled and spattered rain,
Gulls hovered and waves boomed.
Oblivious, particoloured,
The wagtail pecked undoomed.

O wagtail, dressed in black and white,
You wear your life and death
But now you live for crumbs within
The moment and each breath.
15 December 2015

'Pied', 'particoloured'. (*Concise Oxford Dictionary*.)

Time like the Sea 1

A brown photo on Tenby beach
Of my long-dead grandfather:
The moment my aunt detects he's
Swollen with throat cancer.

Cancer of the oesophagus,
The lead 'cure' crept past his chin.
I stare at the brown photo and sense
Time like the sea creep in.

31 December 2015

The brown photo was taken in 1925 at the moment Nicholas Hagger's aunt, a nurse, realised that his grandfather had cancer of the oesophagus.

Time like the Sea 2

Thirty-five years on we
Sit in the same room, each
Munching sandwiches, and we hear
The same boom on the beach.

Thirty-five years on it's
The same place, nothing's changed
But during our journey together
Our looks have been rearranged.

Thirty-five years on we
Have prospered round our spines
And have resisted time, which has
Etched our faces with lines.

Rough sea and a backsuck
Of shingle, then a roar.
I breathe in and out like the waves
And hear time ebb and pour.
31 December 2015

The visit to the first-floor lounge at the Royal Victoria Hotel, Hastings took place on 24 July 2009.

Goldfinch

A goldfinch, red-faced, gold

Wing-bar, black and white head.
You come to my feeder
So rarely. Flash your red.

Goldfinch, I watch spellbound
As you peck at the seed.
Sorry we've no thistles,
Enjoy your passing feed.
31 December 2015

Nuthatch

Nuthatch, with rusty breast,
Neckless with pointed bill,
You climb your streamlined grey
Head-first down my nut grille.

I watch your form in awe:
Straight-line from bill to tail,
All grey and rusty buff,
Your sleekness looks so frail.
31 December 2015

House Spider

A giant house spider
With large black legs squats on
My fawn carpet, quite still.
It's unclean, must be gone.

With a mug upside down,
I cover it and slide
Paper beneath and tilt
And carry it outside.

Spider, you've lived your life
Under my desk's redoubt.
Friendly companion, I
Am sad I've put you out.
28 January 2016

The house spider was of the family *Tegenaria gigantea*.

Fox

Two yards from my window
As dark becomes half-light,
A fox stops, turns and looks,
Red-brown; chest, tail-tip white;

Pointed nose and ears, shy.
It seems to sniff the air,
Then heads down to the stream,
Scenting a vole or hare.

Fox, who lives in my field,
Your wolf's glare hunts for prey
Yet is in harmony
With this dark, dawning day.

How can it be hunters
And hunted are in one
Benevolent system
That cares for night and sun?
28 January 2016

Stag, Trapped

A bucking by wire fence.

Through binoculars I peer.
A stag's antlers are trapped.
It bucks and kicks in fear.

O stag, I will free you.
Exhausted, you sit down.
Two fellows arrive, one
Sits on your back. I frown.

With wire-cutters one cuts
Your antlers free and you
Rise up and bound away
To the forest's purlieu.

Through binoculars I see
Curled wire round your great horns.
O stag, don't wolf our plants
By stealth in these March dawns.

O stag, you roam the wilds
And munch, rut and stand tall,
A king of beasts, branched horns
In harmony with all.
19 March 2016

12. 'Purlieu', British history, 'a tract on the border of a forest, especially one earlier included in it and still partly subject to forest laws'. (*Concise Oxford Dictionary.*)

Epistle to King Harold II of Waltham Abbey and Loughton

I stand before the familiar Abbey
Tower and arched door, but think of the third church
You built, healed by the Waltham Holy Cross.
Norman builders brought over well before

The Conquest built the finest English church
Till Westminster Abbey. Our last Anglo-
Saxon King, you ruled pre-Norman England
(And the terrain of Essex and Suffolk,
The Danish Kingdom of East Anglia)
And held four manors round here, including   10
Lochintuna, my Loughton, which you gave,
Our landlord before the Norman Conquest,
To the canons of your Holy Cross church,
And then you fought the Saxons' last battle
Against the Norman troops, who brought Europe's
Civilization to our land. You stood
For Anglo-Saxon cultural purity
(Like Alfred who opposed marauding Danes,
As Arthur had stood for Celtic-Roman,
And Boudicca for Celtic, purity).   20
England has absorbed all its invaders:
Celts, Romans, Anglo-Saxons, Danes, Vikings,
Then Normans. You are buried somewhere here,
Near the altar of your now buried church.

Now I am retired within your manors
Some nine hundred and fifty-five years on,
The European Norman influence
That swamped you is just as strong. We have paid
Half a trillion in tribute to Europe.
I sit and look across the sweep of trees   30
You once knew, and live among woodpeckers,
Jackdaws, parakeets, foxes, rabbits, carp.
I stroll, pinch lavender and smell fingers,
Admire heather I guard against the deer.
I grow satin roses and herbs in jars.
I have founded and run schools and quested
In Eastern cultures and most nation-states
And have written poems about the One.
I have shown Englishness yield to Europe

And I have welcomed European rule   40
In a masque you might think was treasonous.
I see you walking up my upper field
Which LIDAR pictures show has stone circles
Of Anglo-Saxon huts from your reign's time –
When you ruled over the united lands
Of the East Saxons and Angles' 'South Folk'
(East Seaxna and East Engla Kingdoms),
These woodland meadows of ancient Loughton
And the flat fields round Tudor Otley Hall –
And as I walk to welcome you back in   50
Your old manor and your old lands I know
You have now come to support a World State
Comprising all invaders and invaded
That will ban future conquests and bring peace;
And that you now stand for global culture
With local identity and won't fight
To keep Muslim refugees from watering
Down the Christian culture in which you built
Your church of Waltham Holy Cross. I know
You now see the world's peopled with global   60
Citizens who all treasure local sites,
And that you will greet me with great interest
And want to understand my perspective.
Saxon Harold, anti-European
Who fought the Normans and their French language,
Lord of East-Anglian Essex and Suffolk,
I see you standing near the mower shed,
Having strayed in from the forest, and as
I cross the lawn you approach the fish-pond
And we stand and talk and I feed the fish,   70
Bask in the warm sunshine and cloudless sky
And in the harmony of the universe
That beams not-slaying Norman invaders
And seeing-beyond your Christian Holy Cross
In our new EU and coming World State.

Harold, lord of Loughton and harmony
Between the East Saxons and East Angles,
I am pleased you have left your desperate time
Of nation-states for our Universal Age.
31 December 2015; 1, 28–29 January 2016

Nicholas Hagger writes: "I sat in front of a blank sheet of A4 paper with the idea that Harold II was Loughton's landlord and absolutely no idea of what would appear on the page, and this epistle and its two attitudes to Europe seemed to write itself and come from the beyond."

Harold held the Manor of Lochintuna/Loughton before c.1060 and handed it to Waltham Holy Cross c.1060. He rebuilt Waltham Holy Cross (church 3) c.1060–1066. He was killed at Hastings in 1066 and is thought to have been buried near the altar of his church, Waltham Holy Cross.

29. 'Half a trillion.' The UK has paid £503 billion to Europe between 1973 and 2015, and has received many trade benefits in return.

46. 'South Folk'. Maps of the Kingdom of East Anglia, 6th century to 918, show 'North Folk' (Norfolk) and 'South Folk' (Suffolk).

33

AN UNSUNG LAUREATE
2009–2016

"I, an unsung laureate with truthful eye."

Nicholas Hagger, 'Ceremonial: On the End of a National Era,

The Funeral of Margaret Thatcher'

"I told the class, 'I don't care what dictators there are out there, there is freedom of speech in my class. Outside this classroom there is no freedom of speech, but within it there is.'"

Nicholas Hagger, *My Double Life 1: This Dark Wood*, p.145,

about his lecture room at the University of Baghdad in 1962

The first four poems (written between 1997 and 2003) appeared in *Classical Odes* and are reproduced here as the theme of volume 33 – the feeling of the end of an era and of the modern Elizabethan Age, and the birth of a new European and global destiny – continues their perspective. Their subjects are the sort of subjects a Poet Laureate might reflect but some lines are too outspoken for Laureate poems. Nicholas Hagger was awarded the Gusi Peace Prize for Literature in 2016, and became a Gusi 'Laureate'.

Pastoral Ode: Landslide, The End of Great Britain

I

I wander round this Tudor, timbered Hall.
The setting sun shines spangles in the glass
Of leaded windows set in a brick wall.
I feel it in the air, eighteen years pass
Like the long shadows on the croquet lawn.
In the still evening I detect beside
My open study window and calm scorn
A shifting in the nation, dark "landslide".

Night's shadows creep, the sunlit garden fades.
Eighteen years of a certain kind of rule   10
Are ending. Cold war and armed truce are shades;
In place of missiles, hospital and school.
The country needs renewal, a safe switch
To a fairer society, have-nots
Doing better without hurting the rich;
A new energy, free from backbench plots.

I feel it in the breeze, a mood for change.
The people have turned against long tenure
For a fresh approach, rejecting as strange
Smears, lies, divisions and corrupt behaviour,   20
Impatient with State cuts and expecting
An end to cash shortage and mass pay freeze,
Certain taxes will go down, resenting
Division, splits, scandals and endless sleaze.

The people have forgotten it went well,
How unions were tamed, the pound made strong,
How living standards rose, inflation fell,
The victories won in wars against the wrong,
How privatising, market forces so
Transformed the weather they prolonged daylight   30
Till this illusion that the sun must go
Spread across the land like these shades of night.

A peacock honks from dark silhouettes, tense.
A world government Group has planned to scoff
At and steal our national independence,
To break up the UK by splitting off
Scotland and Wales as European states,
Finishing with the pound, stopping our boom,
Bringing back union strife. A tame press baits
One side with its scandals and foretells doom.   40

The gloom is real, the vision has now gone.
The regicides ditched conviction, belief,
Loyalty to an idea and passion
For the pragmatic posture of a chief
Who linked with personalities and hoped
For human loyalty and was let down
When they, still fighting for an idea, moped
And betrayed him with this pretender's frown.

I think, walking under the early stars
(Looking for a man in a ruff, his head   50
Tucked under one arm), knowing *their* press czars
Manipulate opinion round their dead,
Surely the public cannot trust this dressed
Demagogue who has like a hatched cuckoo
Pushed all the other eggs out of their nest
And opened his mouth to devour and chew.

I rest on centuries' quiet in the Great Hall,
See our nation's history in adzed beams, bide
Time. I switch on the television. All
Exit polls predict a Labour "landslide" –   60
Into the sea towards Europe. I go
To bed, watch a screen and count swings, like sheep,
Of eleven to fifteen per cent. I know
What the outcome will be, and fall asleep.

II

A cuckoo calls. I wake and grope a hand
To the bedside radio and now hear
That this upstart who has said "Trust me" and
Has hatched by policies already there
In the old, reused nest, has won with ease
By a hundred and seventy something seats.   70
The people sought to punish splits and sleaze,
Not give unchecked power to these pious cheats.

139

I walk with painters and a builder, chat
With an electrician and leaded glass
Repairer, who do not refer to that
Result as if nothing has changed the grass.
Bees swarm round their queen on a white post, twined.
A beekeeper lifts them with his bare hand,
Puts them in a box and leaves some behind.
So Providence removes a clustered band.   80

A blazing day and on my lunchtime screen
In the moat room, French windows wide open,
Our Prime Minister calmly ends a scene
And says that he will leave the stage; and then
The pretender arrives and grasps raised hands
That happen to wave issued Union Jacks.
A hired crowd: such "public opinion" bands
Bode fierce manipulation, and the axe.

Late afternoon. A cockerel struts and crows.
Small midges dance above grass by the moat.   90
I sit in the open study windows
And recall a Shetland ram and a vote
At a show for first prize in a rare breed.
Penned in by sycophants, with two curled horns,
That scornful long-haired ram waited to lead.
So had our lost leader waited on lawns.

Wild bees and wasps nest in our viewing mound.
We have a trusting public, who believe
There is no danger in our hillocked ground,
That well-strimmed promises do not deceive.   100
Our new society hums like wild bees
That menacingly buzz to guard their nest,
Which looks harmless in an afternoon breeze
But contains lethal stings that can arrest.

A Bilderberg agenda rules this crowd.
Like actors politicians recite scripts
Under the direction, as from a cloud,
Of a global *élite* in bankers' crypts
Who want a European Union
And urge our politicians to agree   110
To hand their power to bankers to bring on
A single European currency.

I walk past the nuttery urn and stand.
A bunch of Scotsmen now hold all the main
Offices of State in the UK, and
Will give the Scots and Welsh Parliaments plain
Self-rule, break England into regions – eight
Linked to Europe through county councils to
End all national borders and integrate
Our nation in supranational EU.   120

A naive optimism is abroad,
Settling the Irish problem is now right
As if IRA hard men, overawed,
Will surrender, give up their century's fight.
They will seek a united Ireland in
The new United States of Europe, scent
We now have leaders who will not bargain
With realism, but with wish fulfilment.

Here by the moat under a chestnut tree
With candles I ponder. Our nation's gold   130
Will now go to Frankfurt, and there will be
Nothing to back our pound, which must be sold
For inflated euros as we unroll
A Union of fragmented nation-states.
I see a country Rockefellers stole
From Rothschilds while our Englishness deflates.

By hanging fragrant wisteria I mourn
The New World Order's rule, towns ringed by moats,
Motorways where tanks can move in at dawn,
Besiege the people, keep them out like goats   140
If they are driven to the countryside;
Where, hospitals and camps heaped in ashes,
A populist leader with a landslide
Reaches out to a crowd he oppresses.

Indoors I linger on the landing by
My framed seven-foot chart and print of Canute
Commanding the sea to retire. Now my
Nation-state is provinces in a mute
Centralised Europe which floats a slick top
Of grants, policies, laws that all seem strange,   150
Like King Canute I see but cannot stop
The tide that creeps in and wets us with change.

The UK this momentous day has been
Sold to a United States of Europe.
I take no pleasure in having foreseen
On my chart twelve years back the sickening drop
To our civilization's newest stage,
Along with Communism's end. I see
Our tradition invaded and rampage
Like our fishing fleet into slavery.   160

Will the change last or perish with the hours?
The purpling of meadows is seasonal.
The rarest minds, like the rarest wild flowers,
Are ephemeral and perennial.
See a thousand faces droop from stems, blow
Like purple snake's-head fritillary bells
In Framsden's mottled green water-meadow
Where each spring hang transient, perennial smells.

Time creeps as on the face of an old clock.
Cogs turn, pendulum ticks and lowers weights,   170
The long-case hand moves discreetly, tick tock,
Past painted peacocks, floral scenes, estates,
The moon a woman's red-lipped face half set.
The hand ticks with the tyranny of time
And on the hour, with a whirr of cogs met,
The ting-ting-tinkle of a high-pitched chime.

Ducks swoosh by white lilies, quack their advice.
Like Marvell and Voltaire I will retreat
Into my garden, Suffolk paradise,
This end of Great Britain, sit on a seat,   180
Put the moat between myself and the world,
Leave the affairs of State to come unstuck
In an impostor's hands, Euro-flag furled,
And feed chickens and peacocks, and breed duck.

I will retreat into the distant past,
Recreate history as a Tudor knot
And medieval herb garden, contrast
The apothecary's rose and the shot,
Splashed blush-white of Tudor *rosa mundi*,
Learn falconry and Tudor bowls and thought,   190
Study the Virgin Queen's progresses, try
To ignore the dreadful things done at court.

I will keep hawks and bees and watch wheat grow
In farmers' fields by bridle-path and lane,
Listen to the cuckoo where cowslips blow,
See gold fish spawn in splash-ripples like rain,
Look for rabbits at dusk, savour the balm
By ponds aglow with lilies, gaze at stars,
Write odes as if this were a Sabine farm
And ignore conquered ninnies' blind hurrahs.   200
1–26 May, revised 2 July 1997

143

Nicholas Hagger writes: "I was at Otley Hall on 1–2 May 1997, the night of the British General Election, which New Labour won by a landslide. I immediately grasped that New Labour would attempt to dismantle the UK into regions which would be subsumed within a European superstate. I had a sense that a thousand years of English tradition were now at an end. That night and the following morning I digested the implications, walking at night and the next morning in stunningly beautiful grounds. The poem contrasts the peaceful, timeless countryside of Little England with the disturbing changes ahead."

34. 'World government Group'. See note to line 105.

42. 'Regicides', i.e. those who deposed Margaret Thatcher as Prime Minister.

44. 'Chief'. Thatcher's replacement, John Major.

48 (also 85). 'Pretender'. The Leader of the Opposition, Tony Blair.

50–51. Gardeners at Otley Hall report having seen a headless man in a ruff, with his head under one arm.

67. 'Upstart'. See note to line 48.

83. 'Our Prime Minister'. John Major.

105. 'Bilderberg agenda'. See Hagger, *The Syndicate* for details of the Bilderberg Group's world government policies.

135–136. The Rockefellers, US billionaires, and the Rothschilds, European billionaires, share power on the Bilderberg Group. See Hagger, *The Syndicate*.

159. 'Rampage' (intrans.), 'rage, storm'.

166–167. Nicholas Hagger had visited Framsden to view a meadow of purple snake's-head fritillaries on 27 April 1997.

169. The clock was an 18th-century long-case clock, which then stood in Otley Hall.

199. 'Sabine farm'. Horace, the Roman poet, had a Sabine farm. See 'At Horace's Sabine Farm'.

200. In other words, those celebrating New Labour's victory, including politicians, did not realise they were celebrating being conquered by a Brussels-led superstate, and so were 'blind'.

Second Pastoral Ode: Landslide Unchanged,
The End of England

I

The sun shines on brilliant red-yellow pull
Of roses in the rose garden, I stand
Near fallen blue wisteria, wistful
This glorious June morning, sun warms each hand.
All is still, peaceful save for twittering birds
Rejoicing in the early morning calm,
All Nature's exultant, but a few words
Have made my heart heavy in the sun's charm:

News of a "new landslide" in polls that claim
The poorest turn-out since the First World War.   10
It's "crushed" the Conservatives, who've the same
Number of seats as four years back (one more).
They'd reorganised to end division
Among themselves, but the public's concern
On the economy, health, education
Made their Eurosceptic stance seem to spurn.

I wander onto the fresh croquet lawn
To the herb garden and gaze at the knot
That shows a box "8", infinity shorn,
And *fleurs-de-lis* arrows of time. I spot   20
A nest. The cuckoo Blair posed as a dove
To hatch eggs he'd found in the dovecote's shade.
Now, pushed aside, the Tories could not shove
The cuckoo out, retake the eggs they'd laid.

The public was not listening. I recall
Waiting while my car battery was charged
And where I sat a TV by the wall
Showed Portillo, sound off, his face enlarged,
Like a goldfish, his mouth opening, closing,

145

No message. Nothing mattered: Prescott's blow   30
(Left hook), foot-and-mouth, fuel, triple counting.
The public knew its mind a month ago.

By the moat, my roofer, with a hand-tilt,
Hands me twelve Tudor tile pegs from our roof,
Says, "They've been there since the Hall was first built."
I hold pale whittled wood, datable proof.
The Tories left their policies too late;
Like a boxer who had fought by coasting
Till the last round, they were in a bruised state,
Punched groggy, and stood no chance of winning.   40

Now on TV, a shock. Hague stands, no squirm,
And "steps down" to bring a new leader on.
He is exhausted but his voice is firm,
No quaver, no flinching – a strong man gone.
The public wants the euro, the new age
Demands a single currency he'd slay.
Defiantly he has walked off the stage.
Who'll want to lead when there's such disarray?

I wander by the moat, see the tranquil
Reflection of the Tudor Otley Hall   50
On green water – a changeless image, still,
Of our country centuries before its fall.
They had an anti-European skin,
A xenophobic, inward-looking team.
The parties that take the centre ground win,
The ones that move to an edge seem extreme.

A new day has broken through a blue sky,
Wielding a referendum like a knife,
No leader to oppose the euro, vie
Or speak for the traditional way of life.   60
This was the last national election, now

There'll be no England, just nine regions, great
Tax-raisers with autonomous know-how,
With representatives in Brussels: states.

I wander to the Solar corridor
And see my framed seven-foot-long history chart
Predict (in the mid-nineteen-eighties) for
A United States of Europe to start
In 1997. As a sheepskin-
Clad newsman at Arsenal's ground by floodlight   70
Reports a nil-two loss but wants a win,
I take no pleasure in being proved right.

And yet there are benefits: the euro
Will simplify European travel;
And though our nation-state will melt like snow
And Churchill and Montgomery will yell
Out from their graves against our loss of pence
And interest rates now set by Germany
Just as Hitler wanted, that our defence
Is run by a European army,   80

Once again England's at one with the long
European line – Greeks, Romans, untame
Gauls, Visigoths, Franks, Crusaders, a throng;
The mainland stock from which Britishness came:
Celts, Angles, Saxons, Jutes, Vikings, Normans;
Reunited with movements and poets:
Early Renaissance and Romantic spans,
Dante and Goethe. Seen thus, no regrets!

The New World Order's banner's been unfurled,
Rockefellers have prevailed. As I stand   90
By the moat, a world government and world
Dollar now certain, holding in one hand
The twelve wood Tudor tile pegs just been found,

Fixed when the Hall was first built by the moat,
Shivering, I pull the Hall's reflection round
My wobbly shoulders like an overcoat.

II

I ruminate days later, now estranged.
There was no second landslide, the first one
Of 1997 remained unchanged.
I walk by the H-canal in warm sun.   100
The Conservatives were in power seventy years
Of the twentieth century's hundred, resent
Labour stealing their central ground with jeers
And posing as the new Establishment.

Now I see wrong positioning is to blame.
Hague's party was not inclusive enough.
There was no room for Europhiles, their claim
On the economy was too untough.
They should have answered questions that engage,
That keep worried voters awake at night: 110
How to protect parents in their old age,
Their own pensions, rising taxes; their plight.

Blair has reshuffled his Cabinet so
His team reflects his own image, so he
Wins the referendum on the euro,
Takes us into the new State's currency
By stealth through a pragmatic FO man
Who will decide with an "impartial" fist
Rather than through an ideologue whose "can-
Do" judgment would be seen as prejudiced.   120

The bulldog did not bark at the burglar.
The English public was quiet on Europe,
Ignoring Tory alarm as dogma,
Wanting to move forward, to "develop".

By the next election the EU will
Have its own constitution, police force,
Criminal justice, armed forces, treadmill
Business tax harmonization – the sauce!

It will then almost be the single state
With a politically integrated   130
Economy and currency and fate,
That Jospin and Schröder say is ahead.
Europhiles and Eurosceptics have both
Been in denial on Bilderberg's plan
And have vied to keep their Bilderberg oath
To keep the public ignorant of their ban.

This has been one of the last Elections
Britain's held as an independent power.
Too soon we'll be part of a new nation,
Westminster'll be a museum like the Tower.   140
Pensions, taxation and the mortgage rate
Will be decided in Brussels and Frankfurt.
We will have lost control of the debate,
Of our economy, which will soon hurt.

As British taxpayers fund pensions for
Improvident Greeks and Turks who've not saved
And asylum-seekers fleeing from war,
And see a nation-state destroyed, enslaved,
Its revenue paid to East Europe's poor,
The countryside abandoned, Lords torn down,   150
Livestock slaughtered, doddering peers no more;
Voters will wear a disappointed frown.

Resistance is useless; Bilderberg won.
I am living in an occupied land.
Labour panzers hold the streets of London,
The monarchy is frail, will soon be banned.

The BBC puts out propaganda,
And leaves the real news to be deduced.
Devolution's left the UK a blur,
England's State power is next to be reduced.   160

There's a dictatorship of smug and rich
Liberals, who, flushed with power, apply the same
Destructive, permissive policies which
Broke millions of marriages, to their shame,
Abandoned millions of children, set free,
Left their crimes unpunished, blamed on a slum,
Undermined manners and civility,
So our streets are strewn with litter and gum.

An ancient, literate culture's been destroyed.
Tape-recorders, CDs in passing cars   170
Blare out a yelling noise on silent void,
TV-men talk in grunts, in-your-face stars
Tastelessly show nude flesh and flaunt yobspeak.
Pornography vies with guns-and-blood fate;
Pundits dumb down, praise black bands' mindless shriek;
And leaders sneer at rational debate.

Our new dictatorship's abolishing
Our country and our culture in the name
Of liberal progress, and is embracing
The new Europe to general acclaim.   180
The liberty-loving British public
Who are so civilized and tolerant,
And law-abiding, must accept seismic
Changes, and so must I; a recusant.

I must be realistic. By this moat,
Though I lament the deceit of this lot
Who are devious, honest, preachy and gloat,
And the tyranny of Bilderberg's plot;

I must embrace the future, not the past.
I must look forward and secure the best   190
Mirroring of our culture, and forecast.
All hail new Europe like a much-loved guest!
8–15 June 2001

The General Election was held on 7 June 2001. It produced a result that was
virtually unchanged from the Labour landslide of May 1997.
1. 'Pull', 'attraction'.
67–68. 'Predict... for... to start'. The normal grammatical construction is
'predict... that... will/would start', but this alternative includes a nuance. It
suggests that a United States of Europe is set to happen anyway, and that its
start will be in 1997. 'Predict... that' excludes the idea of its starting anyway.
96. 'Wobbly', rippling.
97. 'Estranged', alienated.
117. 'FO man', Jack Straw.
119. 'Ideologue', Robin Cook.

In Westminster: The Passing of an Era

Guards carry the coffin from Westminster
Hall's door and lay it on the gun-carriage,
Draped in lioned flag, her crown on top. And, drawn
By hussars' horses, the stately *cortège*
Moves off. Uniformed men and royals slow-march,
Drums wash, beat. Crowds twenty deep fall silent,
Troops parade to the Abbey, whose bell tolls
A hundred and one times for each year spent.

The Queen walks down the Abbey aisle, ignores
Subjects in black bowing, genuflecting.   10
The coffin-bearers remove guards' busbies,
Bear the coffin into the dark building
And down the aisle to the bier at the front.
The royals sit together, opposite

Royals from Europe's states under stone vaults.
In the monks' quire sly politicians sit.

The service starts with hymns and music sung
By the choir, readings from the classic dead.
I think of the old certainties on show –
The Crown, army, family united   20
And the traditional values of the Church
And a hierarchical society –
As she's buried within a line of kings
As if she'd said, "This is how things should be."

"She warmed all like the sun," the Archbishop's
Said. The service over, the Queen, in black,
Walks up the aisle, heads bob, knees bend as she
Passes. The hearse leaves, coffin in the back,
Six cars process to the Mall. Overhead
A Lancaster, two Spitfires dip wings, keen: 30
She rallied in the war and saved the Crown
After abdication, was a good Queen.

Now the hearse heads for Windsor, the crown still
Visible on the flag inside the glass,
And thousands line the roads, warmly applaud,
Throw flowers, single sprays, as fond memories pass.
An era's passed with this woman to whom
All feel distantly related, at one,
Who lived a privileged grand life and had
The common touch, shone on all like the sun.   40

The Windsor staff are lined up as the hearse
Glides in behind the inner castle gate.
A lavish funeral, a spectacle that's
Relaunched the royals as central to the State
Before the world: a billion on TV,
A sixth of mankind, as if she had said,

"These things were important in my lifetime,
The values that endure and should be spread."

She cleverly planned details of the route
To show the royal family in good light,   50
Her gift towards their continuity
So that the monarchy would grow in might.
She hijacked the agenda from Labour,
Showed the merits of her glittering era,
Defiantly asserted its values
As relevant through a piece of theatre.

They look actors, these costumed haughty royals,
Perfectly dressed, word-perfect in gesture,
Each salute, step carefully orchestrated,
All scripted, nothing left to chance, all sure,   60
Nothing spontaneous, all to be rehearsed,
All carried off as in a well-planned play
Whose theme was the continuity
Of the monarchy in our "modern" day.

This funeral has united all of us
And made us feel a sense of nationhood,
Belonging to something more enduring
Than *Big Brother*, *Pop Idol*, people's Could:
Hysteria, shrieking, the common culture
New Labour wants us to adopt: the Dome,   70
Ephemeral programmes with dumbed-down content,
"Bread and circuses" for our shabby Rome.

The transportation to the lying-in-state
Spoke (through the crown) of the Empire, India
Of which she was Empress; the *Koh-i-noor*
Where it was fought over, Central Asia.
The funeral asserted a strong nation –
The Crown, the Church, army and class or caste;

Affirmed to all the crown heads of Europe
That Britain as a nation-state's not past, 80

But with another meaning or new gloss
Put on it. The glittering of the crown
Was a signal to Olympians who want
A world government like an eiderdown
To cover naked empire, old Europe.
Those royal visitors were being told
By the younger royals, "We're one with you
Now she has at last gone, out with the old!"

Out there republicans look for the end
Of lavishness, smart uniforms, bands' noise, 90
Of ceremonies with perfect timing,
Formality and graciousness and poise.
We have to find new things to unite us,
A sense of European nationhood –
The common culture of knowledge, virtue
And merit I've found in ruins: the Good.
10 April 2002, revised 14, 16 April 2002

The funeral of Queen Elizabeth the Queen Mother took place in Westminster
Abbey on 9 April 2002.
16. 'Quire', old spelling for 'choir'.
96. 'The Good', a Platonic concept.

The Conquest of England

I

I sit and look across the sea to France.
Framed by my window, both sides of the bay
Recede in mist that masks the horizon
Where leaders have been meeting to display
With some secrecy that all decisions

Have been snatched from our side of this calm sea
And dropped beyond the wobbling reflection
Of a moored yacht and beyond Normandy.

There is a new EU constitution
For a new behemoth of three hundred   10
And seventy million folk, one state stretching
From Galway to Gdansk, and German-led.
Chaired by d'Estaing, a convention will tell
What two extremists drafted as our fate:
A new set of rules to unite Europe
And bind all states into a superstate.

Habeas corpus and a thousand years
Of English legal history will be wiped
Out by European law, and we will find
Our foreign/defence policy's been swiped   20
And's now anti-American, our tax
Will rise to Europe's, businessmen will pay
For the ten new, poor countries to catch up:
International socialism has sway.

Each state will make over its sovereignty
And some powers will be delegated back;
But not public health, social policy,
Transport, justice, agriculture, a stack
Of energy, environment and trade
Powers we've lost. Article 9 stipulates   30
The constitution will have primacy
Over the law of all its member states.

Article 46 makes clear, to leave
The EU without permission will be
Illegal. Secession must be approved
By two-thirds of member states. Now I see
A third can strip a seceder of all

Trading rights and cash, currency reserves
Held by the European Central Bank.
We forfeit our savings! This Europe swerves!   40

I scan the papers, digest the comment.
It's a prison clause, the union is not
A voluntary one we're in, it's the end
Of parliamentary sovereignty. I jot:
Our democracy would be abolished,
All would be within Brussels' competence.
I see Putin sitting beside Chirac.
We may be run by Russian "commonsense".

This draft will go before the convention
Of a hundred and five. There'll be a new   50
Treaty of Nice when all the twenty-four
Other states could create – and then pursue –
A union and marginalise Britain
Who, sucked in, could in just nine months deflate
From being liberators of Iraq
To twelve regions in a conglomerate.

Is our future as the fifty-first state,
An island offshore from America,
Independent of Europe, self-contained,
Our currency tethered to the dollar?   60
Our fishing and farming free from quotas?
The American mind first set its prow
From East Anglia and voyaged to Jamestown –
Is it not fitting we should join it now?

But we've not liked its attack on Iraq,
Don't want to share its world hegemony,
Suspect that the *Pax Americana*
Is an oil-grabbing war on tyranny.
The US came in late in two world wars

When we gave it British oilfields as bribes.   70
It ordered us to abort Suez, yet
Expects support for war strikes on poor tribes.

Should we continue alone as we did
When we built two empires and ruled the waves?
We're the motherland for the Commonwealth,
We're still loved – we fed the backward, freed slaves.
Our empire's improved the lives of natives,
Our liberal capitalists expanded,
Created a global economy –
Can we not trade with all and stay ahead?   80

Again, we drive on Bodmin's misty moors,
An undulating green land with some sheep
And distant hills, our pleasant English land:
Sporadic farmsteads, well-cared-for woods sleep;
Granite stones, clumps of gorse, cows in walled fields,
The glory of the English countryside,
Its produce like our pension fund still ours –
I look on it with heavy-hearted pride.

I drive down Devon lanes with buttercups
And green hills smiling in the morning sun,   90
Grass shimmering-green, to an old stone bridge,
Past a horse, farmhouses and a hen-run,
Ivied sheds and trim flower-bordered lawns
To the stannary town of Tavistock,
Walk by the Tavy's weir that froths silk strands;
Abbey walls, arched bridge to the market block.

I taste creamy Brie in the old cheese shop,
Then drive across Dartmoor to Two Bridges,
The English sun warm on my cheeks, hedges
Pinked by wild flowers, up to the tors' ridges: 100
Boulders buried in green, small wild ponies.

We stop and munch our lunch on a knoll. Still,
I hear the cuckoo from a wooded copse,
A nightingale trill from behind a hill.

We turn off for Chagford, a narrow lane
With harebells in the hedgerows either side.
I stop at the Three Crowns, stand in the porch
Where Sidney Godolphin was shot and died,
Savour the remote village and thatched walls.
England, I love your hills and leafy ways   110
Which Montgomery and Churchill defended –
I brim sunshine and a patriot's praise.

II

I stretch out in the warm, late April sun.
A heat wave from the Sahara: blue sky,
Cloudless, a haze above the sea, my cheeks
Warm, shoulders, arms, body, legs and each thigh.
I feel the sun permeating my flesh,
Imbuing it with healing vitamins.
I bask and soak it in, red-brown go in,
See the nightmare that's happened in Athens.   120

On TV, in the Stoa of Attalos,
Near colonnades Socrates and Plato
Spoke from at the height of Athenian
Democracy, our nation's dealt a blow:
Ten new nations are welcomed to Europe,
And (bathos) Blair stands up and speaks for three
Minutes, exalts their new-won freedom from
"Dictatorship and repression" with glee.

Elsewhere in Athens rioters now fight
A street battle in protest against Blair,   130
Calling for peace by bombarding police
With petrol bombs and stones flung through the air.

Policemen fire tear gas, agitators
Put on goggles and ventilators, spread
Across Constitution Square, hurl rocks while
Europe's new constitution's presented.

The ten thought they'd be in a rich men's club
But find a deep division between those
Who hate America – France, Germany –
And those who're with the coalition's pose,   140
Regime change in Iraq. The new boys don't
Want to displease America's rulers
Who liberated them from the Soviets,
But don't want to displease their new masters.

The deepeners are aghast, the wideners
Have linked poor countries with no welfare scheme
For their elderly and improvident
To their tax systems, so rich countries cream
Tax from their bourgeoisie to pay pensions
For Bulgarians, Turks, Cypriots, Maltese: 150
A socialist Europe where wealth's transferred
From the landed to ghettos overseas.

"Democracy, freedom, the rule of law
Unite the EU," Blair says. An imposed
New constitution will abolish all
Twenty-five nation-states, which will be closed
States in a superstate, their assets locked
In Frankfurt's Central Bank. And then? To free
Them two-thirds must vote – or seceders lose
Them with trading rights. Some democracy!   160

He's proposed the new superstate should choose
A President whom the White House can call.
He wants this time-span job: no Parliament
To be questioned by, no Queen and no fall.

I grasp the posturer's attacked Iraq
To create an image that he is pro-
Nation-state while he dumps the pound for: not
Presidential ambition – the euro!

I grasp his "courage" that attacked Iraq
When his party, country, Europe opposed   170
Was to con us into supporting him
While he sold British interests and bulldozed
Parliamentary sovereignty and tax
To be run for the world government's gain.
I grasp he is the quisling of our time,
His betrayal's an indelible stain.

He signs our nation into superstate
With one President, Foreign Minister.
As a wind rustles a field of gold wheat
I hear the British people's quiet anger.   180
There have to be trade union rights – to strike.
Now Britain's voice speaks from the vaults of banks
And must be diminished, and this traitor
Still poses as a hero against tanks.

A new Norman Conquest is in the air.
We are now just one voice in twenty-five,
We're recreating a Soviet Union
In Europe, a new union that will thrive.
Many have tried to end the English power –
Spaniards, French and Germans. Now a Briton   190
Has succeeded where all others have failed.
What can we do? Riot? The glory's gone.

III

Dusk gathers on the land. I look to sea.
It's so calm beneath my evening window.
Beyond the clouds a clear pale azure sky

With hints of pink. Gulls flap, wheel to and fro.
My cormorant has stopped diving for fish.
All is so peaceful, tranquil, this May day.
I look towards Europe, to the skyline,
Disturbed: my country's no more round this bay.   200

Across the newspapers, "Europe sets out
Sweeping new powers" and "EU issues draft
Constitution". On all sides there are fears
Sovereignty's lost. Just "tidying-up"? That's daft!
Blair's had the preamble's "federal" struck out
But a more-than-federal state looms sullen
Like the dark clouds above me, dimming light.
The Sun proclaims, "The End of our Nation".

I read the headlines with numbed foreboding.
Britain ruled from Brussels, two million jobs   210
Will go, Frankfurt will set all interest rates,
Bureaucratic inspectors will, like yobs,
Prowl, scuffle, mug our purse. The Queen will go
Next, the Head of State will be elected.
All Churchill and Montgomery fought for's
Been surrendered as if Hitler weren't dead.

Light fades, the sea turns grey, gulls shuffle, stand
On rocky bar and breakwater and stare.
All the certainties I knew as a child –
Gone. A new legal code, guilty as air   220
Unless proved innocent. A thousand years
Of long English tradition now buried.
I, the chronicler of Britain's decline,
Am sad I was alive when it ended.

And yet this ending was not unforeseen.
Fifteen years back I put the United
States of Europe on my long chart. I wrote

A verse play on a Prince's choice and dread.
Ignored! The Establishment ignored me
And now they're finding out that I was right.   230
I wrote of regions replacing England.
The new treaty's unveiled them to our sight.

I foresaw it and warned an Earl, who leapt
Onto the woolsack in the House of Lords
To object that it's been packed with yes-men
To vote through these constitutional frauds.
Our Prime Minister's in with foreign powers,
Is internationalist, would give our land
Away without a vote – his masters' will.
The Earl's act shines across this murky sand.   240

The light is fading fast, the gulls now sit
On water like ducks, ready to take wing
To their nests in the nearby cliffs, a moth
Flits past my window in its foraging.
A peaceful, tranquil calm but I'm troubled,
I see someone shooting our traitor who
Is doing to our country what Philip
Of Spain, Napoleon, Hitler could not do.

And inwardly I'm filled with a quiet rage
For I'm powerless. What can I do but mewl?   250
Bilderberg have us by the throat, we have
To submit to a time of foreign rule
By diktat as compelling as conquest,
The Queen brushed aside in our Cromwell's swoops,
A revolution that – though mere paper
Constitution – is more crushing than troops.

The dark has gathered, I can hardly see
To write these words in my sea-view window.
The gulls have merged into the twilit mist.

The Queen, remote, aloof, who chose to go   260
And unveil a street sign that lacked planning
Permission and had to be taken down
Instead of Gosnold's statue Ipswich planned,
Is shaken, but's not defending the Crown.

That's at the heart of it, we're all dismayed
At our indifferent Royal Family;
Their independence, which they won't defend,
Should be our guarantee of liberty.
They sneer at us and patronise, ignore,
Look with superior airs and did not heed   270
Our warnings and are now in shock. Too late!
You should have listened long before the deed!

Now snails are creeping on the lamp-lit lawn,
And little flying midges cross the bay
And there's a misty blur on the skyline
Which could be land, Europe floating this way.
It looks like a far bank seen from a ship
In a wide river, and I swear it's France
Drifting towards us: continental drift
Encroaching on our independent trance.   280

I think of wartime England my parents
Knew, the brave land young men fought for and died;
I think how I'm English and wear my birth
As a badge of honour with Essex pride.
I knew we'd be here that election night
Six years ago, but few agreed with me.
They trusted the grinning young globalist
Who'd captivated – captured my country!

The birds have gone, the lights are in windows
Across the harbour, men walk dogs, in awe,   290
Saunter or stand in half-light, unaware

Their future's been snatched as if by a war.
The seaside village with one shop is quiet,
A fisherman is unloading his boat.
All think of the end of a long day's work,
No one thinks of the Channel as a moat.

And I'm a dislocated dissident.
I've opposed those who are running our land,
And soon I'll oppose those who take it on,
French-, German-speakers who have for long planned   300
To confiscate our wealth, spread it around.
Most Europeans do not have our slate,
The provident must fund the improvident.
Thrift does not pay in the new superstate!

The *Earl of Pembroke* and the *Kaskelot*
Have port-hole lights below their six tall masts.
A couple walk across the harbour bridge,
Their footsteps echo as the twilight lasts.
Gull Island shimmers in the glassy sea,
Walkers on the pier look out from a lamp   310
And at a light beyond it on Ropehawn
On the Black Head above a far boat ramp.

And now the crab-pots have been lost to dark
And half the boat that lists as if it fell.
The sheep on the hillside have disappeared,
The outside drinkers are in the hotel.
All's dark and quiet, the roundhouse still under
Flagpole, the battlemented fort and sand
That's Smeaton's harbour's black, but not as dark
As the night that's settled over England.   320
12, 17 April, 27 May 2003, revised 9–12 August 2003

In October 2002 the European Commission gave the go-ahead for the admission
of 10 new states to the European Union. At the same time a constitutional

convention chaired by former French President Valery Giscard d'Estaing proposed a draft constitutional treaty.

10. 'Behemoth', 'an enormous creature or thing, beast' (from a Hebrew word perhaps based on the Egyptian for 'water-ox').

14. 'Two extremists': the two commissioners on the praesidium, France's Michel Barnier and Portugal's Antonio Vitorino.

108. Sidney Godolphin was a poet of the Civil War. He was shot and killed on 9 February 1643, far from his seat at Godolphin in Cornwall.

152. 'Ghetto', 'a slum area occupied by a minority group or groups'.

228. 'A verse play': *The Tragedy of Prince Tudor*.

233. 'An Earl', the Earl of Burford, now Charles Beauclerk, who protested against Blair's constitutional reform of the House of Lords by leaping on the Lord Chancellor's woolsack on 26 October 1999.

250. 'Mewl', 'cry feebly, whimper, mew like a cat'.

260–263. See 'On the Queen's Visit to Ipswich: Dissident' (in *Classical Odes*).

285–286. 'That election night', 2 May 1997. See 'Pastoral Ode: Landslide, The End of Great Britain'.

302. 'Our slate', i.e. the system in which savings are written down and respected.

305. *The Earl of Pembroke* and the *Kaskelot* were ships moored in Charlestown harbour.

311. Ropehawn. Ropehaven is pronounced "Ropehawn" by the local Cornish.

319. John Smeaton, the first self-styled civil engineer who designed the second Eddystone Lighthouse, the Forth and Clyde canal and the harbour at St Ives, built the harbour at Charlestown. He died at the age of 68 on 28 October 1792.

Lisbon Treaty: The End of Great Britain, Demise of a Nation-State

I

Over blue-grey sea a squally day rules.
Curtains of rain conceal Europe's veiled land.
The tide flows in from France and fills still pools
Round bladderwracked rocks, and glistens the sand
As sunlight breaks. A causeway of light draws

Me towards Trenarren's Black Head, and on.
To left all's murk, to right a brilliance pours
Splashing light. Our independence has gone.

On the screen by my window with sea-view
A newscaster says, "The Czech President 10
Has ratified the Lisbon Treaty too."
All twenty-seven European states, leant
On, have ratified. Now I'm living in
A county, not a country; in an E
U with legal personality, spin.
Our laws will all be passed across the sea.

By the anti-French battery cliff gulls soar.
The French and Germans were often conquered.
We English have not been invaded for
Nearly a thousand years, not since we heard 20
That Norman ships were in Pevensey Bay.
We've been a proud nation, our chiefs with guile
Fought for our island's autonomous sway.
And now it's been signed away with a smile.

Two cormorants fish outside the harbour.
O Churchill and Montgomery, please sleep,
Our independence was signed away for
Our rulers promised, but were in too deep,
To seek our consent. Now it is too late.
No referendum, for the people would 30
Have voted No, and the new superstate
Would have been stillborn, all would have been good.

On the hill sheep graze heedless of torment.
The main 'no consenter' who blocked us all
Is trying to be Europe's President:
Tony Blair who led England into thrall
Now seeks his rewards: the Emperor's crown,

More traitorous than if King Harold had wished
To invite Duke William to London town
To take the throne Edward had relinquished.   40

A long curled wave rolls shoreward, and then more.
Can a signed treaty be cancelled next day?
No, for like hard rock it's set into law.
The Treaty of Amiens, which gave away
Too much, was renounced within six months, dashed,
But the ratified Lisbon Treaty's blur,
Like the Treaty of Rome, cannot be smashed
Unless by revolution's sledgehammer.

Dead fish, algae-eaten, strew beach, clog boats.
And now I see the Rotten Parliament –   50
MPs' expenses spent on ducks and moats,
Second mortgages, evaded tax, bent
Family-member staff, cleaning, gardening chores,
Porn films, food, you name it, oh, huge TVs
They corruptly claimed – now has but few laws
To pass, is best by-passed for MEPs.

II

I turn on the TV. A brave young man
Is borne in a *cortège* – he did defuse
Sixty IEDs in Afghanistan;
Flags dipped, flowers placed to veterans' tattoos.   60
England's confused. It feels a nation-state
In Wootton Bassett's homecoming and cars,
And yet it's ceased to share a nation's fate
Now it's under a blue flag, yellow stars.

Now outside the harbour the *Phoenix* waits
For the high tide that will float her in, see
Two masts, fluttering flag, upward prow, crates,
Looking like the *Victory*, or *Discovery*

That took empire to Jamestown when, lithesome,
We'd been a Tudor nation, now for show.   70
England's island's now a floating museum
Like this ship that's as it was long ago.

And now I think of the history I love,
European civilization's roots
In Greece and Rome, its Union above,
This new superstate England now salutes.
All Europe's history's in my country now.
Are not the English migrants from Celtic,
Roman, Anglo-Saxon, Danish and (bow)
Norman tribes in Europe's body ethnic?   80

I work again on a World State, my cause.
I advocate a federal 'hauberk'
World government that will, with new world laws,
Enforce peace and disarmament, and work
To share world resources, solve global stealth
(Climate change), end famine and disease, steer
The banking crisis, redistribute wealth
To end poverty – a good upper tier.

The nation-state is passing, all discern
A time of regions and Unions, and our   90
Sovereignty's been surrendered in return
For a share in the EU's sovereign power.
It's a preparation for a World State
That will bring a peace dividend and lease
A benefit to humankind, a great
New Golden Age: prosperity and peace.

I'm relaxed at our demise, a mere cloud,
Pretext for Blair to try for President
At the end of a thousand years of proud
Independence and law-making well-spent,   100

For I'm reunited with my roots, zones
In the Greek, Roman and Renaissance mind.
Europe's high culture acts as stepping-stones
To a Universalist humankind.

I once stepped across the flowing Rothay,
Tiptoeing across stepping-stones in bliss
In Wordsworth's footsteps where he walked each day
To work in Ambleside's old post office.
I tiptoe across the Channel with kings
To a cultural landscape that not too late   110
Connects me to all humankind and brings
Me to more stepping-stones, to a World State.
5 November 2009; 7–8 April 2015

The Treaty of Lisbon was signed on 13 December 2007 and came into force on
1 December 2009.
44. The Treaty of Amiens of 1802 temporarily ended hostilities between the
French Republic and Great Britain.
69. 'Lithesome', 'flexible, supple'. (*Concise Oxford Dictionary*.)
82. 'Hauberk', 'a coat of mail', from Old French and Frankish words for 'neck
protection'. (*Concise Oxford Dictionary*.)

Zeus's Emperor
(A Mock-Heroic Poem)

Canto 1

Sing, Muse, of empire made from nation-states
By men who yearned for peace and urged debates
On ensuring there would be no more war,
And enmeshed France and Germany in law;
Sing how the Lisbon Treaty created
A European superstate that spread
A call to join it to the still unsure,
Whose expansion filled outsiders with awe;

Sing a New World Order's imperial dreams
To advance their *élite*'s self-serving schemes   10
And of Zeus's Universalist hopes
To create (through some hand-picked philanthropes)
A democratic World State that will rule
Mankind benevolently like a school.
If the UN's General Assembly were
Voted in, then mankind might find a cure
For war, famine, poverty and disease;
And a world superstate could not but please.
Or so Zeus thought, and every empire must
Have an 'Emperor', a President all trust;   20
And the European superstate should –
A United States of Europe – do good
And lead mankind forward to the World State,
A United States of the World that's great.
Sing, Muse, of Zeus's noble ambition
As he seeks an 'Emperor' who will stun.

Otto von Habsburg was Zeus's first thought.
He told Hera: "He's the one I have sought.
He'd make an excellent new President,
He's had huge experience and is well-meant.   30
He was head of the House of Habsburg for
Umpteen years and was, before Hitler's war,
Crown Prince of Austria, Bohemia
And Hungary, also of Croatia.
His godfather was Emperor Franz Josef
From a time when the people were not deaf
To monarchies, who was represented
By the Archduke Franz Ferdinand, shot dead
At Sarajevo. And his godmother,
His grandmother, Portugal's *Infanta*.   40
He was brought up linguistically, to speak
All languages spoken in Habsburgs' sweep:
All languages and dialects – a choir –

In the Austro-Hungarian Empire.
I believe he's fluent in thirty-seven.
They taught them well during the Great War, then.
I've heard he has seventeen Christian names,
Ideal for resonating where he claims
In the twenty-seven states under his rule.
Each state will identify with one. Cool.   50
He's already an Emperor-in-waiting,
Pretender to the Austrian throne, and King
Of Hungary. I repeat, he has been
Emperor and King, and might even be Queen.
I say we appoint him immediately,
Or set in motion a quick victory.
Hermes should approach him without delay.
I'm so excited, more than I can say."

Hera listened with languid insouciance
And finished painting her nails, with a glance   60
At the door dismissed him without comment.
All his enthusiasms came and went.
Then she went straight on to the internet.
Ten minutes on, she briefed, they again met.
"Dearest," she said, lowering an eyelid,
Commanding his attention with timid,
Demure acceptance of all he had said,
"I've been thinking, this Otto's a good head
And would have done wonderfully a few years
Back but alas! Time's intervened and jeers.   70
He's ninety-six, and Presidents somehow....
And he only speaks eight languages now.
There were just fifteen languages spoken
In the Austro-Hungarian Empire then.
Perhaps he had a few words in thirty
When he was a boy but they were clumsy.
He hasn't experienced Germany,
France or the UK, now the central three.

What do you want in a new President?
Do you want knowledge, or a cipher meant   80
To be a vacancy all can pour in
Their prejudices and bigoted sin,
An emptiness that is all things to all,
Who will preside by 'not-offending small'?
What do you want of Europe's superstate?
To be effective or to expand, wait
For time to bring in a world government
That will fill the whole world with good intent,
And meanwhile block the New World Order so
It can't strengthen its hold on Europe's show?   90
If so, you're looking for a man who'll con
The élitist, self-interested wan
New World Order into supporting your
Vision of an anti-élitist, raw,
Democratic World State, someone who'll wreck
Rothschilds from the inside just as – you'll check –
He wrecked the UK from the inside by
Too much borrow-and-spend. You need someone
Who's devious and engages, and has done
Something in the same line, and yet appears   100
Vacuous to allay suspicious fears,
And bland, and a regular kind of guy.
I'm thinking of a man who did well by
Us both in dumbing the UK with smarm,
Who'll take our brief for payment and stay calm.
The man I'm thinking of was made Quartet
Envoy on the same day on which he set
Himself on a new course by resigning
As Prime Minister, for money-making.
He's been PM and's now 'Ambassador'   110
To each powerful Middle-Eastern leader.
He could easily be a President.
Blair's your man, vacuous blandness is his bent.
Send Hermes to propose that he applies

Before a peace plan snatches off our prize –
And before he's sacked as 'Ambassador'
For bland inactivity and *hauteur*.
He's lost a little credibility
Through Iraq but this job will set him free."
Zeus listened, stunned at such a good idea.   120
"Of course," he said, "it is President Blair."
Hera smiled, Zeus now had what he wanted
And she could control him – and the godhead.
Languidly she returned to her *boudoir*
And sat at her mirror, her door ajar.

Hermes found Blair in a Jerusalem
Hotel plotting his envoy's stratagem,
New casting out of devils into swine,
To bring peace to Israel and Palestine
Close to the Rothschilds and Rockefellers,   130
A Syndicate role to stop massacres.
Since he arrived the Mid-East had got worse
But undeterred, reluctant to coerce,
He placed full hope in his diplomacy
Which worked in Northern Ireland famously.
(He had excused the IRA's dissent
And crimes, and let them into government.
It was simple, really. And now Israel
Should release Palestinians from gaol
And let them share the running of one state –   140
He was patient and was prepared to wait –
But could retain Israeli settlements
On the West Bank, which were no more than tents.)
Rothschilds, pleased he talked to the other side,
Hoped Israel would continue in her stride
And, Hermes knew, would willingly consent
To his applying to be President
Which would distract, give Israel breathing-space
To move on before he resumed the case.

None of this Blair knew when Hermes appeared   150
In his mirror, sporting a Grecian beard,
And said: "I last saw you when you were still
PM. You'll recall I said, 'If you will,
Do the groundwork for the Lisbon Treaty
For Brown to sign and implement neatly,
Then you'll be considered for high office
In Europe's new and coming synthesis.'
You did. I bring a message from Zeus. He
Sees you as talented, wants you to be
President of the European Council,   160
Effectively (to put a spin on skill)
President of Europe, or Emperor.
You could be the first Emperor and draw
And shape the EU towards its next stage.
The Syndicate will welcome such a sage
And gifted, and experienced, man as you
Governing and directing the EU."
Blair's eyes had widened. "You speak as I've thought,"
He said to the image his mirror brought.
"I'd certainly like to apply." Hermes   170
Nodded and faded. Blair pondered, at ease.

                          Canto 2

Now in his mirror rose a startling scene.
He saw Napoleon as in a dream
Being crowned Emperor of the French in
Notre Dame Cathedral in an ermine-
And-velvet coronation mantle filled
With embroidered golden bees found and milled
From regalia in Childeric the First's
Merovingian tomb – a scene that bursts
In from a cold December Sunday in   180
1804. Napoleon (no grin)
Solemnly placed a laurel crown as worn
By Roman Emperors on his own head, torn

From the Roman Empire, gold laurel wreath,
And then took from the altar, waist beneath,
The new 'Charlemagne crown', ignored the Pope
So he would not have to accept the dope
As his overlord, crowned himself and sat
On his imperial throne, an autocrat –
This conquering soldier unexpectedly   190
Crowned himself as he owed his power to 'me' –
With sceptre, sword, ring, orb, both ornaments
And regalia, with Charlemagne's 'incense'
From twelve candles held by twelve French virgins
(Who'd been hard to find in Parisian inns
After the social revolution there)
All round Charlemagne's coronation chair.
Napoleon looked to the empires and ranks
Of the Romans, Merovingians and Franks.
And all over his coronation robe   200
Of velvet that would be known round the globe
Imperial bees in gold and 'N' that broke
From a wreath of olives, laurel and oak.
David, commissioned, was given an order
To paint in Napoleon's absent mother.
According to the tallies of the banks
All cost over 8.5 million francs.
A new dynasty, like the Frankish Kings'
And Holy Roman Emperors', now springs.
Three hundred thousand French died for a vow   210
To overthrow the Bourbon throne, and now
The monarchy was back with a new name:
'Emperor', not 'monarch', but just the same.
"Vivat imperator in aeternum,"
Proclaimed Pope Pius the Seventh, now glum.
"May the Emperor live forever." Full choirs
Sang, *"Vivat"* and *"Te Deum"* filled the spires.
Blair watched transfixed. The Emperor of France
Had had all this, but this was just a trance

Beside what Europe's Emperor would see,   220
Expect at his coronation, surely?
Napoleon led campaigns, dominated
Europe and in a *coup* became the head
Of the French State – First Consul – and then court
Emperor and King of Italy, fought
The coalition until Waterloo,
And was twice exiled to an island's few.
Blair led campaigns in Afghanistan, hurled
Troops at Iraq, dominated the world
While PM in the UK, had to stop,   230
And now should be President of Europe.
Napoleon was Emperor of the French
But Blair, as Emperor of Europe, would wrench
The laurels from Napoleon's hangers-on,
He would be better than Napoleon.
Charlemagne, Napoleon and now Blair.
A grandeur (that was grandiose) filled the air.
A bubble of megalomania
And self-importance? No, but some *hauteur*.

It had long been suspected by Farage   240
That there had been a deal, that those in charge
Of the EU, especially Barroso,
Would reward Blair for wanting the euro
In the UK, waiving Britain's rebate
And declining a referendum's date
By making him President (with new powers)
Of the European Council. He still glowers
At the thought, but there is no evidence
Of a deal, which Barroso calls nonsense.
Was there an unspoken understanding?   250
Was there a look, a glance, a posturing?
Let's give Blair the benefit of the doubt
And say there was no plan to give him clout.

⌐ Behind this Europe, as under a stone
 A toad squats, squats behind the Council's throne
 The true kingmaker, the Rothschild empire
 Which controls (to Zeus's alarm and ire)
 One hundred and eighty-seven central banks
 Under the English-and-French-merged bright ranks
 Of Concordia BV led by David   260
 Rothschild, who like an ancient chief druid
 Controls French, Belgian and Continental
 Rothschilds banking through the international
 Rothschild and Cie Banque, and banking elsewhere,
 Including N.M. Rothschild's English flair,
 Through Rothschilds Continuation Holdings
 AG, and numbered among several 'kings'
 Rothschilds' puppet and creature Sarkozy,
 French President. Two years previously
 Sarkozy, at Rothschilds' bidding, had launched   270
 (Once the wound of his departure was staunched)
 A campaign for ex-Prime Minister Blair
 To be the EU's President with clear
 Support from Brown, the new English PM
 And other EU leaders. But, ahem!
 The Tories and Liberals, despite applause,
 Declined support, and Iraq dogged his cause.
 The German Free Democrats' leader's plea
 Was for someone from a smaller country.
 Blair became a Catholic to cement   280
 His credentials for being President.
 Now Rothschilds estimated to be worth
 Five trillion dollars, the highest on earth –
 Five thousand billion against Gates' forty,
 Way off the top of the rich hierarchy –
 Wanted a new European chairman,
 Not a chief, and began to renege on
 An EU President, and downgraded
 The role to the Council. They went ahead

And sought a nonentity who would do   290
Their bidding, give them more control of new
Oil and gas supplies. They wanted a weak
President, not a strong one, who would speak
From the ground of the Centre-Right, and found
Herman Van Rompuy who'd support a round
Of new EU taxes, having once worked
(Or, more truthfully, like a spider lurked)
In Belgium's Rothschilds-controlled central bank.
He spent a day each month in a 'think-tank',
In a monastery, and he wrote haikus.   300
Him now did the kingmaking Rothschilds choose.
At the end of October Sarkozy
Held a private interview with Rompuy
At an EU summit in the EU
Parliament chamber, Brussels. Merkel, too –
Creature of Rockefellers, power behind
Post-war Germany's Marshall Aid, and kind –
Crossed the room to him and then left with him.
Rompuy was now the Chosen One, a whim
Of the self-interested New World Order   310
Who had him down to chair their own dogma.

In November Rompuy was invited
To a secret dinner – a lavish spread
At Château de Val-Duchesse, a landmark
Where the Treaty of Rome, midwived by Spaak
And Robert Rothschild, was born – by Vicomte
Davignon, ex-Commission VP, prompt
And front for the secret Bilderberg Group
Who told him what they want (over the soup):
A world federation and EU tax.   320
Then Rompuy stood and said that's what he backs.
He understood that he must chair meetings,
Build consensus and smile out warm greetings,
An international representative

Who'd work for his masters and would not give
Cause for concern or seem to contradict
The Syndicate's wishes, or cause conflict:
A Mr Nice who's a safe pair of hands
With the Syndicate's agenda and stands,
One of five candidates who were all grey;   330
But it was clear where Rothschilds' preference lay.
Alerted, Hermes gatecrashed the dinner
And reported to Zeus on the rupture.

Zeus was aghast that the New World Order
Might own the President and manager
Who'd bring in *his* World State, chief Blair, who should
Be conning the *élite* of all he could,
Shifting its oil and gas from bankers' grasp
To humankind's ownership and hand clasp,
And asked Apollo how best to detach   340
Rompuy from Rothschilds, what scheme he could hatch.
Apollo said, "Someone should tell him he
Should be a full-time haiku poet, free
From the distractions of a President.
I will find someone to write an urgent
Sonnet flattering his skills and haiku.
Leave it to me. I will soon know just who."
Soon after his screen showed *Armageddon*.
He was absorbed in *jihad* with his scone,
An epic poem on a grandiose scale   350
About the War on Terror, will Bush fail?
He asked Hermes to get a sonnet penned,
To ask the Muses who they recommend.
Calliope told Hermes: "It's hopeless.
English poetry is in such a vast mess.
The poets – poetasters rather – claim
To be original but, to their shame,
They plagiarise in irregular lines.
Few know about sonnets, or what refines."

Euterpe, near at hand, brought her laments: 360
"Hardly anyone's any good at sense.
Few know about Belgium or the haiku.
What English poet writes on the EU?
You might as well go to Selfridges where
The celebrity Jordan's bust and hair
Are promoting her book, in bikini
With four cross-dressers, to a crowd for she
Sells more books in a day than all poets
Sell in a year. But her books are rosettes,
They're all ghost-written, she's not scratched a word. 370
The whole thing's preposterous, quite absurd.
She cannot tell a haiku from a hike,
She wouldn't know Van Rompuy from a bike.
You couldn't do worse than approach Hagger.
He dwarfs Rompuy in quantity and purr.
He knows about Belgium and the EU.
He was in Japan, he'll know the haiku.
An Apollo bust stands in his garden,
And Apollo's reading his works again.
He couldn't be English Laureate as 380
He's not got a national outlook, he has
A Universalist perspective that's
International and can do Europe's spats.
He's the Muses' amanuensis when
We send him inspiration, and he's then
Under Apollo's control. He's invoked
Dante and met Pound, he can write a cloaked
Address to Rompuy, flatter his haikus.
Take Apollo, and these words from his Muse."

So Hermes and Apollo made their way 390
Past the bust of Apollo in bright day
To the spiral stair to this poet's room,
His study where he sits in tranquil gloom
And gazes on Henry the Eighth's deer park.

Here Apollo greeted him, "Hi skylark,
For you look down from high, see unity."
He passed on Euterpe's message. "Rompuy
May end up chairing Europe for Rothschilds.
You don't want that and nor does Zeus. The wilds
Are his true love, he really wants to write   400
Haikus about Nature. Praise his insight."
He laid some haikus on his desk like gold.
Our poet looked, then shook his head, left cold:
"He's such a Syndicate supporter he
Can't be dissuaded, President Rompuy.
You need to focus on a true World State,
This diagram's structure – it's not too late."
He handed Phoebus *The World Government*.
Lines and boxes showed what a World State meant;
Also *The Secret American Dream*   410
To show what Obama could do and scheme.
Later Apollo showed the diagram
To Zeus, who was shocked but then claimed, "I am
The originator of Hagger's 'chart'.
I sent it to him to inspire his art."
Apollo, the inspirer, shook his head.
Zeus's spinning threatened to leave truth dead.

Zeus was dismayed Rompuy had edged out Blair
And watched with horror and mounting despair
As the Spanish PM Zapatero   420
Met Brown, the British PM, with a blow
At Belgium's Zaventem Airport: he asked
Brown to drop his "pointless" campaign, unmasked
Now, for Blair to be President. Support
For Blair now drained away during a fraught
Meeting of EU socialist leaders.
The EU now agreed (through its hagglers)
The Centre-Right should hold the presidency,
The socialists the foreign ministry.

At a dinner that night to celebrate   430
The Berlin Wall's fall, for each member-state
Twenty-seven representatives dined on
Sea bass and fine wines and discussed who shone,
Which candidate to choose as President,
What the High Representative's role meant.
Hermes, disguised as a waiter, now tried
To spike the wine and cloud judgements, sharp-eyed,
Egged on by Zeus, who still championed Blair
But had no more influence than thin air.
In vain! For in that Brussels dining-room   440
The Machiavellian plotting and wine-fume
Ended in nominations, a clear choice:
Rompuy for President, man of soft voice,
And Lady Ashton for the other post,
British like Blair, who was now but a ghost.
The New World Order were delighted now
They'd a hireling for their agenda's plough.
There was a toast, then rejoicing and mirth:
Two pygmies for roles that straddled the earth.
Rothschilds could now expand their trade, conspire   450
And extend their Franco-German Empire.
The appointments were announced and a press
Conference at Justus Lipsius, smoothness-
Led Council of Ministers building. Each
Seemed shocked, Ashton had no acceptance speech.
She was the Treasurer of CND
At the time of the Falklands War, and she
Now had seven thousand staff and salaries,
And a hundred and twenty embassies.
Rompuy surveyed the scene, now Emperor.   460
Dazed eyes, glazed, gazed out at the daunting blur.

Canto 3
Zeus was furious that he'd not had his way.
He was shocked, angered and filled with dismay

At the nonentities who'd rule Europe
And appalled that the New World Order's scope
Would be more powerful than before. Now none
Could con it into supporting his one
Democratic, philanthropic World State.
Depressed, he was now beyond all debate.
He was comforted by Hera who, too,   470
Was dismayed that her way had proved taboo.
Both had supported Blair as Emperor,
And both were overruled by a mobster.
Zeus felt, 'I'm not as powerful as Rothschilds
Who are kingmakers out there in the wilds.'
Blair ruefully learned that he'd been surpassed
By a man of less flair who he'd outclassed.
Rothschilds had stage-managed the appointment
Of two pygmies, who'd do what they present:
President Whatshisname, Baroness Who.   480
Merkel and Sarkozy could now pursue
An increased federal, protectionist threat
Against the Anglo-Saxon free market
In a Franco-German Empire controlled
By the ex-East-German Stasi agent's hold
Of Merkel, protégée of Kohl (a man
Who prolonged Rockefellers' Marshall Plan),
Who in June criticised Rothschilds' control
Of central banks and a French bail-out's dole;
A Franco-German Empire that's co-run   490
By Rothschilds and Rockefellers, and spun
In the Bilderberg Group – scant British say.
Barroso thought Blair close to Bush's way
And though he was a good candidate for
Rothschilds and pro-Turkish enough (though raw)
For Rockefellers, Blair did not oppose
Like Merkel, who was an outspoken 'rose',
Rothschilds' control of global usury
And was less federalist than Van Rompuy.

Giscard lamented: where was the stature 500
Of George Washington in our new leader?
December the first, the Lisbon Treaty
Was implemented by Emperor Rompuy.

Now pygmies sat in giant seats, and three
Controlled – Barroso, Ashton and Rompuy –
The new superstate. Yet still Merkel towers
Above the distribution of new powers.
The banking crisis and bail-outs, and then
Problems in the eurozone. Things worsen.
Zeus seemed to have lost control of mankind, 510
Man seemed quite beyond what Zeus had in mind.
Zeus was appalled that the potentially
Totalitarian New World Order's free,
Too mighty. He tried to lead it astray
Through Blair, now had to find another way
Of bringing in a World State to devour
The Syndicate's and New World Order's power.
"That seer Hagger told me," Apollo said,
"A partial World State could be created
By Obama." Zeus said, "I do agree, 520
I must deal with the US. Look, I see...."
Zeus extended Hagger's seven-foot-long chart
Over his knees and peered beyond his heart
At twenty-five civilizations down
And sixty-one stages across his frown
And tried to grasp how history works, its sprawl
Through civilizations that rise and fall.
At last Zeus got the chart the right way round
And now shared with Apollo what he'd found:
"On Hagger's chart, the next stage of the North- 530
American civilization set forth
Is a Universalist one. I've read
The Secret American Dream, which said
That the US, not Europe, is our route.

Instruct Obama to speed up, transmute
The world and implement the chart's next stage
So a democratic World State can cage
In the dictatorial New World Order's
EU and absorb it in its pastures."
So Zeus took his history from Hagger's chart.   540
All the gods now relied on human art
But Zeus's initiative petered out.
Obama dithered and was filled with doubt,
He sided with, to Apollo's dismay,
The Freemasonic New World Order's way.

Zeus sat in dejection and told Hera
"As Rompuy, not Blair, is my Emperor,
I have to accept that my power's failing.
It's not as absolute as in my spring.
The chief god lives forever but grows old   550
(In a way of speaking), mind patched with mould.
It is a relatively recent trend
That the chief of the gods can no more send
His vision of the future via Hermes
To human minds that make sense just as bees
Make honey from thyme; that he has lost power.
We gods, no longer all-powerful, just glower.
The true Emperor is kingmaking Rothschilds
Who have supplanted us out in the wilds."
Hera comforted him: "That's too extreme,   560
You're still more powerful than the sun, you beam
And the earth goes on doing what it should.
You send a thunderbolt and burn a wood.
You used to send thoughts into human minds
But few now see your Light which they think blinds.
It's not your fault that men cannot receive
Your visions. My dearest, you must not grieve.
You're still the order in the universe
Which couldn't function without you as nurse.

Men aren't as deep as once they used to be   570
And so they're ignorant of your energy.
The New World Order will not have its way.
The coming World State will soon hold its sway.
Rothschilds think that the UK's been absorbed
By a Franco-German Empire that's daubed
It, that Blair sold Britain down the river,
Conned by the promise he'd be Emperor.
The New World Order thinks it's doing well
But what is ahead only you can tell."
Now Zeus perked up, his confidence restored,   580
And said, "I'll put those Rothschilds to the sword."

Blair'd implemented the Syndicate's stark
Wish – and Rothschilds' – by invading Iraq
Believing Saddam had WMDs.
Did he lie to the British people, please,
Or was he taken in, did he not check?
Or did the intelligence crash and wreck?
Such questions were considered by Chilcot.
Zeus was sad that Emperor Blair could not
Cause the New World Order the mayhem he   590
Inflicted on Britain via Iraq's spree.
Blair failed to bring peace to the Middle East
As Quartet envoy, and his flair decreased.
By the time he resigned from the Quartet
The Middle East had become a world threat.
During his eight years of pursuing peace
Unfortunately warfare did not cease.
Two wars between Israel and Hamas blipped,
Civil war in Syria, *coup* in Egypt;
ISIS occupied large parts of Iraq   600
And Syria, spawned from his post-Saddam dark.
The reputation he hoped to rescue
Was now demolished by war and curfew.
For eight years he held court in luxury,

In the Emirates' Palace, Abu Dhabi,
A Hotel in whose foyer it's routine
Gold bars are dispensed from a cash machine.
A Representative of the Quartet –
The EU, US, UN, Russia – yet
Without a secretariat or staff   610
He's cost the British taxpayer – don't laugh –
Sixteen thousand pounds a week – what a dream! –
To pay for private jets and house his team
Of eight Metropolitan police there
(Not counting four who guard his four homes), near
His hotel suite and view of the Persian
Gulf (seven thousand pounds a night) where he'd plan.
His peace meetings with dozens of leaders
Were mixed with filling his private rosters
Of clients who would pay millions of pounds   620
For his advice, on contract, that astounds –
Short of potential conflicts of interest
With his unpaid role as one of the best
International envoys, for talking peace
Works best when peacemakers can sell a lease
Or strike a commercial bargain that they
Won't want to be sidelined by war's delay.
Asked for a twenty-minute speech on how
To feed the poor at a conference, he – wow! –
Demanded a three-hundred-and-thirty-   630
Thousand-pound fee to talk on the hungry,
According to Stockholm's Eat Food Forum,
Enough to strike a million starving dumb.
He'd contracts all round the globe, and had ten
Properties that need protecting, amen!
He'd dined with billionaires and heiresses –
Li Bingbing, best of Chinese actresses
And friend of Wendy Deng Murdoch (divorced
After he visited her home unsourced);
And Ofra Strauss and Belinda Stronach,   640

And charity donors who watched his back.
So Blair would busy himself, now he could
Not be Emperor, by doing lots of good.

Meanwhile, the new Emperor could not control
The banking crisis and eurozone's role.
Now Zeus hoped his World State would clear the mess
The Franco-German Empire'd made, and press
The EU and US, through the UN
And Ban Ki-moon, to outflank and weaken
The self-interested Syndicate that sought   650
To imprison the world within a fort.
Zeus knew its totalitarian style
Could be vanquished by democratic guile.

Alas, gods are no longer all-powerful.
If we want world peace, then we have to pull
Our weight and do it for ourselves. Self-help!
When life gets hard it doesn't help to yelp.
We can't count on the gods delivering.
The gods, like politicians, are struggling
To convince themselves they're still in control.   660
Sometimes they can help, sometimes they console.
Zeus had been buffeted by two world wars,
Umpteen Cold-War skirmishes and old scores.
Man's slipped the leash and rampages beyond
Zeus's control, many seek to abscond.
Hera was right in what she did profess:
Zeus can't be blamed for mankind's waywardness.
Zeus's loss of power is not down to him,
But to increasing ignorance of dim
Mankind, that is no longer living right.   670
Man's inner sky is now an endless night.
But, and this is crucial, Zeus can still send
Inspiration in Light to dawn and blend
In opened souls, and so his hand-picked few

Continue to transmit what he would do,
Plans for future initiatives and works,
Light-coded messages, the mystic's perks.
Politicians do not open their souls
As they quibble and bicker on their goals,
And so Zeus is cut off from world leaders   680
As if those who should be guided partners
Have had their phone line cut and receive no
Instructions or guidance, are left to go
About their business without divine aid
And blunder and fall down though on parade.
Zeus keeps his links with mystics' inner eye
Which receives and decodes Light like a spy.
And so, and this is really important,
The mystic's become Zeus's confidant.
Mystics, not politicians, instigate   690
And receive the vision of the World State.
A mystic's inner eye can glimpse two new
Elected Presidents in the EU:
The Commission's Juncker and Council's Tusk
Who replace Barroso, and Rompuy's dusk.
It is an indisputable truth and right
That there's a Law of Order, and with Light
And a struggle on Zeus's part, right will
Prevail and good will triumph – just be still.
Zeus' ordered plan for a World State must   700
Inevitably make the world more just
Even though Zeus has lost his confidence
And depends on the mystics to make sense –
Even though Zeus has forgotten the plan
And to remind himself now has to scan
Works by mystics he claims to have inspired
Like Hagger's chart and World-State books he Fired.
23–27 November 2009; 30 March, 1, 9–11, 13–18 April, 12–13 June 2015

Herman Van Rompuy was declared President of the European Council ('EU

President') on 19 November 2009.

295. Herman Van Rompuy, shortened to Rompuy in some later lines.

689.'confidant', 'a person trusted with knowledge of one's private affairs'. (*Concise Oxford Dictionary.*)

Royal Wedding

I

Guests throng the tree-lined aisle in morning suits,
Field maples make a leafy avenue.
Royal and Abbey ushers show them to seats,
Ladies' hats sloped to side in fashion's sway.
No Blair, snubbed for his comments in his book,
No Brown, shunned for saddling Britain with debt;
No Syrian envoy, disinvited for
The shooting of reformists in marches.
The best and worst strut styles like peacocks' tails.
British designers compete, and the dress   10
Will be copied by midday and mass-sold.
The Speaker's wife's in barmaid's see-through lace
And high heels that dwarf him three inches more.
Beckham, who lobbied FIFA with the Prince
For the World Cup but lost out to Qatar,
Has pinned his OBE on the wrong side
And should not be wearing it here at all.
His fake-tanned wife is dressed in navy blue.
Johnson has hired his suit from Moss Brothers.
Oh no, why's that loathsome, podgy slob here?   20
Because he crooned at Diana's funeral?
He's cut off his mother as his partner
Took offence at some remark that she made.
The Prime Minister strides in tails, thank God.
His wife's hatless but for a spangled slide
That's glittery, shiny, multicoloured,
A flower set in crystals in wind-blown hair

That hasn't seen a hairbrush in a week,
To defy convention at this wedding,
A national occasion for doing things right.   30
And the two frumps with fascinator hats,
Too tall to fit in the car that brought them,
Couldn't someone have told them how to dress?
Now the Prince in resplendent red tunic
Removes his hat and gloves, treads red carpet,
An Irish Guard Colonel with Blues-and-Royals,
Black-tunicked brother beside him, and then
His father and (to a fanfare) the Queen
In a yellow coat with matching bonnet,
Who process down the aisle beneath Henry   40
The Third's vaulting a hundred and two feet
Above them (to be higher than the church
Where French kings were crowned, one up on the French).
Look, here comes Diana's nemesis, who
She saw as hoary wolf, hunter of prey,
Who will become our next Queen, not Consort.
And now at last, veiled, lace-shouldered and train
Nearly three metres long – a chic, stylish,
Classic dress designed by Sarah Burton
Of Alexander McQueen's fashion house,   50
Its lace sewn in Hampton Court by ladies
Told it was for a period drama,
Who washed their hands every half hour and changed
Needles every three hours to keep them sharp –
Our cynosure, our ex-commoner bride,
A bouquet of Sweet William and myrtle,
Lily of the valley, hyacinth, ivy
Symbolising gallantry and marriage,
Happiness, constancy, fidelity;
Veil held in place by a Cartier halo   60
Platinum-and-diamond tiara lent
By her Majesty as 'something borrowed',
Smiles down the aisle, steadied by father's hand.

Cameras stray to the low cut at the front
And figure-hugging back of the slim dress
Worn by her blushing, or not so blushing,
Sister, chief bridesmaid. Cameras, turn back.
Three tiny bridesmaids and two red-tunicked
Page-boys behind, she stands beside her lord,
Who says blandly, "You look so beautiful,"   70
Before the ancient pavement that displays
The universe's medieval spheres,
The *sacrarium*, the choir screen behind.
The Queen looks glum, stern and expressionless.
She reigns by looking blank, unrevealing,
Through her profile on stamps and coins preserves
The continuity of our free speech,
Remote, aloof, aloft and Germanic.
The bland couple stand at the front, back-view
Ciphers on which their subjects project love.   80
Introit and hymn now sung, and welcome given,
The Archbishop elicits vows and winds
The stole that's round his neck, binding their wrists,
And a commoner has become Princess,
Latter-day Anne Boleyn, plucked from her small
Village, Bucklebury, to become Queen.
A hymn, the lesson, *Romans* chapter twelve
From US *Bible* – "Do not be haughty" –
Read by the bride's brother; then an anthem.
The Bishop of London begins the address   90
With Catherine of Siena's "Be who God
Meant you to be, you'll set the world on fire".
He says, "In the spirit of generous God
Husband and wife give themselves generously
To each other. In spiritual life, the more
We give of self, the richer we become
In soul, become our true selves and reveal
Spiritual beauty. In marriage we seek
To bring each other into fuller life.

Thus we wean ourselves from self-centredness.   100
We transform our partners but must not seek
To re-form them, for as Chaucer once wrote,
'When mastery cometh, the god of love anon
Beateth his wings – and farewell! he is gone.'
The fruits of the spirit are love, joy, peace."
A celebration of the sanctity
Of Christian, not celebrity, marriage:
If Simon Cowell married Katie Price
Would such crowds line the route and wave small flags?
Sexual attractiveness, hedonism   110
And perpetual drama may not make for
Lives worth living despite applauding crowds.
They make four hundred-and-fifty-year-old
Vows in the name of the Supreme Being,
In a church built a thousand years ago.
The couple's party go behind to sign,
Then after motet and hymn, end prayers
And blessing, they process back down the aisle
Turning to left and right with radiant smiles.
After photos she'll lay her bouquet on   120
The Grave of the Unknown Warrior just as
The Queen did sixty-four years previously.

II

Bells ring out as they leave the Abbey for
An open landau, train folded away,
And ride with bobbing Horse Guards at their back,
Waving to the crowds at least twenty deep,
The front row having slept on the pavement,
Past the window from which Charles the First stepped
In Whitehall Palace to be beheaded.
Passing the Cenotaph the Prince salutes   130
White hand to peaked cap as the crowd waves flags.
Britain at war in Afghanistan, now
In Libya, has a young Colonel Prince

And will Gaddafi's hit men shoot him down?
Suicide-bomb the landau, crash a plane?
The landau jolts into Horse Guards and turns
Into The Mall, more carriages behind.
Crowds wave flags for a country racked by debt,
Facing deep cuts with scarcely any growth,
Legacy of Labour's mismanagement,   140
But all are cheering for a never-was,
A make-believe romance, Cinderella,
The first Queen Catherine since Catherine Parr,
A Ruritanian fairy-tale and reign
After the Queen and the next King have died,
When he's in his sixties like his father
In thirty-five years' time. Look, there's no rain,
And what relief as their landau enters
The safety of Buckingham Palace gates
And all disappear inside, to emerge   150
On the balcony, crowds all down The Mall,
A million cheering as they both act out
A rehearsed public kiss (timetabled for
One twenty-five, scarcely spontaneous)
And look up: a fly-past, a Lancaster,
Spitfire and Hurricane, and a new wave
Of two Typhoons and two Tornadoes in
Diamond formation low over their roof –
And has Gaddafi paid a lone pilot
To crash into the royals and pay us back   160
For NATO's laser bombing of his base
In Tripoli with bunker-busting bombs?
The Queen, edgy, heads into the two doors
And all vacate the balcony for within.
Now Big-Society street parties start,
Feasting on sausage rolls under bunting.

III
The pageantry is over, and the pomp

And circumstance is done, and the British
Have shown to one-third of the world's subjects,
Two billion, the family that they have   170
For one thousand years elevated as
Head of State above party skirmishes.
This marriage will perpetuate the line,
Inheritance will rule us, not merit.
The line is guaranteed, in thirty years
When his father dies, this couple will reign.
Many feel the monarchy costs too much,
There are too many to support, there should
Be a republic after the Queen's death.
And where are the republican voices   180
That were promised, with guillotine to scream
"Off with their heads"? Arrested by police,
Who sealed the route with anti-bomb machines
At either end, including the Abbey,
And kept away al-Qaeda, Libyans
And Irish who'd attack our royal line,
And seized fifty-six anarchists as well.
I think of the English nation's follies.
We've asked the Saxe-Coburg-Gothas to reign
And they've learned English, call themselves Windsors.   190
And we have forgotten their foreignness
And project our wish they should be English.
A grand day out and a significance,
A more down-to-earth, long-term monarchy.
Has this fresh, young, new face in military
Costume renewed the monarchy which glues
The military and the government?
Or was this the monarchy's dying gasp,
Each scene false, rehearsed, manipulated?
The next King's life was overshadowed by   200
His first wife and will be by this couple
And opinion will now swell that the line
Should skip from the Queen to her young grandson.

Has the monarchy renewed itself in
A new generation with theatre skills?
Will it avoid ostentation and waste?
A republic would have come faster if
This Prince had wed a Duke's daughter, but now
We see this couple's Herculean task.
Will this Saxe-Coburg-Gotha marriage save   210
The nation and lessen class divisions?
Can they really preserve the monarchy
And reunite the disparate voices
By being more fun and more like ourselves,
When England's no longer self-governing,
Having ceded power to Europe, devolved
Power to Scotland where separatists want more?
Sovereignty is in Parliament, but still
There's an illusion that the monarchy
Is sovereign throughout the UK's extent   220
And defies Europe, which makes all the laws.
Politicians have bartered sovereignty.
The bouquet's on the Grave of the Unknown
Warrior now the wedding photos are done.
The Prince has said his bride will be known as
Princess Catherine, upstaging Camilla,
And there was no prenuptial agreement
As he trusts his wife and our future Queen.
Now this bland couple must win many hearts
And glue the fragments of our dwindling State,   230
Paper over the fissures, cracks and splits,
After the Queen's, and then the King's demise
And preserve our ancient unity, roll
Back history to Victorian times and sway,
And cement the solidness of the State.
29 April 2011; 5, 28, 29 August 2015

The marriage of Prince William and Kate Middleton took place in Westminster Abbey on Friday 29 April 2011.

Epistle to Gaddafi

I did not know, going to work that day
In my green Volkswagen Beetle, that you,
Gaddafi, led the revolution I
Encountered in the early-morning streets
In your turquoise Beetle, which mirrored mine
(Replicated in the fawn Beetles you
Routinely set to watch me by my gate);
Another instance of your reflecting
My buried self and characteristics.
Active underminer of my musing   10
And *alter ego* who blocked my free will,
Whose *coup* I held responsible for my
Own damaged ego (hence I knocked your cap
From your head when you came to where I worked),
You also had your henchman arrest me
One night and announce my execution.
Staring at the muzzle of a Luger
I said my writing would outlast your reign.
And you having announced that you would bomb
Your own people in Benghazi, NATO's   20
Air strikes have made you flee in a convoy.
And now, after I dreamt you were hiding
In a storm drain, I find my dream was right
For I have seen your killing on TV:
A fierce mob dragged you from a pipe and thrust
A bayonet up your buttocks, spilling blood,
And beat you and then shot you in your head
And threw your body on a pick-up truck
To be displayed to people filing past,
Spitting, in a Misrata meat-chilling room.   30
And now I have appeared on Sky TV's
Lunchtime news and have talked for eight minutes
(Before a studio's lights and Autocues)
About your *coup* and how, despite that night,

I survived you. And by now the black flag
Of who you meant you would bomb, al-Qaeda,
Flies over the court-house in Benghazi.
You overthrew King Idris's order
And now the aftermath of your foul rule
Is anarchy, rule by roadblocks manned by   40
Two hundred and fifty militias
(Soon to be a whopping eighteen thousand)
And no recognised central government
So your weapons stores have been ransacked by
Al-Qaeda and ISIS. Now there's chaos
As East-African refugees pour in
To squash in crowded unseaworthy boats
And be smuggled across Europe's borders.
A row of black-clad IS men have lined
Egyptian Copts on one of your beaches   50
And beheaded the lot beside the tide
So the sea turned crimson with Christian blood.
O, what happened to the sandy beaches
Where so often I took a picnic lunch
And sunbathed on a sweltering afternoon
Cooled by the breezes from the sea, in dunes?
And what happened to those who sat with me?
Swept away as if by a tidal wave.
I was caught between you and patriots.

Gaddafi, your legacy's a failed state   60
And a country riven by civil war
And the oil reserves you stole through your *coup*
Are now in the hands of terrorists who
Want to destroy Europe, behead and maim,
Seeking to restore the seventh century,
As a quick way of reaching Paradise.
It would have been better for Libya,
And for us all, if your bold *coup* had failed
That morning I drove my Beetle to work

And found no other cars out on the roads –   70
And though I had already been approached
To serve my country as a patriot,
I would have avoided my war on you
And remained within my literary life.
You distracted me, Gaddafi, *alter*
Ego and man of action hidden within
The contemplative poet I've tried to be,
And all I've done since, my forty-four books,
Was done by suppressing that active self
Whose release at the time greatly pleased me.   80
You were my buried self, Gaddafi, so
I now acclaim your overthrow and crow
I triumphed over you, though secretly
I am a little sad to see you go
For we had a weird bond, and I am now
A follower of your abstemiousness
(From circumstance, not following your lead),
Your puritanical 'no alcohol'.
You lived in the world of action and dragged
Me from my dreaming into politics.   90
But you were disciplined and self-controlled
When our paths crossed (though subsequently you
Took to drugs and indulgence, and abused
Many girl students with your tyrant's power)
And I have subsequently become both.
You had a destructive impact on me
But also, weirdly, a creative one.
I emerged from the Libyan desert
A deeper man than when I entered it
And I acknowledge your unwitting role   100
In bringing to birth my determined soul
That lives in harmony with all Nature.
Idea: October 2011. Written: 16 December 2015

Nicholas Hagger encountered Colonel Gaddafi several times in 1969–70.

Gaddafi was overthrown and killed on 20 October 2011.

13. 'Damaged ego'. "The actual process of individuation – the conscious coming-to-terms with one's inner centre (psychic nucleus) or Self – generally begins with a wounding of personality, and the suffering that accompanies it. This initial shock amounts to a sort of call, although it is often not recognised as such. On the contrary, the ego feels hampered in its will or desire and usually projects the obstruction onto something external. That is, the ego accuses God, the economic situation, or the boss, or the marriage partner of being responsible for whatever is obstructing it." C.G. Jung *et.al.*, *Man and His Symbols* (Picador, 1964), p.169.

Changelessness like a Fanfare: Trumpeting a Jubilee

1.

A thousand boats progress along the Thames
Led by gilded *Gloriana*, a rowbarge
Whose eighteen Tudor-style oarsmen toss oars.
A floating belfry swings eight bells on large
Wheels, peals answered from land by pealed church bells.
Rowing-boats, shallops, skiffs follow, cocklers,
Herring drifters, kayaks, tall ships and tugs,
Steamers, oyster smacks, cutters and cruisers
From Canaletto's 1747
'Thames on Lord Mayor's Day' – recreating then.   10

2.

A million line the banks and cheer the show,
A pageant with the largest flotilla
To sail on the River Thames since King Charles
The Second brought Catherine of Braganza
With "a thousand barges and boats" Pepys saw
In 1662 to wow his bride.
And on a royal barge with two thrones, decked
With ten thousand flowers, her Duke at her side,
Stands she who's thanked for sixty years – again –

Of selfless reign, in four hours' wind and rain.   20

3.

The Thames Flood Barrier, closed, slows the river.
An orchestra's 'Rule Britannia' 's a feat.
Tower Bridge raises its roads in steep salute.
At her Silver the Queen reviewed a fleet
But it's been sold and now we have these skiffs.
Wet street parties with patriotic grit
Signal with flags that all have united.
More than four thousand beacons have been lit,
The first in Tonga. The Empire's in pieces
But she is still Queen of sixteen countries.   30

4.

A concert outside Buckingham Palace:
Loud tuneless rapping and unfunny 'jokes'.
Our culture has collapsed to clunking din
And inane words shrieked in screeches and croaks
(And vacuous questions presenters preen).
The Duke is in hospital, we are told,
Her Lord High Admiral who stood four hours,
With cystitis brought on by the Thames cold.
Two dozen 'celebrities' strut and prance
And deafen. The ear-plugged Queen looks askance.   40

5.

She stands on the stage, above each tribute.
Her heir kisses her hand and begins fond-
-ly, "Your Majesty – Mummy," as all roar.
She lights the last beacon with a diamond.
Crowds line the streets as she drives to St Paul's.
Victoria (without Albert) could not climb
Its steps in 1897, stayed in
Her carriage for the whole thanksgiving time.
The Archbishop praises *her* selfless joy.

She drives to Mansion House in a convoy.   50

6.

A 'Jubilee' is a 'rejoicing', comes
From Hebrew '*yobel*', a 'ram's-horn trumpet'.
A trumpet fanfare from heralds, all rise.
She descends Westminster-Hall steps, slow yet
Sure-footed though eighty-six years old, past
Where Charles the First was tried and condemned. Grey
Liverymen and politicians sit
At round tables near where her parents lay
In state, and Churchill. The Master Mercer,
Before the English dishes, welcomes her.   60

7.

Thousands of servicemen stand in the streets
As her landau leaves Westminster in rain,
Footmen in gold livery and black caps;
As her Horse Guards' hooves clop-clop their terrain
Into the Mall where crowds thirty deep cheer.
Flags hang between the trees, red guards with black
Busbies on heads make sure her landau's safe.
By her waves her heir's wife (fifteen years back
A pariah who spoiled what might have been),
Facing her heir, a statement she'll be Queen.   70

8.

A quarter of a million fill the Mall,
A river of flag-waving and a cheer
As she stands on the palace balcony
With her heir and his queen, and *his* young heir
And future queen. A fusillade of shots.
A Dakota's roar speaks for wartime folk:
A Lancaster and four Spitfires drone past,
And nine Red Arrows trail red, white, blue smoke.
She unites all, presents a dynasty:

The assured succession of the monarchy.   80

9.

The first Elizabeth and Victoria
Presided over their growing empires.
Her sixty years have witnessed their decline
To dwindling austerity in the shires.
The times have swept away a class system
For money, talent and celebrity.
Her televised thanks are brief and formal.
She unites diverse races silently.
She reigns by saying nothing, showing no
Feeling – which her stamp-and-coin heads forego.   90

10.

She's seen twelve leaders steer her realm through wars –
Cold, hot – fought secretly and by brave troops.
She's seen a Great Power slump while lives have eased
And now hands on a crown that's cheered with whoops.
What of the future? She will hope to reign
Longer than Victoria's sixty-three years.
Will all then still cheer her less-silent heir?
Or will there, when Scotland's left him, be tears?
This Jubilee trumpets a changeless air
Amid change that may fade like a fanfare.   100
6, 10 June 2012

The Queen's Diamond Jubilee was celebrated on 5 June 2012.

Isles of Wonder

The world has come to London for the Games
And our islands are showcased to the world.
The sixty-five thousand spectators see
Red Arrows trail red, white and blue smoke, then

On screen a flight from the River Thames' source
In Kemble, Gloucestershire, skimming meadows,
Sweeping past the Battersea Power Station,
Big Ben, the London Eye, under bridges,
Past the Thames Barrier and through Tower Bridge,
Past where traitors were beheaded by axe,   10
Into the stadium. Four Olympic rings
Ascend on balloons, a tuned bell is rung.
A boy sings 'Jerusalem', and below
Are countryside pursuits, Merrie Englande
In a green and pleasant land, a country
Idyll where, in harmony with Nature,
Happy farm workers toil and stand and herd
Seventy live sheep among chickens, geese
And cows with maids beside a water-wheel
And a shire horse that ploughs a field, beneath   20
Fluffy white clouds, by cricket and football,
Maples, weeding and wheat fields. Now Brunel
(In a carriage drawn by white cart-horses,
Wearing a stove-pipe hat) as birdsong fades
Brings the Industrial Revolution,
Declaims: "Be not afeard. The isle is full
Of noises." Now drummers beat and the word
'Pandaemonium' flashes up on a screen.
We see Milton's chaotic hell, Jennings'
Coming of the machine, and the factory   30
Workers replace farmers, urban rural.
Smokestacks rise from the ground, by a great wheel
Workers hammer. Fiery smoke. Now bells peal,
Suffragettes join dancers, the music slows
And war dead are recalled in solemn tone.
But now a band in brightly-coloured suits
And Chelsea pensioners, and pearly kings
And queens, and Jarrow protesters – and now
A colliery band recalls vanished coal.
Now a fifth Olympic ring has risen   40

And a rain of fire deluges dancers.
Now on a screen James Bond escorts the Queen
To a helicopter and, waved on by
The alive statue of Winston Churchill,
Above the stadium they 'parachute out'.
Below the Queen arrives beside the Duke.
Now doctors and nurses wheel trolleys in
Bearing patients, the beds spell NHS.
Small children bounce and somersault on sheets,
Which form a crescent moon for *Peter Pan*   50
And other British favourites like *Alice*,
Read as bedtime stories. Now the London
Symphony Orchestra plays British film
Scores. A young girl gets ready to go out:
Tube lines are reflected on the huge crowd.
She meets a boy in a nightclub, and songs
From films play on a screen about their love.
The founder of the World Wide Web is shown.
(A Britisher). On screen the seventy-day
Torch relay. The torch is on a speedboat,   60
And is brought in. Before an orange disc
Dancers show the struggle of life and death.
The athletes' parade begins and amid
The flags of two hundred and four nations
I think of the British celebrities
We have just seen and then deliberate
On all the British inventions missed out:
The train, jet engine and television,
Penicillin and the English language.
And now at last the cauldron's set alight.   70

And I have watched with interest and dismay
For I've been shown our nation's new feelings
And have seen my compatriots secure
In our post-imperial identity,
The imagination's stronghold and seat

Of our popular culture's liberty.
A world audience has just been stunned by fire,
By garish images and shallow songs.
In our land, objectivity has gone,
Emotion and sentimentality,   80
Fantasy and feel-good wishful thinking
Have taken its place, and a warm-hearted
Humanist, joyful image of ourselves.
This 'bread and circus' will have wowed the crowd,
But where is our deeper history, our roots,
And where is the deeper life of the soul,
That sees past what an island people's done
And conveys what the poets know: the One?
And what the Greek athletes knew: that the soul
And mind control the body from within   90
And are in harmony; that will to win
Pushes body beyond its limits so
The striving self derives fresh energy
From the inner force deep within the mind,
The soul that receives power from the One.
And where is the oneness of humankind?
I am full of wonder that what's missing
Once could be found in now abandoned aisles,
And is now in the harmonious gaze
That fills all Nature with Light and One-der.   100
Idea: 27 July 2012. Written: 13 December 2015

The opening ceremony of the London Olympics was held on 27 July 2012. The
title comes from Shakespeare's *The Tempest*, 3.2:
  "Be not afeard. The isle is full of noises,
  Sounds, and sweet airs, that give delight and hurt not."
29. Humphrey Jennings, *Pandaemonium, 1660-1886: The Coming of the Machine as
Seen by Contemporary Observers.*

Ceremonial: On the End of a National Era,
The Funeral of Margaret Thatcher

I

The procession starts at St Clement Danes.
The coffin draped in Union Jack, now grand,
Is placed on a gun-carriage and drawn by
Six dark horses behind a dirging band
That head for St Paul's, slow-march down the Strand.
Twelve-deep crowds clap, some boo, turn backs or frown,
Some shout "Waste of money" and "Dead, dead, dead".
Some are just curious, some shout hecklers down.
To muffled drums troops line the streets, heads bowed,
Big Ben's chimes in a silence that is loud.   10

A half-muffled bell tolls the *cortège* in.
The bearer party of ten servicemen
Carries the coffin up the west steps flanked
By red-coated Chelsea Pensioners, then,
British music on organ, all stand till
She is laid on the bier under the dome.
Her grandchildren bear her insignia –
Garter, Merit – on cushions, brought from home?
Heads of State, diplomats, the Queen and Mayor
Listen to the bidding, bow heads in prayer.   20

A lavish near-State funeral paid from
The public purse for a party leader.
Some say she earned it by the seventy-five
Billion rebate she saved the taxpayer.
But opinion's divided, some would have
A private, not a ceremonial, end.
Anthem, address, prayers, commendation, hymns.
The coffin is borne out, all mourn a friend.
A carillon of muffled bells peals years,
A roar of "three cheers" outside moves to tears.   30

Pallbearers place the coffin in the hearse.
Crowds cheer and applaud as she makes progress.
I recall the chaos in the country
The year she took power to clear up the mess:
Unions rampant, their workers quick to strike,
The dead unburied, rubbish filling squares,
Inflation high, tax 98 per cent,
IMF bail-out for financial scares,
The country called 'the sick man of Europe'.
She jumped each fence in turn at a gallop. 40

II

She knew exactly what had to be done.
She reformed the unions, tore them to shreds;
Trounced the miners and Soviet-backed Scargill
Who saw prime ministers as trophy heads;
Cut back the State, shed jobs and privatised;
Spread share- and property-owning, and won
The argument – her reforms weren't reversed.
Capitalist miners now lived in the sun.
She won the Falklands back, this Iron Lady,
And told Europe: no more hegemony. 50

Her conviction smashed post-war consensus
And the hold of aristocrats who'd thrived.
She carried through a revolution, cured
The sickness of her people, and revived
Its energy with new small businesses
Free from union control and State constraint,
Restored the country's standing, a free Way
Followed by enslaved East Europe. A saint?
She won the Cold War when the wall came down.
More time and she'd have cast off Europe's crown. 60

But, 'infallible', she was brought down by
The poll-tax riots and Europe's strong will

To rule all nation-states from Brussels through
A Parliament, Commission and Council
Of Ministers, to which her 'no no no'.
The pro-European Bilderberg Group
Met at La Toja. She'd blocked Europe's bank.
Word went out and the pro-European troop
In her party ' knifed' her, to her distress.
She stood in tears wearing a blood-red dress.   70

I have seen the future that her 'friends' saw,
A united Europe of nation-states
Subsumed within a new union's empire,
A Great Power in talks and UN debates.
I who thumped the unions admire Europe.
Many hate her lack of compassion for
The wrecking of communities that she
Ruined with reforms, left a million poor.
For Operation True Blue some wear red,
Joyfully sing, 'Ding dong, the witch is dead.'   80

III

I read in my *American Free Press*
That she attended a Trilateral
Commission meeting, stayed silent and left,
Said in anger she'd never yield at all
"An ounce of national sovereignty" to
An international organisation:
The Bilderberg and Trilateral goal:
To euro-ise every Euro-nation
And dollar-ise the West and set up one
Currency for the Pacific region.   90

And so, though undefeated by Labour,
She was dethroned by Bilderberg's allies
In her party who mounted a challenge
And urged her to resign and lose the prize

For not winning outright at first ballot.
I see this funeral as the final scene
In an era of national pride that spanned
From Empire, Churchill and the Falklands 'queen'.
Its ceremony spreads an illusion,
It makes us feel we're still a proud nation.   100

Now I must again take a balanced view.
She was no wicked witch or saint or spiv.
She had to reduce union and State power.
It was *it*, not she, who was divisive.
As the hearse carries the coffin away
And thousands applaud her and few oppose
I see her smiling assassins loiter
On the west steps, and sense the absent foes.
I seek to reconcile conflicting fray:
Those who loved her and those who stayed away.   110

Behind division there is harmony:
$+A + -A$ = zero,
Or 0: the world, oneness and unity.
Pro-Europeans plus national Euro-
Sceptics are one in a uniting State.
I, an unsung laureate with truthful eye,
See each regional and each nationalist
Consensus-conviction under the sky
Of one World State whose voted-in World Lord
Will bring a fresh perspective to discord.   120

17–21 April 2013

The funeral of Margaret Thatcher took place on 17 April 2013. It reputedly cost
£3.6 million and harked back to the funeral of Winston Churchill in 1965.
20. 'Bidding', 'bidding-prayer, one inviting the congregation to join in'.

Reflections by the *Mary Rose*

I. Seamen Preserved in Silt

I pass the carrack's hull and starboard side
And rows of bronze cannons suggesting forts,
Stamped HI, *'Henricus Invictissimus'*,
And guns on carriages near open ports;
The bell inscribed in Latin 'I was made
In the year 1510'. The *Mary Rose*
Was rebuilt after Henry created
His own Church and had to threaten his foes.
She plied the Channel and North Sea to warn
The French and Scots: Henry treats you with scorn.   10

The Cowdray painting shows the French fleet in
The Solent fire on English ships. Henry,
Appalled that the Isle of Wight is burning,
Watches on horseback in front of Southsea
Castle as Carew's flagship turns to fire.
Wind catches her sails and she heels over.
O look, the gun ports are still wide open.
Through the lowest row of ports pours water.
She sinks into Eocene clays that spread
And settles into the silted seabed.   20

Anti-boarding nets on the upper deck
Trap crew in ropes, and of five hundred men
Only thirty-five were saved. The master
Carpenter's chest can be seen once again,
And some of the two hundred tools retrieved:
Mallets, augers, planes, adzes and rulers,
Axes, hammers, handsaws, spokeshaves, gimlets,
Chisels and whetstones of six carpenters.
I see the skull found on the orlop deck,
His tools beside him in this capsized wreck.   30

I see the ship's surgeon's chest and stoneware
Jars, shaving and bleeding bowls, and pewter
And wood canisters, lancets to bleed veins,
Pre-made herb-soaked bandages, urethra
Syringes for venereal disease
And a trepan for drilling into skulls.
The crew had thirty or more healed fractures
From cast-iron shot rather than feeding gulls.
His surgery was limited: he prised,
He bled, amputated and cauterised.   40

I see the master gunner's chest and tools:
His linstock that held a smouldering match
To the touch-hole to ignite gunpowder,
Wood tampions to seal powder chambers' hatch;
His priming wire that kept touch-holes clear in
Breech-loading bronze cannons wedged for firing
And wrought-iron muzzle-loading guns so good
At gashing ships' sides and swift reloading.
I see a gunner's skull that never feared,
And his reconstructed face and long beard.   50

We go down to the lower deck and see
The cook's galley where four hundred were fed:
The two brick ovens where birch logs were burned
And joints of beef hung from barrels roasted.
In the cauldrons of broth that lay on top
Floated muslin sacks filled with greens and peas.
One bowl has a carved name: "Nye Coep cook".
This wooden ark blown about on the seas
Had two roaring fires straddling its keelson
Where all was smoke and smells in dark that shone.   60

I see how the men ate: the officers
Lived in cabins with chests, wore leather shoes,
Clothes trimmed with silk, had pewter tableware;

The men had turned wooden dishes for stews
And drank from wooden bowls, wore simple clothes,
Went barefoot, slept on the hard deck in bits.
Daily rations were a gallon of beer,
Two pounds of beef some days, one of biscuits,
A quarter of a fish, a pint of peas,
Two ounces of butter and four of cheese.   70

I go by lift up to the upper deck,
See the mast-top (or crow's nest) to spy hills,
A gentleman's chest with a leather pouch,
A quartermaster's chest; see pikes and bills,
Anti-boarding weapons, and an archer's
Quiver, arrows and longbows that could fire
Twelve arrows a minute. In the Admiral's
Gallery, the Captain's plates. I admire
His condiment flasks and status riches:
His sturdy leather shoes and rosaries.   80

II. Tyrant

This flagship deep in Solent silt that sealed
Nineteen thousand artefacts from the gnash
Of oxygen and gnaw of breathing mites
That attack wood, like the Pompeian ash,
Is our Pompeii: it trapped a lifestyle
In a few minutes, preserved for divers
A workplace, living environment for
Mariners, soldiers, gunners, officers.
We know how Tudors used each bowl and tool
In this 1545 time capsule.   90

The ship sank on the nineteenth of July,
My wife's birthday (on which this tour smiles dreams).
It was built in the year of Otley Hall,
1510, and down-timbers and crossbeams
Recall the carpentry of that old home.

Gun ports with lids were cut into her sides,
Deck heights were raised to take more heavy guns:
A troop-ship now gunboat riding on tides
To defend England from each neighbour's shore
With which *he*'d be permanently at war.   100

This ship was a symbol of Henry's power
With seventy-eight guns when she was launched,
Ninety-one at the end and built for war,
Manned by men used to having war wounds staunched.
He inherited an England at peace
At seventeen, and just five ships; next year
He ordered two warships – this one was one;
Had fifty-eight when she sank. Without fear
He looted monasteries to raise his fleet:
"A tyrant" Popes would scowl and wives would bleat.   110

He was a self-interested monarch
And bellicose husband with skilled outbursts,
First marrying, then snubbing Catholic Spain.
He put his own and England's interests first.
His warship diplomacy speaks to us.
He was an anti-European, rather
Like our Eurosceptics, and a Scotphobe.
Four hundred and sixty-eight years later
We too abominate all French, each Scot,
But make war with referenda, not shot.   120

The heir to the victor of Agincourt
And his son, crowned in Paris King of France,
In his young mind and keen to lead English
Chargers, canter over French lilies, prance;
Henry fought France throughout his reign until
His siege of Boulogne provoked the Solent
Battle, in which the *Mary Rose* was sunk,
A deed that spoke terrorists' argument:

'A ship sunk in retaliation for
Invading and besieging, bringing war.' 130

And looking at the curved starboard ribcage
I think of the common men who were found.
A hundred and seventy-nine seamen
From ten to over forty, all renowned;
Some malnourished in childhood, some with healed
Fractures or battle injuries or strains
From heavy longbows or handling large guns.
They worked and put up with their aches and pains.
They sacrificed their health to earn a wage
As seamen serving a King in this cage. 140

III. Patriotic Harmony

From the Solent I drive to the Sandbanks
Millionaire's row next to the chain ferry
To the Isle of Purbeck and Studland Bay,
Sit in sun on my hotel balcony
And then have my back rippled with soothing
Hot stones in Harmony Spa, and half-snooze.
I dine by the sea looking out towards
The tumbling rocks of Handfast Point and muse.
I fork crab courgettes near the fishermen.
Tudor warships dip, lean and rise again. 150

I think how Henry dined with the Admiral
The night before the sinking and – the coin
Drops – grasp how the biggest-ever French force
Tried to take and turn into a Boulogne
Portsmouth with two hundred and twenty-five
Ships and thirty thousand men, and attack
Eighty ships and twelve thousand men. I praise
The patriotic King for fighting back
To preserve England from the Catholic rod,
Seamen and King 'in harmony with God'. 160

20 July 2013, revised 2–8 August 2013

Nicholas Hagger visited the *Mary Rose* on 19 July 2013. The *Mary Rose*, the flagship of Vice Admiral Carew, sank in the Solent on 19 July 1545. More than 450 sailors died. Some 19,000 objects have been retrieved from a time capsule of how the Tudors lived their everyday life.

11. Cowdray painting: an engraving commissioned by the Society of Antiquaries of London in 1788, copied from a contemporary painting from Cowdray House depicting the attempted French invasion of Portsmouth in 1545. It shows Henry VIII with his land army encamped on Southsea Common as the *Mary Rose* sinks.

59. 'Keelson', the central internal backbone of the ship where the galley was located.

66. 'Bits', 'naps'.

151–152. The Admiral was Viscount Lisle, and Henry dined on the *Great Harry*. It was Vice Admiral George Carew's flagship, the *Mary Rose*, that sank.

The Lion and the Unicorn: Plebiscite in Scotland

"The lion and the unicorn
Were fighting for the crown;
The lion beat the unicorn
All about the town.
Some gave them white bread,
And some gave them brown;
Some gave them plum-cake,
And drummed them out of town."

Tudor nursery rhyme

I. Evening

I wander to the lily pond and carp
On what may be the United Kingdom's
Last day, our family of four nations
Which ruled a quarter of the world, and drums
Three hundred years of empire and commerce.

My mind is on the polling in Scotland
Whose leader resents Westminster's control,
Wants independence from our common brand.

I see the conkers strewn across the lawn.
It's tight and one poll put Yeses ahead.   10
Three Union leaders panic, roar, rush north
And vow to give more powers, filled with dread.
The last night of the Proms plays Union songs –
'Rule Britannia', 'Land of Hope and Glory' –
And after the Union anthem all sing
'Auld Lang Syne' with crossed arms – as one last plea?

It's been done wrong. The question should have been
'Do you want to stay within the UK?'
Supporters of the status quo would then
Have voted yes, not no – a positive say.   20
It should have been two-thirds, not half, to win
With under-eighteen voters barred and nilled.
The unicorn has twisted the campaign
To sever UK ties, not nation-build.

If yes, a border like Hadrian's Wall:
No currency, pound down, recession's threat,
Years arguing and dividing assets.
They'll want their share of oil but not of debt
And plan to default on the deficit.
They dream of cancelling Trident, of slic-   30
-ing tax, of better health and free food banks.
They dream of a socialist Paradise.

I stroll past windfalls to the rose garden
Whose twelve rose beds describe a Union flag
Round a plashing fountain of three Graces
And Aphrodite, and I mourn, feet drag.
I stare at crazy-paving paths and sense

A Union's fracturing to federal states
As even if No win there'll be Home Rule;
For all four nations devolved power awaits.   40

I describe a circle round the fountain.
If the Noes win, the Union will have changed.
England, like Aphrodite, has had three
Attendants who will now be more estranged.
States expand and form unions that decay,
Like the Soviets', into federations
Or pass into others' United States:
Unions like the EU devour nations.

Bees hum in my knot-garden's lavender
Round the pre-Union four-boxed, endless knot   50
Based on Elizabeth the First's prayer-book
And twenty-five herb beds, a lush green spot,
All fixed in structure, seemingly changeless.
Separatists would break this box hedge's span.
The Union's devolved powers can make our isles
A federal United States of Britain.

We are in a time of unions, and yet
Thirty-six nationalist separations
Can be found on the fringes of Europe,
None successful, yet each rebels and guns.   60
Nationhood's passing into unions,
Nation-states group into regional sways.
As dusk fades into dark I understand
That unions triumph over breakaways.

II. Morning

I wake at six. The count's gone through the night.
The Noes have won fifty-five:forty-five.
I feel relief, and yet I'm not surprised.
I thought as much, and now my hopes revive.

The polls seemed tight as the old kept silent,
Intimidated by young Ayes they snubbed.   70
The old voted for status quo, not change.
The Union stands, the separatists were drubbed.

At seven a.m. the English lion stands
In Downing Street and roars what he has vowed
But growls the English must have the same terms,
Home Rule for England, in tandem and proud.
No Scotch MPs should vote on English laws
As English MPs can't vote on Scotland.
The West Lothian question that's defied
Four decades must in four months become banned.   80

Labour are dismayed, they would lose forty
MPs if English Home Rule were to bind.
They have called for a constitutional
Convention which will take a year to find.
First Scotland, then a year later, England.
Home Rule for England is a trap to make
Labour appear anti-English when they
Block it so their majority won't break.

I go to the gym and from the walker
See the Yes leader's resigned, his dream now   90
Gone. Bitter and disillusioned, he says
That some No voters were conned by the vow.
He says that he is surprised at the speed
Of the reneging and its arrogance.
He's handing over to a young leader
Who'll find other routes to independence.

A *coup*? There could be a unilateral
Declaration of independence now
As "No voters were tricked" and as the new
Devolved powers could make Scotland seem, post-vow,   100

Effectively independent when all
The older Scots have died (to mounting cheers).
There will be a "neverendum" approach
That could bring independence in ten years.

The Yes vision is a beguiling one:
All your dreams come true and no price to pay,
Escape London's rules, limitless welfare
From unfound oil for ever and a day.
It paints all three Union party leaders
As self-serving, hurtful and similar,   110
Not interested in Scotland, remote.
It's stirred demands for powers in each quarter.

Half Scotland wants to leave the Union,
Be itself and an EU region, free.
England is too large to be a region
In a federal EU, and so must be
Broken up into regional fragments
If no referendum removes Britain.
And our four devolved nations may become
States in a strong European Union.   120

Tories want an in-out referendum.
Labour does not, is ahead in the polls.
The Tories want to cap immigration.
Barroso says it's illegal, extols
Free movement of people as EU law.
He says the PM wants to stay within
The EU, and drives voters to UKIP
To give us Labour; no in-out; and spin.

III. Afternoon: Future
Now I can see Europe hopes there will be
A Labour government in the UK,   130
No referendum and a strong Union,

No swift devolution for England's say,
No sudden United States of Britain.
The PM must back down or be removed.
The Scottish plebiscite will win new powers.
In Europe the Union will be approved.

And if this can't be achieved, then England
Will pull away to its own devolved powers.
The UK will fall apart into states,
A United States of Britain that glowers.   140
With half its trade with Europe, it won't leave.
Its fragmentation brought on by Scotland,
A Balkanised England will sink within
A United States of Europe it can't stand.
20–21 September, 18–20 October 2014

The referendum for Scotland's independence took place on 18 September 2014.

Caliphate

"He came to Abu Bakr, may Allah be pleased with him, with a severed head, and Abu Bakr condemned it.... Abu Bakr said, 'So you follow the way of the Persians and Romans? Rather, do not come to me with a severed head.'"
Sunan ibn Mansur 2490, referring to Hazrat Abu Bakr al-Siddiq, the first caliph of Islam (632–634), during whose caliphate Mesopotamia and Syria came under Islamic dominion

I

On screen I watch a black-and-white command-
And-control centre disappear in smoke.
Air strikes on fourteen targets: the US
And five Arab monarchies bomb and choke
Islamic state fighters in Syria.
Raqqa is hit by Tomahawks fired from
Warships and Stealth fighter jets. Refugees

Flee north, IS troops swarm, behead and bomb.

Fifty nations in a coalition
Now degrade this caliphate that has spread   10
Through Syria and Iraq, wants the Levant
And fills the entire Western world with dread.
Three hostages have been beheaded by
An Englishman in a black mask, a brute
Who wields a knife on video, each kneeling
In an orange 'Guantanamo' jump suit.

A year ago the British Parliament
Was recalled over strikes on Syria. Fraught,
It voted to stay isolationist,
MPs questioned which side they should support.   20
They nearly came in on ISIS's side.
We British then retreated from all fights.
But the menace has spread unchecked since then
And mixed with Khorasan's al-Qaeda-ites.

Like a seventh-century army ISIS spread
Unchecked down to Tikrit and shot prisoners
In Saddam's palace grounds, hissing "Persians"
(Saddam's scaffold snarl) at Shiite soldiers.
They've come out of the second Iraq war
And Zarqawi's al-Qaeda-in-Iraq.   30
They have rampaged through the north, displacing
Two million and beheading in the dark.

These Sunnis and their foreign conscripts drove
Thousands up a mountain in gruesome heat.
They swept into Mosul and rule through fear.
US-trained Arab troops are in retreat,
Only Peshmerga Kurds stop their advance.
They drive trucks captured from Iraq's army
And Allied planes target the defences

Round a dam that could flood Baghdad city.   40

Shiites and infidels are told, "Convert
Or be killed." And now the new caliphate
Seeks to revive the Ottoman Empire
That stretched through Spain and reached Vienna's gate.
The Caliph Harun al-Rashid ruled all
Muslims from his high-cultured Baghdad court.
Now Abu Bakr al-Baghdadi calls
In a Mosul mosque for worldwide support.

His cry is "Forward to a new Dark Age
Of Shariah law and Mohammed's globe".   50
He studied at the University
Of Baghdad after me, wears a black robe,
Black hat and beard and has been photographed
With Senator McCain, not in disguise,
When he was in al-Qaeda-in-Iraq.
His background's as mysterious as his rise.

Some say he had Jewish parents and's known
As Shimon – Simon – Elliot, a spy
For Israeli Secret Intelligence
Service, ISIS. Some wonder if he's sly-   60
-ly gathered twenty thousand of the worst
Terrorists in one territory so they
Can be bombed and wiped out, so Israel can
Expand from Nile to Euphrates and stay.

Greater Israel, Herzl's and Yinon's plan,
Can be won by breaking neighbours' backbones –
The Iran–Iraq war, which crippled both –
And by splitting Iraq into three zones,
Sunnis, Shiites and Kurds, which ISIS seeks
And Allied bombing is bringing to be.   70
Were three beheadings flaunted to provoke

The West into carving Iraq in three?

Is the caliphate not religious but
Political? Will it expand Israel?
Is ISIS led by a Mossad agent?
His twenty thousand soldiers who assail
Are Islamic fundamentalists like
'Jihadi John' the beheader, and so
We must see ISIS as a murderous force
And wipe it off the Levant as a foe.   80

II
There's fighting just three miles west of Baghdad.
Hordes swarm and menace the capital's space
Which is to be their caliphate's new seat,
Restoring Harun al-Rashid's power base.
While missiles rain on their dug-in trenches
Their fighters swamp defending troops and pound,
Marauding and beheading as they pass.
Missiles also require troops on the ground.

They're one mile from the centre of Baghdad:
In Mansur, where I lived, and in Caliph   90
Mansur's Round City on the western side
Of the brown Tigris, and make cruel mischief.
The Baghdad I knew and its Rashid Street
With Turkish balconies and stalls and stench
Is on the cusp of a catastrophe:
The Fall of Baghdad. I shudder and blench.

I lectured at the University
Of Baghdad three decades before Abu
Bakr, the leader of ISIS, learned there.
I spread Churchill's vision of one state's glue   100
To Sunnis, Shiites and Kurds, and I know
That executions in Saddam's palace

224

Grounds in Tikrit to shouts of "Persians" is
Saddam's revenge on Shiite killers' hiss.

This is the third Iraq War in twenty-
Three years and marks a generational
Clash between two old civilizations:
Between an extremist Arab rabble
Of barbarians like Mongol hordes who're bent
On spreading early Islam – Shariah, veils,   110
Death – and Westerners who spread rule of law,
Freedom, democracy, justice's scales.

IS has entered Syrian Kobani.
Its black flag flies above a ruined fort
A few hundred yards from Turkey's border,
Europe's frontier, a visible onslaught.
The barbarians are pressing on Europe,
The clash of civilizations is red
Beneath the smoke that hangs above the town
And screams as the townsfolk are beheaded.   120

The IS fighters wade in blood, fighting
A proxy war for Sunnis who oppose
The expansion of Iran, armed with better
Weapons than Kurds' and with pitiless prose.
Air strikes and willing troops will not prevail,
There must be a back channel to talk needs
With the odious enemy that beheads
And deal with it in words as well as deeds.

III

Like Romans attacking barbarians
We perpetuate our *imperium*   130
And hope we are spared Varus's defeat,
Loss of three legions and opprobrium.
The struggle with the beheaders will, like

225

The Romans' struggle with the massing hordes,
Last for decades. We have to contain them
And confiscate their tanks, guns, knives and swords.

And so I ignore Abu Bakr's links.
If he's an actor who recites and dupes
By rote in a mosque I don't want to know.
I focus on his fanatical troops.   140
Unless we strafe and take the offensive
They'll capture Baghdad, behead, crucify
And target Westerners in Europe's streets –
Unless we train ground troops to occupy.

Epilogue
Saudi TV claims US airplanes bombed
An al-Qaim bunker's IS meeting
For tribal elders to pledge allegiance,
Wiping out ten, maiming forty, wounding
Abu Bakr, tribesmen say, and 'Jalman',
The masked executioner from England,   150
'Jihadi John'. Troops clear hospital wards,
Mosque loudspeakers call blood donors to band.

Now Abu Bakr's been driven with 'John'
To a captured Syrian army barracks
In Raqqa with a sub-ground hospital,
Demands "volcanoes of Jihad" like tax.
IS has beaten four armies – Iraq's,
Kurds', Syria's, Syrian rebels' – but its head,
With sixteen high command killed, nine injured,
Has now nearly been decapitated.   160
27 September–18 October, 9, 10, 14, 16 November 2014

Abu Bakr al-Baghdadi (named after the second caliph) became leader of al-Qaeda in Iraq in 2010. After breaking away from al-Qaeda and leading a desert *Blitzkrieg* across Syria and Iraq he proclaimed himself 'Caliph' (successor to

Mohammed) of a new 'Islamic State' (IS or ISIL, known in the Arab world as the terrorist organisation Daesh). On 21 April 2015 it was announced that he had been critically wounded in an American air strike near Al-Baaj on 18 March 2015. He had allegedly suffered spinal damage caused by heavy shrapnel injuries requiring continuous care and was allegedly no longer in command of ISIL. The leadership passed to his deputy Abu Alaa al-Afari, who was killed in a US air strike in May. ISIL was by then past the zenith of its power, which al-Baghdadi had masterminded. Al-Baghdadi's whereabouts were unknown.

According to an allegation wrongly attributed to Edward Snowden (the American defector to Russia), Abu Bakr al-Baghdadi is Simon Elliot, the son of two Jewish parents, an actor and Mossad agent who was filmed with Senator McCain in 2007, when McCain held a meeting with al-Qaeda in Iraq. It is possible that the photograph was doctored to include both McCain and al-Baghdadi. This story was spreading in Baghdad in 2016.

98. 'Three decades before'. Nicholas Hagger lectured at the University of Baghdad in 1961–1962. Al-Baghdadi was a student at the University of Baghdad in the 1990s.

109. The Mongols conquered Baghdad in 1258, and the arrival of the Golden Horde Mongols in Egypt resulted in many Mongols becoming Muslim.

118. 'Red', 'bloody'.

149, 151. 'Jihadi John' had a *nom de guerre*, Jalman al-Britani. His real name was Mohammed Emwazi.

Churchill 50 Years On: Great Briton

I

I'm back as a child under eiderdown.
Outside a whine cuts out, I count the strafe.
At ten there is a distant blast, I smile.
It's not our house that's been hit, I am safe.
There is terror up in the blacked-out sky,
Indiscriminate flying bombs that kill.
One man protects us, shields our frightened heads:
My MP, our PM, Winston Churchill.

When France fell he stood up to Germany.
He had not been PM a month but he   10
Did not surrender as many assumed,
Called us to fight alone and remain free,
Offered blood, sweat and tears. The Blitz was so
German ships could invade us and subdue
Without threats from the air. He stood between
Us and the bombers, and sent up the Few.

I'm back before the war memorial.
Bare-headed Churchill speaks to us. I am
So near I could reach and touch his right arm.
He tells us he is leaving for Potsdam.   20
There he will learn he has been voted out.
Now I'm back on the High School's top step and
He stumps up with his stick and hat and smiles
And signs my album, beams and shakes my hand.

His coffin is borne upstream on a launch.
I see the Thames on black-and-white TV;
The only commoner of the century
To receive a State funeral. I see
Crowds line the embankment in silent awe.
Cranes dip their jibs in homage as the boat   30
Approaches our leader's last landing-stage,
A vanished UK once again afloat.

II

Nearly fifty years on I take my seat
To hear Boris Johnson talk on Churchill.
He climbs onto the Imperial's stage,
Hair dishevelled, and bumbles on the thrill
His family got from Churchill's speeches.
"He used short and Anglo-Saxon words, he spoke
With Ciceronian polish, he did not
Extemporise. He mesmerised all folk.   40

"He was born when the British Empire was
Seven times' the extent of Trajan's Roman
Empire, and wanted to keep it going.
He said different things at different times on
Europe – wanting to be absorbed within
A united Europe or be remote.
He was consistently for free trade as
It put cheap food in each working man's throat.

"He was the most highly-paid journalist,
Was taken prisoner in the Boer War   50
And famously escaped. He fought in four
Continents and killed men. I am in awe.
He left the Tories in 1904,
Became liberal, invented the tea break,
Went from Minister to the trenches, then
Returned to the Tories, a party rake.

"After his blunder at Gallipoli,
He got the Yanks in on both wars." I think,
'By handing over all our oil in North
Iraq, then Saudi Arabia,' and blink.   60
"But his greatest achievement was to stand
Up to Hitler in May 1940
After the fall of France. What made him make
That choice not to give in, to remain free?"

III

Now the re-enactment. The *Havengore*
Follows the route of the funeral upstream
And bears a wreath that's cast into the Thames
By Parliament, like a repeated dream.
It holds a V, the victory sign he made
Bow-tied, in hat. His finest hour, the throng   70
As he announced Germany's surrender.
Sweet Thames, run softly, till I end my song.

Crowds line the banks and bridges to witness
His recreated last journey, in awe
Of a great Briton who led a vanished
UK to victory in one-sided war
With the courage to stand for what is right.
A new generation is learning how
Nearly the British came to be conquered,
And speak German as their first language now.   80

Before Hitler blitzkrieged Poland, Churchill's
Career was haunted by failures that irk:
Gallipoli; Norway; French surrender;
Defeat and headlong retreat from Dunkirk;
The Blitz – German bombers' penetration;
The fall of Greece; Singapore; Tobruk's fall.
Soviet troops and American Lend-Lease
Enabled him, and Britain, to survive it all.

Who was the greatest Briton? Churchill thought
Alfred the Great, who beat the Danes, prinked pride   90
And, King of the West Saxons, called himself
'King of the Anglo-Saxons', unified
England as the heptarchy's overlord.
Elizabeth who fought off Spain with skill
And set England on a Protestant course?
Newton? Shakespeare? Many would say: 'Churchill.'

IV

By 1939, distrusted for
Twice changing parties, he thought his career
A failure, yet next year was a symbol
Of national unity, Britain's role clear: 100
A grandiose final chord, loss of empire
And the collapse of British power – yet he
Founded the noble European idea
And pointed to our EU destiny.

He helped found the Welfare State, invented
The tank and RAF, shaped Iraq's sand,
Israel and the Middle East, three times saved
Civilization – in two world wars and
In the Cold War. Is history made by
Great men or a force? Like the Thames drifting   110
Under bridges, history flows through stages
And bears great men as its slow currents sing.

Borne from imperial to European stage,
He witnessed the Age change as staid post-war
Britain gave way to TV, affluence,
Rock 'n' roll, tower blocks and permissive law.
Suez and Profumo shook the Empire,
Macmillan's fall ended the 'Old England'.
Born a Victorian, he towered on,
An obsolete Colossus but still grand.   120

Churchill was a soldier who saw action
In India, Sudan and against Boer threats;
A politician who held office in
Liberal and Conservative Cabinets;
A journalist, historian and writer
Who won the Nobel Prize for Literature.
I hail a man of action and of thought,
A many-disciplined, great character.
31 January, 1 February, 3 April 2015

34. Nicholas Hagger heard Boris Johnson on 23 October 2014.

On Richard III: The Last Plantagenet

I. Bosworth Field
The sun glints off the swords this August day
As Richard the Third, on a grassed hill's spur,

Leads nobles and foot-soldiers thundering down
Into the valley where Henry Tudor,
The pretender, resists the mounted knights.
French mercenaries, outnumbered two to one,
Fight hand-to-hand, hack, club and sever limbs.
The king heads for Tudor, horse mired, outrun.

On foot and shouting "Treason" as nobles
Desert him, the king is hacked with nine blows   10
To his head and a pointed weapon's thrust
Through his skull's base (as 'his' skeleton shows).
His body's stripped and stabbed and flung naked
Over a horse, hands bound, and like a slave
Ridden to Bow Bridge whose stone hits his head,
And he is flung into a shallow grave.

It marked the end of the Plantagenets
And of the Wars of the Roses. Now known,
Henry Tudor, citing his descent from
John of Gaunt, seized the crown and took the throne   20
As Henry the Seventh and took as bride
Elizabeth of York to unite – tame –
Both York and Lancaster. His Tudor spin
Blackened the last medieval king's name.

Shakespeare, funded by Henry's granddaughter
Queen Elizabeth, presented his view
Of a usurping monster who murdered
His way to the throne by killing his two
Nephews when Lord Protector, both Edward
The Fifth and his brother, declared to be   30
Bastards ineligible for the crown;
Then attendants and chamberlain: a spree.

Was Richard a serial killer or king
With enlightened, reforming pious looks

Who set up chantries and abolished press
Censorship, lifted restrictions on books
And printing-presses, a great warrior
Who did more in his 777-day reign
Than any other great monarch, and was
The victim of a Tudor smear campaign?   40

Six murders within his own family
Including his wife and son, it is said.
He had the motive, to obtain the throne.
Henry the Sixth and his son too? *His* dead?
Usurpers always killed predecessors
As did Henry Tudor. No proof or clue,
But we must judge by standards of the Age,
Not modern standards as Ricardians do.

                        II. The Finding of the Bones
A Ricardian fan looking for Greyfriars
Monastery near Bosworth, where monks took in   50
And buried Richard's corpse, in a car park
Near Leicester cathedral had goose-bumped skin,
A hunch she was standing above his grave,
And when three years later at her behest
A skeleton was unearthed, she, amazed,
Claimed her intuition had been sound – blessed.

The skeleton of a 'crookback' was found
To have a curved spine that reduced his five-
Foot-eight height by a foot, caused by severe
Scoliosis, a deformed spine – what drive;   60
Right shoulder higher than the left, thin arms
But none withered. It *was* small and was hacked
With nine blows and a pointed weapon's thrust.
Roundworm's eggs in gut.... Is it him, in fact?

DNA tests showed this man had blond hair,

Blue eyes and a round face, whereas paintings
Show Richard's black hair, brown eyes and thin face.
DNA shows its descent from the king's
Female line, but not his male line. Was this
Broken by illegitimacy, is   70
This not Richard but a cousin or else
Someone who died of similar injuries?

The Queen's distanced herself from the find, her
Website brands a "usurper king" – Richard.
The broken line suggests adultery,
And might show John of Gaunt was not Edward
The Third's son but a Flemish butcher's boy
And Henry the Seventh's descendants from Gaunt
Have no right to the crown, nor the Tudors,
And our royals may not be royal – may just haunt.   80

I see on TV the *cortège* depart
From Fen Lane farm, the Bosworth battlefield.
A service at the Heritage Centre,
The oak coffin on a wheeled bier, its shield;
Then in a hearse to Leicester and Bow Bridge
On a gun-carriage drawn by four horses.
The box of bones nears the old Cathedral.
Crowds line the route and throw on white roses.

'Richard the Third' lies in repose and will
Soon be laid in a tomb as was his wish.   90
The bones' too-early carbon dating has
Been adjusted as he ate many fish.
Is *he* in this coffin or has Leicester
Used bones to grab a tourist industry?
I'm not sure what can be known of these bones
And fear nothing is known with certainty.
22–23 March, 8–9 April 2015

A skeleton identified with 99.99% certainty by Leicester University as Richard III's was dug up in a Leicester car park in 2012 and reburied in Leicester Cathedral with ceremony in 2015. The carbon dating on the bones placed them as 1430–1460 or 1412–1449. This was adjusted to 1475–1530 because this person ate a lot of fish. But technically the carbon dating and the Y (male)-chromosome DNA do not match the bones with Richard's dates of 1452–1483.

38. '777' should be pronounced 'seven seven seven'.

On Thomas Cromwell's Ruthlessness

A quiet Cromwell played by Mark Rylance.
We sympathise as wife and two girls moan
And die of sweating sickness in one night.
(Documents show they died, at times unknown.)
Loyal to Wolsey, a silent watcher,
He tells Henry the Eighth his strategy
In France is wrong, and's asked to help divorce
Catherine of Aragon immediately.

He plots and schemes from stillness, and intrigues
Votes in parliament that help Henry's plan.   10
But this self-effacing, thinnish Cromwell
Contrasts with Holbein's portrait of a man
Full-faced and with a double chin and eyes
That stare into the distance, and quite lacks
The forceful personality that closed
And dissolved monasteries as ruthless tax.

Wolsey asked Cromwell to help him survey
Six monasteries to be converted, all
For the use of his Cardinal's College
At Oxford, and to dissolve thirty small   20
Religious houses to fund building works
At his college and at his grammar school
In Ipswich, projects anticipating

The dissolution of monastic rule.

I read about the actual Cromwell, how
He sat beside the rack, tortured a lot
Suspected of still being Catholic
And ordered executions – the Abbot
Of Glastonbury who was hanged on the Tor;
How he threw twenty thousand nuns and monks   30
Onto the streets to beg and divided
Spoils between Henry's chests and his own trunks.

The real Cromwell, like his murderous time,
Was savage and ruthless to line his own
And Henry's crates with the wealth of the Church,
Proceeds from each gold chalice, precious stone.
Like ruthless Richard the Third he murdered
His way to power and must be understood
Within his time and not modern outlooks
Superimposed from today's genteel 'should'.   40

I have known this anonymous Cromwell
Who lurks in shadows of affairs of State,
Proscribes books, undermines launches, denies
Publicity, urges all to be late.
I've seen him whisper threats, tinker with plans
So his masters keep hold of the rainbow,
Control democracy for hidden power
And perpetuate its rule's *status quo*.
26 March, 8 April 2015

Enigma

"The King hath note of all that they intend,
By interception which they dream not of."

Bedford in Shakespeare, *Henry V*, 2.2, 6–7

I

I hear about the secret war hidden
Till 1974 of which none spoke:
How nine thousand, working at Bletchley Park,
Billeted in nearby homes, in shifts broke
The German forces' Enigma ciphers.
Thirty thousand or more machines conveyed
Instructions from the German high command
To U-boat commanders – plans Hitler'd made.

We are shown a map of 1901:
Scores of copper cables link states, endure   10
Under the sea, then Marconi's wireless
Makes contact instant but far from secure.
The Enigma machine disguised the words,
A commercial machine patented in
1926, and adopted by
The army and the Nazi war engine.

We are now shown a four-rotor machine.
It looks like a black typewriter – no page.
Each day the code changed, and a sender, told
By a code-book, encrypted a message: 20
Put in plugs as instructed, and then pressed
A letter, lit up another, its twin
And turned one of four wheels a notch. After
Twenty-six letters the next wheel clicked in

Twenty-six studs and springs and wires and plugs.
There were three times ten to the power of one
Hundred and fourteen ways of setting up
An Enigma machine, amounts that stun,
More than the atoms in the universe
(Ten to the power of eighty), a new mode.   30
The Germans thought the war would be finished
Before the British arrived at the code.

Three Polish mathematicians monitored
Wireless traffic in the nineteen-twenties
And learned the Germans were using machines
To encrypt and then decrypt messages
Whose codes they broke in 1932
By maths and 'bomb', heads bent over their bench.
They destroyed their base before the Nazis
Found it, but first showed the British and French.　　　　40

All Germans in Norway used one code-book,
All in France another, all on U-boats
Another. Each code-book was changed each month.
The wiring at top and bottom plugs gloats:
Gave ten to the power of 114 ways
To decode. In BP's huts 6 and 8
Men sat with headphones over intercepts
To find Enigma settings used that date.

They distilled messages from 'Ultra', got
English translations to the field unseen.　　　　50
In May 1941 a U-boat
Was captured with an Enigma machine
And documents, so BP could break codes.
A four-rotor machine, circulated
Next year, was introduced and could not be
Read till another U-boat was boarded.

I handle the machine, see how settings
Give six letters and then convert to more.
I touch the keys and ponder how bright men
Decoded complex messages, in awe.　　　　60
In the Battle of the Atlantic I
Intercept U-boat codes, moved at the drives
Of those first computer men who shortened
The war by two years and saved countless lives.

II

I see Bletchley Park's gables and chimneys
And where Code and Cryptic (the SIS)
Was first housed, go to the stables which were
First occupied by Turing, then progress
To the dilapidated Hut 6 where
Decoders worked on each Enigma page   70
In one of three tiring round-the-clock shifts
At the start of the new digital age.

Hut 11, room of the British Bombe,
An electro-mechanical 'warhead'
That worked 1.5 times 10 to the power
Of 20 times before it repeated
Itself. (There are 9 times 10 to the power
Of 21 stars in the universe.)
I see Enigma machines on display
And the Lorenz and Tunny, which immerse.   80

Now I at last confront the Colossus,
The world's first electronic computer.
Semi-programmable, with two thousand
Five hundred valves, it looks a wall-filler,
A floor-to-ceiling 'telephone exchange'.
I nod to Tommy Flowers, hard-working sage
Whose machine-building genius delivered
Britain into a new digital age.

And now to Hut 8. I find Turing's room
With his mug chained to the radiator   90
Near his plain desk, and muse on his stature:
Our digital age's bright creator.
I wander through the mansion musing on
The necessity for nationalism's grind
Against Hitler, but the necessity
Of being at one with all humankind.

III

In the bookshop I pick up *Secret Days*
By Asa Briggs, just published – he's 90.
I buy it and that evening read that he
Worked for the last two war years at BP   100
Decoding the Enigma intercepts,
A short walk from Turing and Hut 8's clout.
He worked all his time in the new Block D.
His wife did not know till this book came out.

A guide tells me Masterman, my Provost,
Had to leave BP out of *The Double-*
Cross System – about the Twenty (XX)
Committee which he had chaired – and, careful,
Turned German agents round to take back home
False information: D-Day would be won   110
In the Pas de Calais, not Normandy.
I'm in the Masterman-Briggs tradition.

I visit Briggs in his great Lewes home.
He sits at the large kitchen table in
Pyjama top and sweater "immobile
By land, sea and air," his face much more thin,
Having slimmed after having DVT,
A head of hair though nearly ninety-four.
I thank him for urging me to write down
My Double Life, narrate *my* secret war.   120

I ask him, "How many transcripts a day
Did you decode? Forty?" He: "More, I should
Think. But I should have written *Secret Days*
Earlier. Winterbotham's book was not good."
I say, "In 1978 I should
Have urged you to write your book when you told
Me to write mine." "Yes, but it took a year
For me to leave Sussex, all was on hold."

I talk of Masterman's interest in me,
Of our Hollis, a KGB hireling?   130
He tells me, "Pincher asked me to trawl through
Worcester's archives on him. I found nothing."
He talks of Masterman's difficulty
In getting his book published. And then his.
My protector signs my *Secret Days* "On
A very special visit to Lewes".

I think of men I've known, who knew BP:
Red-faced Angus Wilson, Harry Beckhough
Who received near El Alamein BP's
Decoded texts on rice-paper somehow,   140
Which he passed to General Montgomery's
Liaison Officer, who passed them on
To the General, who read the intercepts,
Then chewed and swallowed them till they were gone.

I leave and reflect on an enigma.
We need to defend our realm and police
All dictators, but be one with mankind.
It is a riddle: how can war bring peace
When mankind is a unity and must
Love under a world government, not fight.   150
The real enigma is: the nation-state
Has had its day and world government's right.
30 September, 1 October 2011; 19–21, 24 April 2015

Nicholas Hagger attended a themed weekend on 'The Secret War' in
Northampton from 30 September to 2 October 2011, and handled and operated
an Enigma machine in the Northampton Marriott Hotel. He visited Bletchley
Park on 1 October. His visit to Asa Briggs took place on Friday 24 April 2015.
45. '114', pronounced 'one one four'.
107. 'XX', pronounced 'ex ex'.

Stability: On an Unlikely Conservative Election Victory

I. Exit Poll

Our General Election, a long campaign
And eleven opinion polls forecast
The top two parties neck and neck, and see
A Labour–SNP agreement classed
As of the losers, led by the unions
And nationalists bent on seeing the end
Of the UK and of austerity,
Who'd scorn the deficit, tax, borrow, spend.

Ten o'clock, as the polling-stations close
News channels flash the exit poll on screen   10
Based on 22,000, the Tories
Are the largest party with 316
To Labour's 239 and Lib-Dems' 10.
The party of responsibility
Might make new links and see the rescue through,
Retain their grip on Labour bankruptcy.

Has there been a late surge to the Tories?
Have eleven opinion polls been wrong?
A mean-spirited, envious campaign,
Miliband's resurrected class-war 'song'.   20
Large houses are deemed 'mansions' to be taxed
And the tax must be sent up to Scotland.
Elections are won from the centre as
Foot and Kinnock learned – and now Miliband.

The poll's strapped above the BBC's square.
On the news channels leftist leaders scorn
The stark figures: "If true, I'll eat my hat."
All urge caution in fog like a foghorn.
Miliband carved vacuous promises
On a 'tombstone' to stand in Downing Street's   30

Back garden. What *hubris*! Triumphalist!
He's mocked as a Moses in myriad tweets.

Long after midnight I scan the TV.
If they have more than 310, the Tories,
They'll govern on their own and take their chance
That their Queen's Speech will be backed by MPs.
Leftist guests claim Miliband will govern
Though he's 50 seats behind, it is said,
As the Tories have no majority.
I yawn at speculation, go to bed.   40

II. Majority

Morning TV. The exit poll was right.
The Tories are forecast one seat below
An outright majority and they will
Be able to rule as a *de facto*
Government. The nightmares have receded,
The unions and Scot Nats making threats.
The Tories can complete the rebuilding
Of the economy and pay our debts.

A huge swing to the Scottish Nationalists,
To the Conservatives from the Lib Dems,   50
To UKIP and Greens who'll have one seat each.
Will the Scots wreck what Westminster condemns
Or exert influence as third party?
Will the Tories achieve 326 seats?
If not, will there be instability?
Will a thin majority bring defeats?

The people had a choice between Labour
Led by the unions and SNP,
Interest rates put up by the IMF;
Or the Tories and new stability.   60
Will there be blue-on-blue battles ahead

Again over the EU, the left's fight
For decency, the poor, equality –
Will 'one-nation' Tories move further right?

The British electorate *are* still wise.
They put recovery before hand-outs,
Borrowed cash our grandchildren must repay.
Their communal common sense weighs and doubts.
Now a Tory majority of twelve
Is forecast. They'll be a moderate team: 70
It will be a weak government and won't
Be able to do things that are extreme.

The Tory vote has confounded the polls.
They have three hundred and thirty-one seats.
The Scottish lion has roared in a landslide.
How will the Scots work with Tory '*élites*'?
There's talk of anti-austerity riots.
Balls, who wanted our wallets, has lost all.
The Lib Dems have now been decimated.
Miliband, Clegg, Farage – three leaders fall.   80

Five years ago the Lib Dems joined a pact,
A Coalition, in the State's interests
To rescue us from Labour squandering
And the deficit they left, that still tests.
They slowed down all the cuts out of fairness,
To shield the least well-off and now they're scorned.
Two leaders in a sunny rose garden
And now one's gone from losses, who's unmourned.

It's said the electoral system's a fraud.
UKIP's more votes than the SNP's hauls.   90
Five million UKIP and Green votes – two seats.
Proportional representation calls.
'Core-vote' Labour moved left from the centre

With class-war raids on our wallets. We knew.
There'll be a one-year negotiation,
Then a referendum on the EU.

It's as if the electorate has said,
"We don't want the Liberals braking, to slow
The clearing up of Labour's deficit,
And we don't want Labour back to borrow   100
And make another mess to be cleared up.
We don't want Scottish Nationalists to drain
148 billion pounds from the UK.
Tories, clear up the mess, we're great again."

Scotland will vote to stay in the EU
And if it seems the Scots will lose that fight
Then, now in effect a one-party state,
They may call a new UK plebiscite.
We need a vision of prosperity
For all the UK – Scotland, Wales, Ireland   110
As well as the long-suffering English.
Chaos has been banished, the UK's grand.
7–8 May 2015

The British General Election took place on 7 May 2015.
12. '316' pronounced 'three sixteen'.
13. '239' pronounced 'two three nine'.
34. '310' pronounced 'three ten'.
54. '326' pronounced 'three two six'.
103. '148' pronounced 'one four eight'.

In St Petersburg: Thoughts in Hermitage

I. Hermitage
In the eighteenth century Catherine the Great
Began opening the Winter Palace's

Staterooms for musical evenings she called
Her 'hermitage' as she could forget riches
And all State affairs, and show her private
Collection of paintings, drink coffee, view
With her guests, a tradition I observe
By attending a concert in the New
Hermitage which will blend baroque splendour,
The imperial home, art and high culture.   10

We leave the ship and in immigration
Queue so my face and passport can walkway
Past a banned list of eighty-nine EU
Citizens and MPs announced that day
By the Kremlin, and, though I'm all over
The internet, I survive scrutiny
For past anti-Soviet activities.
The FSB – renamed part-KGB
For passport control – aren't as efficient.
We're driven to the Hermitage event.   20

We enter the Winter Palace and now
I walk through Greek and Roman busts and climb
The much-gold-leafed Ambassador's staircase,
Pass through to the small Throne Room where, in prime time,
Peter the Great stands beside Minerva,
Through the 1812 gallery, on through
To the large Throne Room, see the two-headed
Eagle, then pass to the Small, then the New
Hermitage added for the public, walk
Past Leonardos and Rembrandts – and stalk.   30

And now in the Italian Skylight Hall
I take a seat as the State Symphony
Orchestra of St Petersburg files in
Behind a candelabrum candle-tree.
The young conductor leads off with Mozart

And as the violins, drums and trumpets roar
I grasp I am sitting by Mazzuola's
Sculpture showing a goring by a boar
And twisted Adonis's dying gasp.
I think of Nicholas and the Bolsheviks' clasp.   40

Fauré, Rossini, Mascagni, Glinka,
Then 'Prince Igor' (of which I once sang part,
"Sing we praises to our glorious Khan"),
Tchaikovsky and Strauss. I sit near the heart
Of the Tsars' winter home and recall I
Worked for the USSR's rule to cease
And, once double-o, now slowed to hermitage
By advancing old age, I make my peace
With benevolent Tsars' autocracy
Which fell to seventy years of tyranny.   50

St Petersburg, gateway to Paradise
Named after the keeper of the gates' key.
Peter the Great's loved for Westernising,
Opening to Europe. Gorbachev should be
Too as even more a Westerniser,
For ending the Soviet Union's reach,
Shutting down the KGB, setting free
Fifteen Republics, bringing in free speech,
But he's reviled for "a mistake that's dire",
For "breaking up the Soviet Empire".   60

II. A Moderate Stance
In the Cathedral of Peter and Paul
I stand among forty Romanov tombs
Near the heart of an imperial Empire
Putin wants to restore, with force that dooms
Gorbachev's *perestroika* and *glasnost*.
I worked to free Europe from Soviet's yoke
And stand against the latest bans and am

At one with what the moderate Tsars awoke,
Who combined freedom with autocracy
And gave to Russians firm stability.   70

Still within the Peter and Paul Fortress,
I walk to Trubetskoy Bastion, which tells
Of the Tsars' political prisoners held
In some seventy identical cells.
I seek Dostoevsky's cold, hermit's room.
I study each unglazed barred window, high,
And iron-framed bed. In the exercise yard
On whose cobblestones prisoners had to die
I walk in protesters' footsteps, aglow,
And think it could be me tramping through snow.   80

And in the Cathedral of the Spilled Blood
Where Tsar Alexander was shockingly
Killed by terrorists of The People's Will,
I think successors of the KGB –
Ended but part-revived as SVR –
Might spill my blood with a bomb, break my bones,
And I am pensive for I can foresee
My blood may too seep onto cobblestones.
I stand where a Tsar stood and faced terror.
I too have faced terror and may face more.   90

I scan Kronstadt island, the main base for
Russia's Baltic fleet. I could also be
Banned from entering Russia for my past
As an ex-double-o, still an enemy.
Granted I did not vote for the EU's
Sanctions against this expanding regime
That hopes to reverse Gorbachev's freedoms
And restore the Tehran Agreement's scheme,
But I was part of the fight to expel
The Soviets from East Europe's citadel.   100

I, a hermit thinking about the Tsars,
Stood in a Tsarist cell and now devote
Thought to all prisoners who suffered (such as
Nechayev of whom Dostoevsky wrote)
For freedom that, when it arrived, became
A worse Communist tyranny's wrong way.
I may find I've stood for freedom of speech
Too blatantly, too honestly, and may
Learn I'm in breach of some law and must dwell
In a similar British prison cell.   110

There is a relief in speaking freely.
Too long I've hidden behind a poet's mask.
It's time to take issue with all who would
Renew the Cold War, reinvade and bask
In Soviet territories, Estonia
And West Ukraine, and with those who'd spread war
Across the Middle East. And so I take
My moderate stance beside the Tsars whose law
Resisted terror and mob tyranny
And maintained stable life so most were free.   120
31 May–2, 10 June 2015

Nicholas Hagger visited the St Petersburg Hermitage on 31 May 2015.
18, 85. The KGB was closed down by Gorbachev in 1991 and replaced by two
organisations, the FSB and SVR.
37. Giuseppe Mazzuola's 'The Death of Adonis'.
71–80. The first Peter and Paul Fortress, which held Dostoevsky (in cell no.9 of
the Alekseevsky Ravelin), was demolished in 1872 and replaced by the present
two-storey building of 69 similar cells, two punishment cells and an inner yard
in the Trubetskoy Bastion.
104. Dostoevsky's Pyotr Verkhovensky in *The Possessed* was inspired by the
revolutionary Sergey Nechayev.

In Tallinn: Premonitions of War

In Tallinn we drive to the Upper Town
Past Fat Margaret and reach the Maiden's Tower
And from the Kiek in de Kök Bastion peer
Down at the Lower Town's kitchens, which cower.
The medieval wall recalls the time
The town thrived in the Hanseatic League,
Was occupied by Germans and Russians,
Though in the EU's not clear of intrigue.

For Russia overflies with its aircraft.
Our guide says, "They could invade any time   10
By land, sea and air. There are one million
Estonians, Russian-speakers are forced – I'm
Glad – to learn our language and they've appealed
To Moscow. Russian troops may be sent in
Disguised as militias as in Ukraine.
We hope that NATO will protect our skin."

I walk in the Song Festival grounds where
Three hundred thousand Estonians crammed. All
Sang national and patriotic songs
In their Singing Revolution to call   20
For independence from Soviet rule.
Our guide asks: "Which is better to have had,
Nazis or Soviets? Would you prefer
Bubonic plague or smallpox? Both were bad."

In a manor house I eat cake and watch
Two girls in national costume play kannels,
Two-thousand-year-old versions of zithers
With strings plucked like a harp's flowing sound-swells.
One explains the meaning of what they wear.
I can tell their youth by the red bands in   30
Their skirts, and the married sport an apron.

They are proud of their ethnic origin.

"We did so much for Poland's nationhood,"
A Russian guide said, "now we're blamed for that.
It's not fair, we feel humiliated."
But madam, it's history's 'tit for tat'.
The Russians called the British 'imperialists'
After we'd let a quarter of the world learn
Their nationhood, and were thanked with insults.
You suppressed with your tanks – now it's your turn.   40

In March thirty-three-thousand Russian troops
Rehearsed the sealing of this Baltic and
The capture of Denmark's Bornholm island,
Sweden's Gotland island and the Aland
Islands from Finland so the Russians can
Seize and protect and have a land route through
Estonia, Latvia and Lithuania
To their Kaliningrad missiles – a *coup*.

They'd also invade part of North Norway
To protect their interests in the Arctic.   50
If they re-enact this military
Exercise for real, they'll quickly unpick
Gorbachev the Great's *perestroika*
('Restructuring') and *glasnost* ('openness'),
British-style freeing of speech and markets
For a coming New World Order's *largesse*.

I pass the ex-Russian submarine base
And think of the Russian Baltic fleet's sprawl
At Kronstadt that can steam to Estonia.
Will NATO risk nuclear war for so small   60
A nation of just over a million?
Russian tanks are five hours away, it's plain
They can quickly take Tallin and open

A second front to distract from Ukraine.

I ask the Ukrainian captain at 'drinks',
"Is Russia expansionist?" He's not thrilled.
"Part of my country has been occupied.
Two thousand Ukrainian soldiers were killed
Because the Russians are in East Ukraine."
The British, needing cuts, will arm in name   70
And repeat their nineteen-thirties' mistake.
Time will tell if overflying's a game.

So I muse on premonitions of war,
On small nations that are alarmed and cower
From a threatening neighbour poised to invade,
That resents its reduced imperial power
And to restore its lands, lowers like storm clouds
That spatter rain and whip up mountainous seas.
But all conflicts, like waves, are reconciled
And calm returns like morning's sparkling breeze.   80
3, 11, 29 June 2015

Nicholas Hagger visited Tallinn on 3 June 2015. He writes: "The previous
March, less than a couple of months before my journey, there had been a
Russian military exercise involving 33,000 troops to rehearse the capture of part
of North Norway to protect Russian interests in the Arctic, and of Bornholm
island from Denmark, Gotland island from Sweden and the Aland Islands from
Finland, which would allow Russia to seal the Baltic and isolate Estonia, Latvia
and Lithuania with a view to linking Russia to its retained exclave of
Kaliningrad on the Polish border, where missiles capable of bearing strategic
and nuclear weapons were being transported."

Chaos in Iraq

A grim scene in Tikrit, getting on for
Two hundred prisoners kneel in a long line

On what looks like wasteland, not palace grounds.
IS executioners shout – consign –
"Persians" and fire into their backs. They fall.
Saddam on the gallows asked masked hangmen,
"Are you Persians?", scornful word for 'Shiites'.
It's his revenge, in his palace grounds, then.

IS, once al-Qaeda in Iraq, brought
The Sunnis back above all other groups.   10
They've split Iraq into three warring states,
Sunnis against Shiite and Kurdish troops.
Churchill's Iraq united all three, I
Helped weld them in Baghdad, all had their say.
Kassem's authoritarian structure held
Hostile factions together in my day.

When Saddam fell the police structure fell.
There's now a vacuum IS has filled.
Al-Baghdadi, once a student at my
University of Baghdad, strong-willed,   20
Emerged as Caliph in seventh-century dress
And had 'Jihadi John' behead prisoners.
Twenty Syrian pilots submissively
Knelt to be beheaded as if actors.

I Google Simon Elliot and find he
Has Jewish parents, is an actor. Track,
He's shown sitting with Senator McCain,
The same man in Mosul's mosque, garbed in black.
Is al-Baghdadi a Mossad agent?
Has he split Iraq into three, a long-   30
Standing Israeli goal of fifty years,
And called twenty thousand zealots who're wrong

To come to a new Spain and be wiped out
In sectarian warfare, by US drones.

And now he's done his work has Israel moved
Him back home to Israel with "broken bones"
And "being paralysed in an air raid"?
His whereabouts are unknown, but all feel
That whether its leader's acted Caliph
In black garb or not, IS fights for real.   40

All IS below leader spread Sunnis
Throughout Iraq and Syria and behead
Ethnic minorities like Yazidis
And raze pre-seventh-century ruins they dread
Such as Hatra as history 'began'
With Mohammed. IS fighters and fans
Scorn culture and past civilizations,
Are fanatics and new barbarians.

Saddam boasted he'd chemical weapons
To impress Iran who Iraq had fought.   50
The West overheard, recalled Halabja,
Deposed him, then found his tally was nought.
Gaddafi said he'd massacre Libyans
In Benghazi who had al-Qaeda's grouse.
After he was deposed their black flag flew
From the flagpole on Benghazi's court-house.

The West, obsessed with deficits and cuts,
Does not want to be involved in a new
War in Iraq and its strikes from the air
Are no match for what ground fighters can do.   60
The West's resolve peters and needs to be
Strengthened if it's to maintain global power.
US hegemony is in decline
And cries out for a leader of the hour.

The West has bestridden the free world like
A Colossus, enforced peace on all mess.

Colossal Liberty still holds her torch
To welcome in the poor and the homeless
To the American dream of plenty.
The West cries out for Liberty to sweep   70
Away chaos in Iraq and impose
A *Pax Americana* that all keep.
6–8, 11 June 2015

29. According to an internet rumour wrongly attributed to Edward Snowden, Abu Bakr al-Baghdadi, the head of the Islamic State (or ISIL, also known as ISIS), was a Jewish actor named Simon Elliot and Mossad agent. See note to 'Caliphate' for more details.

Watcher and Two Carts

A card from Ricks, a Vorticist image:
A 1900 card of a dark wood,
The bridge at Boldre in my publisher's
Hampshire and two horses and carts. All's good:
A 'serf' toils in the river cutting reeds
And loading them, watched by a sitting man
In a cloth-cap, and all is murky gloom.
The two carts are my two books and.... I scan.

I toil in fourteenth-century conditions
And on the eighteenth-century bridge and way   10
Ricks sits, watching me toil and load bundles
Of reeds, my poems and from a past day
My 'bolder' memories of my double life
In two books like open carts by my graft,
And my laborious, medieval way
Is measured by Neoclassical craft.

But then I think the watcher is a spy
And I am watching the two men who toil.

The watcher and the carts show secret work.
The watcher's me, not Ricks, the reeds are spoil.   20
The card shows a time before my Provost
Joined Worcester College in1908,
When life was simple and rural, and no
First World War had men watching for the State.

I think how my Provost invited me
To sherry to consider secret work,
My duty, and swore me to secrecy.
I could not break his confidence and shirk,
Could not tell Ricks but had to choose two peers
And tell them what my new career might be.   30
He might have headed me off from the call,
Like Kitchener's pointing, to serve my country.

I think of the rural world of Hardy
And Barnes and of communities that shone.
I think of a rooted, simple, toiling
Life in a wood, by a river, now gone.
Now I have described my secret bundling
I have a sense of '*nunc dimittis*' furled.
I am soon ready to depart now I
Have shown the carts and watcher to the world.   40

25, 27 October 2015

Nicholas Hagger had sent Christopher Ricks copies of *My Double Life 1: This Dark Wood* and *My Double Life 2: A Rainbow over the Hills*, which reveal his four years' undercover work as a British intelligence agent. Ricks sent him a c.1900 Barrie 'picture card' of a dark wood, two horses and carts and a watcher on 19 May 2015. Like a Vorticist image it triggered rushes of association at several levels. A month after this poem was written, *The Poems of T.S. Eliot*, the annotated text edited by Christopher Ricks and Jim McCue, came out in two volumes. Nicholas Hagger was now the watcher of *his* two carts (as Ricks knew he would be when he sent the card).

28. 'Shirk', 'shrink from, avoid, get out of (duty, work, responsibility)'. (*Concise*

Oxford Dictionary.)

38. 'Furled', 'roll[ed] up and secure (a sail, umbrella, flag)', i.e. for the time being. (*Concise Oxford Dictionary*.)

Oxford Bait

I park in a lay-by and read reviews
Of Bate's book on the 'unauthorised' life
And hundred thousand pages of journals
Of Ted Hughes – consent was withdrawn by his wife
Who had asked in vain to see what he'd written.
I drive on to the college orchard gate
And in the porter's lodge collect my pack,
Take bag and evening dress to my room and wait.

I find contemporaries by the long room,
Stand sipping tea, wearing a college tie   10
Among familiar faces. Open-necked,
Bate greets me warmly and soon tells me why
He could not quote lines written long before
Hughes knew his widow, to whom in his will
Of three handwritten and unwitnessed lines
He left his estate when terminally ill.

For an hour Bate addresses us while we
Sit on chairs in the long room and I hear
The rattling of a college begging bowl.
Afterwards he tells me that there's a clear   20
Distinction between letters for private use
And letters that have a public interest.
He cannot quote Hughes' private letters now
His widow owns them after his bequest.

Down by the lake I encounter Hookie
Who was Ambassador in Iraq when

Saddam invaded Kuwait. I describe
My Baghdad from thirty years before then.
Outside the door that leads up to my room
I meet Miles who is ninety and believes   30
In ether whose electrical charges
Contain life's substanceless network that weaves.

We all attend chapel in evening dress
And listen to the choir's medieval
Antiphons among Neoclassical
Pillars, take in each Neronian mural,
Walk to a thronged reception in the long
Room, sip champagne and I see Bate weave through.
I say Ricks has reservations about
Hughes' poems. "So do I," he says. I knew.   40

"The ghost of a pentameter should lurk
Behind free verse, Eliot said," I say.
"Hughes is too free sometimes. D.H. Lawrence
Was too free in 'Snake'. They're on the same way."
"I've reservations," he says. "Read the book
And write and tell me what you think of it."
A more polished, questing poet, I walk
Up steps to hall and find my year, and sit.

I am a few seats from where I once sat
The college entrance exam, writing on   50
This table, facing the marble fireplace.
December light from the high windows shone
Behind me so my paper was in gloom,
Three-hour papers for a week, then *viva*.
Only four in our hundred would get in.
Some sixty years have slipped by like water.

Coffee's served. Bate rises and speaks, and says
Removing panelling has muffled sound.

He shares his plans to improve acoustics.
The college is in great demand, renowned.   60
He sits down to applause. After farewells
I rise, head out, locate my car at peace
And drive back home for I have to be up
At four-thirty to catch a flight to Greece.
25, 27 October 2015

Nicholas Hagger returned to Worcester College, Oxford for a Gaudy on 3 October 2015. The Provost, Jonathan Bate, had an 'unauthorised' biography of Ted Hughes being published, which acted as 'bait' that drew him back.
25. 'Hookie'. Nickname for Sir Harold Walker, British Ambassador to Iraq in 1991.
28. 'Thirty years before'. Nicholas Hagger lectured at the University of Baghdad from 1961 to 1962.
44. D.H. Lawrence's 'Snake' begins: "A snake came to my water-trough/On a hot, hot day, and I in pyjamas for the heat,/To drink there."

Symposium: Averting a Nuclear Winter

I. World State

Plato's symposium, 'drinking together',
Had men talking in turn of love with weight
Followed by musical entertainment,
And his 'Republic' was an ideal State.
We modern international *philosophes*
Are to found a new World State and declare
War illegal, begin disarmament:
A new 'Republic' in Athenian air.

I drive from Athens airport to the Bay
Of Phaleron and am shown to a room   10
With a panoramic view of the sea,
Of Salamis, Aegina. On that spume
Theseus sailed to seek out the Minotaur

And the Persian fleet, menacing, appeared.
It's between the walls of Themistocles.
I leave my bags and drive on to be cleared.

Under the pediment of the City
Of Athens Cultural Centre I climb
Steps and, within, stairs to the first floor where
I register. I've arrived just in time.   20
Igor greets me with a Russian bear-hug
And a Polish *philosophe*, keen to please.
My Chinese assistant then walks me round
To statues of Plato and Socrates.

I make my way to the Georgian Centre
Where, to singing and food, I meet some more
Of the world's professors of philosophy.
Next morning in a ground-floor room next door
I meet Raoul and Timi and discuss
The coming World State, and sit in a hall   30
Upstairs to hear greetings: each speaks in turn,
I listen to their voices rise and fall.

All day the *philosophes* present in turn,
End to applause and then interpreters
Convey their words in first Russian, then Greek.
I am to be Chairman (Igor avers)
Of the Constitutional Convention.
Next day I sit on high and think of dates
When George Washington chaired and got approved
The Constitution of the United States.   40

I'm chairing in a new Constitution
For the Universal State of the Earth.
The Head of our Earth Bank explains the new
'Tero' he will issue and bring to birth.
At last I read the 'Declaration' out

And it is passed upon a show of hands.
I have (with Igor) brought into being
A new World State that now covers all lands.

II. Disarmament

Now we delegates climb aboard a coach
In Omonia Square, Igor's next to me.   50
He tells me how Aristotle differed
Inhabitants from 'citizens' and key
'Aristocrats', the best educated
'Philosopher-rulers' of highest mind.
The State's political party will work –
The Citizens of the Earth – for mankind.

He tells me how he came to found the World
Philosophical Forum – he read (I smirk)
Of the World Economic Forum at
Davos – and how he found his best-known work   60
On dialectical materialism
In Engels in the Soviet era.
A "KGB man" found his first PC.
(How come he got it from such a handler?)

We reach Mycenae, and again I pass
Through the Lion Gate I loved when seventeen
And climb the citadel to the palace,
Locate the two small rooms that once had been
The bathroom where, the night that he returned
From Troy, his wife stabbed Agamemnon while   70
He washed. We drive on to the '*tholos*' tomb
Of Agamemnon, in the beehive style.

On the coach we have discussed the Supreme
Council of Humanity's membership:
I am its Acting Chairman now the new
World State's been adopted, it's in my grip.

We stop at the Palamidi fortress
And I am given a purple cyclamen.
In Nauplion, I lunch with Igor by
The harbour walls I know are Venetian.   80

We pass Tiryns and reach Epidaurus.
I stand in the theatre where I slept, a feat,
In a sleeping-bag when I was nineteen,
And share the President's central stone seat
With a curved back with Igor as Paris,
The actor who brought down the Light last year
In Plato's Academy, declaims Greek
With Doric words whose each whisper you hear.

A cramped study at the Georgian Centre.
Igor shows me his website's visual aids   90
That end with a nuclear explosion
And cloud that blots out the sun for decades,
A nuclear winter of minus fifty
Centigrade, and says of humankind's plight,
"We need disarmament." I now see I'm
Part of a plot to disarm Russian might.
9, 26–27 October 2015

Nicholas Hagger attended the World Philosophical Forum's annual conference and symposium in Athens from 3 to 9 October 2015. He writes: "I had been invited by Igor Kondrashin, and I chaired the Constitutional Convention of international philosophers to found a new World State, the Universal State of the Earth (USE). At the beginning and end of the conference I visited the Georgian Centre, which promotes the culture of the ex-Soviet Republic of Georgia."

24. The statues of Plato and Socrates are outside the Academy of Athens, the university.

38–40. George Washington chaired the US Constitutional Convention in 1787.

44. The new World State's currency was to be the 'tero'.

63. 'PC', 'personal computer'.

79. 'Nauplion', pronounced 'Nafplion'.

The Sorrows of Allah, The Nameless One
"Not in my name"

You point your guns into the air and fire
At baled-out parachutists floating down
And chant *"Allahu akbar"* as if I
Wanted you each to wear a murderous frown.

But know that I have always stood for peace
Ever since I led you from the nights' chill
Of desert tents to a caliph's palace.
I cringe when you invoke me as you kill.
25 November 2015

A Russian plane was shot down by a Turkish Su-24 after straying briefly into
Turkish air space. Jihadists in Syria fired at the two parachutists chanting
"Allahu akbar", killing one.

Thoughts on Syria: Rush to War

And now a rush to war. Two years ago
The UK, anti-Assad, nearly placed
Itself on ISIL's side, and now we're set
To bomb IS fighters, and in such haste
That Parliament's debate must last one day,
Not two. What new information's emerged
That's caused this 'self-defence' and planes to wait
On stand-by to bomb Syria when urged?

A majority: the Shadow Foreign
Secretary sided with the PM's threats   10
And now the Typhoons in harm's way circle

Above Raqqa looking for new targets.
And I, above white clouds, nearing Berlin,
The Allies' target when I was a child,
Empathise with our pilots tasked to kill
ISIL's leaders so Syria's reconciled.

The safety of our nation is at stake.
We must disrupt a foe that can attack
At any time, and our precision bombs,
Laser-guided, and drones, can set it back.   20
And Syrian troops may enter the *débris*
But civilians will be blown up, so why
So hastily? Do they know more than's said?
We cannot forget politicians lie.

I think of news I heard, that the IS
Have captured a Syrian laboratory
And are on the verge of nuclear knowledge.
Is this IS trying to oversee
A nuclear bomb small as a cricket ball
That will release to winds what never fades: 30
Radiation that can contaminate
The green belt round London for four decades?

And what of IS use of mustard gas?
After two Iraq wars an inspector
Sought weapons of mass destruction – in vain.
Saddam used mustard gas in Halabja
And killed five thousand Kurds. We never found
His stock. Did it pass via his old henchmen
To IS, who have used the gas four times?
Are they planning to use it in London?   40

Russia, the US and France are bombing
Syria already, the UK Iraq
But not Syria (as if a football team

Sought to score from their half and make their mark).
The UK only have twelve planes to send –
Some bombings and what reconnaissance yields.
The big hoo-ha in Parliament will make
Little difference on desert battlefields.

Putin's accused the Turkish leader's son
Of buying cheap oil from IS convoys.   50
Russian planes have filmed hundreds of lorries,
One downed by Turks' evidence-hiding ploys.
So Turkey's buying oil seized by IS
With EU cash to keep the refugees,
Which IS is using to fund the war.
And Turkey's double-dealing, if you please.

IS will be decapitated though
Their head hides in tunnels, beneath human shields.
Some of the Free Syrian Army will be
Ground troops to go in as IS power yields.   60
But nation-states are fighting nation-states,
A supranational force can legislate
For all countries to enforce peace, once war's
Been declared illegal by a World State.
3–5, 12 December 2015

1. 'Two years ago'. The British Parliament refused to bomb Syria on 30 August 2013.

34. 'Inspector'. The British scientist and authority on biological warfare employed by the British Ministry of Defence and formerly a United Nations weapons inspector in Iraq, Dr David Kelly, who died on 17 July 2003.

39. Four times. IS used mustard gas four times in Marea, north of Aleppo, in and after April 2015.

45. 'Twelve planes'. Initially the UK sent 4 Tornado jets from Akrotiri, and soon afterwards 2 more Tornado jets and 6 Typhoons.

At Berlin's Kaiser Wilhelm Memorial Church

A Christmas market by Kaiser Wilhelm
Memorial Church the Allies bombed. From cold
I wander through the front tower's vestibule
And blink at the ceiling mosaics' gold,
And at the walls' marble reliefs, salvaged
From the removed ruins. All's well, no strife:
Christ Pantocrator peers down, the legend
Says 'I am the Way, the Truth and the Life'.

On the ceiling I see the procession
Of the younger Hohenzollerns, with Queen   10
Luise and her husband Friedrich Wilhelm
The Third, their son Wilhelm the First, here seen
Wearing a cloak of imperial crowns;
His older brother Friedrich Wilhelm
The Fourth, his son Friedrich the Third and then
The Kaiser of the First World War – and realm.

Kaiser Wilhelm the Second and his wife
Auguste Viktoria, in court regalia:
The Kaiser wears an ermine cloak and sports
A turned-up moustache, looks like a soldier.   20
Further along the ceiling, the other
Side of an altar, process the elder
Hohenzollerns in balanced piety.
A dynasty under Christ and altar.

How could Kaiser Willy, with this Christian
Lineage, start the Great War, the whine and whop
That ended the old stately, sedate world
And killed eighteen million and wrecked Europe,
Causing the settlement that twenty years
Later brought in a new round of mad war   30
That would ruin this magnificent church

Whose sumptuous mosaics fill with awe?
5, 11–12 December 2015

Nicholas Hagger visited the Kaiser Wilhelm Memorial Church, Berlin on 5 December 2015.

Collapse of the Old Order

Images scream from screens, of rubble in
Syria and Iraq after air attacks
By Assad, rebels, the US, Russia,
France, the UK and Arab states in wars
Self-interested nation-states working
Within the UN cannot solve. All show
Buildings caved in, ruins, streets filled with stones,
The *débris* of institutions, houses
And homes where families camp and scrabble
Under girders and salvage from piled bricks,   10
And from which many refugees have fled.
Gaza, Libya, Yemen, Afghanistan
Have more destruction and dereliction.
I wander through the West and see similar
Devastation, though not as tangible.
I see the collapse of an old order,
Shattered banks still functioning in ruins,
Broken capitalism and fragmented
Socialism, all nation-states damaged:
Unstable regions in the eurozone   20
Crying out against grim austerity
In Greece, Italy, Spain and Portugal,
And France in turmoil, and Europe's borders
Swamped by a tidal wave of refugees
From an epicentre of bombed-out homes
In war zones and Africa's crop failure.
Europe, which kept peace for seventy years,

Is threatened by its borders and exits.
I see totalitarianism heaped
In Libya, Burma and great China,   30
Despots standing in ruins, the starving
Pleading for food and foreign aid that fails
To reach them. I see monarchies totter,
In all the world's countries the suffering
Of war victims, the poor and the diseased,
Refugees from pandemics, drought, famine.
And everywhere governments' deficits
And indebtedness rising each second,
Talk of another financial crash and
Future displacements caused by climate change.   40
In all the world's capitals I see streets
Heaped up with *débris* from the old order,
Disused 'isms' that collapsed from decay,
Colonialism, decolonisation,
Self-determination, relativism,
Collective security and NATO,
Internationalism as the UN
Can't solve the world's problems in assemblies,
And superpowerdom: the US holds back.
I see the rubble of the nation-states   50
That send aircraft to bomb and drone-attack
But, each operating from self-interest,
Have no vision of a peaceful era.
Everywhere I look, on each continent,
Is a heap of problems, collapsed *débris*,
The rubble of old thinking which has failed:
Wars, property, disease and famine, the earth
Neglected as the richest get more rich.

O Tennyson, I need you at my side
As I dream of a clearance of the piles   60
Of the nation-states' ruined commandments,
Summon a Federation of the World.

O Christ, I could do with your long-promised
Second Coming, for you could now proclaim
The unification of humankind,
A paradisal war-free, peaceful Age.
O King Arthur, asleep in the Welsh hills,
I could do with your immediate return
To oversee (once you have overcome
Your shock at seeing the mess mankind's in)　　　　　　70
The reinstatement of an ordered earth
On the principles of your Avalon.
But I, the poet of humanity,
Can only dream of universal peace
And hope that influential men – the Head
Of the UN, the US President,
The ex-President of the European
Council and my future King, for instance –
Can come to my help with direct action.
I call for the UN to be transformed　　　　　　80
Into a United Federation –
With a supranational authority
That at a federal level will declare
All war illegal and enforce world peace
And disarmament with a peace-keeping
Force – and turn democratic so the world
Is represented in an Assembly
And a higher Senate and Commission.
I have presided over the drafting
Of a Constitution for a World State　　　　　　90
And now call for such a World State to be
Debated at a Constitutional
Convention of the UN's delegates
To the General Assembly and voted in.
Then famine, disease, poverty, like war,
Can be declared illegal and resolved,
And the ruins of the earth's old thinking
Can be cleared away so a new order

Can preside over good living for all.
I see a conference on climate change 100
For every nation-state throughout the world
Reach agreement in Paris, but know well
Not enough's been made legally binding,
A UF can declare more illegal.
I see UN leaders meet five-yearly
And recognition that the World Wide Web
Has made possible a broad UN-based
World State of the kind I chaired and founded
In Athens – exploring what can be done
To reconstruct the shattered old order. 110
I am a poet and have dreamed great dreams.
I am a poet whose statecraft has dreamed
(An amanuensis of the beyond)
A new order and universal sway
That will bring in a universal peace
And rehabilitate all refugees,
Rescue all ruin-squatting humankind
From the destruction of the old order
And restore all to a worldwide paradise.
15 December 2015

Epistle to the Chancellor of the Exchequer

It's a time of austerity and you
Are putting up our taxes as you see
It as a badge of honour that you fight
The next election with the deficit
Paid off, and so there can't be any new
Borrowing, tax-and-spend's anathema.
So how've you had a give-away budget?
Where did you find the wherewithal to lift
The abolition of mass tax credits
That even swell the income of MPs? 10

My younger brother who worked for the Duke
Of Westminster and ran the Grosvenor
Estate tells me, the answer can be found
In the Bank of England Asset Purchase
Facility Fund's annual report, page
Seven, which I find online and print. I read
The Asset Purchase Fund's operations
Are indemnified for loss by H M
Treasury and so any surplus is
Due to H M Treasury. The report   20
Says, "This arrangement is accounted for
As a derivative," enough to put
Most people off, my brother sagely says.
I ask, "What does it mean? What's going on?"
Sitting by me in Canto Corvino
Forking arancini and sipping wine
In booming London's Artillery Lane,
He says: "The Bank of England created
Three hundred and seventy-five billion pounds
Of new money (quantitative easing)   30
And lent it at minimum lending rate,
Now 0.5 per cent, to the Asset
Purchase Fund, which is kept separate from
The Bank of England. The Fund then purchased
Gilt-edged debt in the open market at
An average yield of some 2.85
Per cent, earning it a current margin
Of 2.35 per cent. The Treasury
Then guaranteed the Fund against all loss
That would occur if minimum lending   40
Rate goes above 2.85 per cent.
(Most gilts could be sold back to the market
Before then, but that is most unlikely.)
H M Treasury required all profits
Should be paid to the Exchequer, and there
Was a bumper first receipt by H M

Treasury, which stands to pay over each year
2.35 per cent of three hundred
And seventy-five billion pounds, a tally
Of 8.81 billion pounds a year   50
That has to go on to the Exchequer.
This sum funded the give-away budget
And the tax credits whose abolition
Was blocked by the House of Lords." And so, though
You preach a language of austerity
You have created a secret fund from
Quantitative easing that brings in eight
Billion a year so, though Scrooge, you can seem
Generous like Father Christmas, full of gifts.

It has to be said (let us speak plainly)   60
Politicians spin 'dreadful' into 'nice'
So voters will approve of what they've done.
I understand you must ameliorate,
But you have hidden the transaction in
The Fund's annual report, behind the word
'Derivative' which glazes over eyes,
And you know the Bank of England should not
Be printing money (an inflationary
Pressure) while imposing hardship upon
The masses who pay burdensome taxes.   70
My brother continues his exposure:
"The Treasury guarantee is covered up
In the notes to the accounts of both the Bank
Of England and the Asset Fund. H M
Treasury and the Bank of England direct
Enquiries to the Issuing Department
And the Debt Management Office, neither
Of which is transparent about all this.
So the UK government's debt is now
Three hundred and seventy-five billion   80
Pounds more than disclosed, since quantitative

Easing's not included in National Debt.
If it were included, National Debt
Would rise by nearly 25 per cent,
Which would alienate capital markets
And force the cost of all borrowing by
The UK government to rise." I frown.
I do not want the cost of borrowing
To rise and trigger a new recession.
I grasp the three hundred and seventy-five   90
Billion might be a contingency fund
In the event of a British exit
From the EU, on which you'd have to draw
If reduced trade with Europe leaves a hole.
It may serve as a 'staying-in-Europe'
Fund to tide you through the referendum.
And so, though shocked at hidden borrowing
Created by Rothschilds' Bank of England,
I understand I must keep my lips sealed.

But I castigate your deceptive lack   100
Of transparency which serves the national
Cause but prints money while preaching 'austere'.
A clever man, to serve the best interests
Of our nation-state you can't be sincere
And are cut off from human honesty,
And what you've done smacks of hypocrisy.
I, too, to serve my country, have appeared
Other than I was, so I sympathise.
But I, more than most, can detect a vice
That must be condemned: failure to be straight.   110
O Chancellor, the country's in good hands
But transparency's a virtue that seems
Incompatible with running a State.
I have to say, you're trapped in a deceit
That isolates you from all humankind,
And seeing where your scheme has led you I

Know I would rather be a poet than
A Chancellor who manipulates Banks
And Funds and thus operates covertly.
And at such times I'm glad I turned my back   120
On corridors of power for fields and trees.
Your concealed borrowing's of national
Importance and, though shocked, I must keep quiet
To serve my country, I must condone spin
And as a patriot must ignore vice:
Falsehood, deceit, lying, hypocrisy.
Your system's safe with me, I will not tell.
But I expose vices in crafty works
(Whose double meanings involve some deceit
And can be castigated as unstraight).   130
As poems don't have a wide readership I've
Hidden your secret in poetry few will read.
25–26 January, 3 February 2016

Nicholas Hagger visited the Canto Corvino restaurant on 23 January 2016 and had a conversation with his brother, Jonathan Hagger.

In its annual report of 2011/2012 the Bank of England Asset Purchase Facility Fund, which is separate from the Bank of England, reported on p.7 that the Fund's "operations are fully indemnified for loss by H M Treasury and in return any surplus from these operations, after deduction of fees, operating costs and any tax payable, is due to H M Treasury. This arrangement is accounted for as a derivative under IAS 39."

This entry reflected a transaction. After April 2012 the Bank of England created £375bn of new money and lent it at minimum lending rate (MLR), then 0.5%, to the Bank of England Asset Purchase Fund which purchased government gilt-edged debt in the open market at an average yield of 2.85%, earning a margin of 2.35% (2.85% minus 0.5%). H M Treasury then guaranteed the Fund against any loss which would occur if MLR goes above 2.85% and required that any profits should be paid to the Exchequer. There are references to the Treasury guarantee in accounting jargon in the notes of the accounts of both the Bank of England and the Bank of England Asset Purchase Fund. The Treasury and Bank of England direct enquiries to the Issuing Department and the Debt

Management Office, neither of which has been transparent about the guarantee.

Thus UK government debt is £375bn greater than disclosed, since quantitative easing is not included in National Debt which, if it were included, would rise by nearly 25%. This would have a negative effect on capital markets and would therefore increase the cost of government borrowing.

Politicians are required to use such hidden methods in running governments, but such schemes set them apart from decent human values and the virtue in terms of which Nicholas Hagger condemns human follies and vices.

The British Chancellor of the Exchequer at the time was George Osborne.

128. 'Crafty', 'crafted, made in a skilful way', 'cunning, artful, wily'; 'cunning or deceit'. (*Concise Oxford Dictionary*.)

34

ADVENTURES IN PARADISE
2010–2015

In Iran: Persian and Shiite Empires

I

I fly to Tehran. The War on Terror
Is at its height. I'm the only tourist,
Come to know the Shiite angle. Pictures
Of the Supreme Leader looking earnest,
And Khomeini in the airport. I'm met
And driven past the US Embassy where
Anti-American slogans scream on
The outer wall. In the bazaar all stare.

I fly to Shiraz, am driven through green
Vegetation to Hafez's garden   10
And marble tomb near orange-trees, under
A dome, poet of love and wine; and then
Past a Sufi *dervish* lost in the One;
Go to Sadi's tomb and rose-garden, free
Persian poet of mankind's oneness, sit
By brown trout in a spring and drink rose tea.

We drive to Persepolis' deserted,
Broken columns and doorways, past riches.
I stand where Xerxes the First's throne once stood
When he, and Persia, ruled thirty countries.   20
I stand before the Gate of All Nations,
I look at wall carvings and grasp that they
Influenced Pheidias's Greek marbles
Through news brought by Persian troops' fearsome stay.

In Pasargadae I see the ruined

277

Sixth-century-BC palace of Cyrus
The Great, and the room where he and Darius
Slept on carpets and cushions; and, rapturous,
Stand before Cyrus' tomb on a flat plain
As high as a two-storey house. It's good.   30
I swat mosquitoes. Here Herodotus
And Alexander the Great came and stood.

I pass an ancient cypress tree as old
As the Great Pyramid. In Yazd I stay
In a garden hotel, see a mosque and
Zoroastrian fire-temple, then away
On to the Towers of Silence, circular
Stone walls on hills where the bodies of dead
Zoroastrians were laid out on stones for
Vultures to pick them clean where they were spread.   40

I lunch at Meynob's *caravanserai*,
Then drive to Isfahan and walk in snow
In Imam Square. I trudge to the Shah mosque,
See under the dome a golden rose 'blow',
The One spreading out into the many,
And the message of peace around its base;
I look at the Sheikh Lotfollah mosque and
The palace balcony where the Shah'd pace.

                    II
I drive to Natanz through flurries of snow
And look in on a Husaynieh, a place   50
For mourning Husayn, Ali's second son,
Third *Imam* to the Shiites, well-known face.
The villagers huddle round leaping flames,
They invite me to eat with them that night.
I wonder if this place will soon be bombed
Along with the nearby nuclear site.

We approach the snowy nuclear site.
I point my camera and click. My guide's scanned
A hump on a hill, points. "It's dangerous,
It's a restricted zone," he scolds, "they've manned   60
Machine-guns. Look." We drive along a fence
For two miles. The anti-aircraft guns jar.
If there is no nuclear program there,
Why are machine-guns trained upon our car?

We stay in Kashan in a small hotel.
I dine near eight hostile men who're bearded,
From Afghanistan, from the Taliban.
Next morning I visit a Safavid
Pavilion in an earthly Paradise.
Four water-channels – 'rivers' – intersect.   70
I see the Shah's balcony, where he viewed
His garden Paradise that was perfect.

Behind the Jamkaran mosque I locate
The stone well with a waist-high cover, calm
With a steel grille through which people have dropped
Messages to the hidden twelfth *Imam*
Who's hidden in a cave beneath the mosque
Since 874 and after anarchy
Will come back up in a Second Coming.
I peer down but there's nothing I can see.   80

I enter the Jamkaran mosque and sit
Cross-legged near black-turbaned *mullah*s dressed
As the Prophet's descendants. At the heart
Of Iran's hostility to the West
And of the Greater Shiite Empire, I
Ask the Light to block nuclear conflict's toll
And a clash between civilizations,
And the Light shines brightly into my soul.

In Qom I visit Khomeini's low house.
I climb steps and turn right into a room   90
Where a *mullah* sits over the *Koran*:
Khomeini's living-room/office in gloom.
I soak in the austere simplicity.
Here he made decisions to execute
Many "corrupters of the earth" before
His revolution's firing-squads – a brute.

III

I drive through the Zagros mountains and reach
Hamadan. I go to the round brick tomb
Of Esther, the heroine of *The Book*
Of Esther, the Jewish orphan whose bloom   100
Reputedly made her Amestris, wife
Of King Xerxes the First, and saved from harm
Her Jewish community and cousin.
A Jewish monument within Islam.

I go on to the Achaemenian
Ganjnameh and climb slippery steps deep
Under impacted snow and ice, past stalls
With lanterns, to the foothills of the steep
Mountain slope ankle-deep in snow, to two
Rock inscriptions by Darius and Xerxes   110
The First, proclaiming Ahura Mazda
Gave them the right to rule, despite the Medes.

I go to the tomb of Avicenna,
Muslim scientist and author beside
Of a hundred and thirty books. I bow
To eighty new herbs he identified,
I bow to his poetry, philosophy,
Music, economics, mathematics,
Physics, astronomy, medicine and law –
Universalist breadth and depth and mix.   120

Back in Tehran I tour the White Palace,
The Shah's summer palace and French ambit.
I see the Louis-the-Sixteenth settee
Where the Shah met the CIA's Kermit
Roosevelt to remove his Prime Minister
Mossadeq. I relive his opulence,
Note the luxurious *décor*, the wavy
Lines in the marble floor: extravagance.

I go to Khomeini's Tehran house in
A poor district, look through glass at his spare   130
Living-room and his paltry possessions.
A walkway leads to a Husaynieh where
On a raised platform he announced decrees
And executions above on TV,
The faithful sitting on carpets below.
I bow to his simple austerity.

The Persian ruins of Persepolis;
Then the Shiite tradition of the well
And the Hidden *Imam*'s Second Coming;
Then Khomeini's revolutionary hell;   140
And now the nuclear program at Natanz;
And the Greater Shiite Empire in bits
Of the Mid East – all can be seen to form
A pattern that reconciles opposites.
9 February, 6–7 April 2015

Nicholas Hagger travelled in Iran from 13 to 20 January 2007.
103. Esther's cousin was Mordecai.

In the Galapagos Islands: The Purpose of Evolution

I

The Galapagos Islands which inspired

Darwin's theory of evolution. On
The ground outside Baltra's tiny airport
Seven seals sleep in the bus shelter. Tired, wan,
We drive to the port, an inflatable
Plies to our small ship and teak cabin. Each
Unpacks and puts on a wet-landing suit.
We take the inflatable to a beach,

Playa de las Bachas on Santa Cruz,
A sandy coral beach with laval rocks,   10
Low scrub, a prickly pear. Brown pelicans
And blue-tailed boobies overhead, in flocks;
Blue herons and brown noddies. I walk past
Red Sally Lightfoot crabs, a turtle's nest;
Pink flamingos, iguanas crawl to swim.
In scrub, yellow mangrove warblers congest.

By inflatable to Pinnacle Rock,
Bartholomé. Frigate-birds circle, see
Galapagos penguins, brown pelicans.
I see where Darwin's *Beagle* moored when he   20
Studied these islands only three to eight
Million years old, short evolution span.
Small-ground finches flit, as a sea lion sleeps
A lizard licks its flies, in Nature's plan.

We sail to Sullivan Bay, Santiago,
Where Darwin camped. Sea lions sleep wearily
On black volcanic sand. We walk on black
Rope-shaped lava a hundred and twenty
Years old. I sit by escutia and watch.
A Galapagos mockingbird flies by,   30
Iguanas eat algae. Stormy petrels
Skim low over the water with keen eye.

I cross to Puerto Egas, take the trail

Darwin took up the volcano in mist.
Galapagos hawk, semipalmated
Plover, oystercatcher and whimbrel twist.
Boobies dive for black-tailed mullet, a smell
Of breeding snakes, a tattler bird and nest.
Noddies pick food from a pelican's mouth.
A yellow-crowned night heron with gold crest.   40

I ask Gino, our naturalist, "What drives
Evolution?" He says, "Self-improvement."
But how do new-born creatures know how they
Must improve themselves with instinctive bent?
I say, "There is an orderly system
All creatures keep going, it does not fuse.
Lizards lay eggs and then depart. They hatch.
Some live, some die, the system continues."

II

What impels evolution? Why are there
Thirteen species of Galapagos finch   50
And only one species of human? We
Go on to Sombrero Chino and flinch
A path through sea lions and their pups. Red rock
Supports candelabra cactus. I muse
On red sesuvium. Then back on board,
We dip and roll through swell to Santa Cruz.

We walk from Puerto Ayora port through
Prickly-pear – *opuntia* – cactus. Each peers
At the eleven species of tortoises
That have endured three or four million years,   60
And six saddleback tortoises nearly
A hundred and fifty years old. I see
Sad Lonesome George, the last of his species
And, in Spielberg's film, model for ET.

Creatures adapt to their environment.
A starved finch fed on cactus adapted
And became a new species, 'cactus finch'.
In the Darwin Research Station I spread
The self-organising principle before
An Ecuadorian botanist: "What preens   70
Finches and tortoises to improve, adapt,
And become new species?" "It's in their genes."

A self-organising mitochondrial
Principle in genes transmits its planning,
Blueprints for adapting and conveying
Transmutations to successors, shaping
New species. I muse on inheritance
Of acquired characteristics as I
Bus up to water-basking tortoises
In their natural habitats, highlands-high.   80

The universe came from a point, and all
Species from one cell. What caused it to split?
Need for survival? Like turtles that crawl
Up beaches, hide eggs from any frigate.
Young turtles hatch in cool of night and crawl
To the sea, safe from frigates if no sloth.
Are they born with this survival instinct?
Is it in their DNA's plan for growth?

We moor off Floreana where once Drake
And Darwin's *Beagle* moored, shouts now silent.   90
We land in Post Office cove where pirates
Left letters, and on Punta Cormorant
See shearwaters, pink flamingos, Nazca
Boobies and yellow-crowned night herons' crests.
We reach a beach where thousands of stingray
Feed on ghost crabs, and find the turtle nests.

III

Again I ponder the great mystery.
Turtles hatch below sand and wait until
The cool of night before burrowing up,
Crawling for the sea safe from frigate's bill.   100
A frigate-bird makes slow swoops, looking for
Newly-hatched turtles to seize and devour.
There's a system and each creature's given
A plan for survival in its birth hour.

Self-organising and self-improvement
Are in each egg, larva, foetus and heir.
We wet-land on a deserted coral
Strip, Gardner Bay, on Espanola, where
Sea lions lie on the sand and mockingbirds
Hop on our bags, seek water near my fist.   110
On Punta Suarez between iguanas
A tame mockingbird perches on my wrist.

We step across boulders and reach a cliff-
Top where young albatrosses learn their skills,
Waddle, lurching from side to side, and run
To take off while others clack beaks, cross bills
In a mating dance. A red Hood larva
Lizard picks grubs from one's back, feeds and grooms.
Albatrosses, boobies and swallow-tailed
Gulls soar, and a fountaining blow-hole booms.   120

We pass finches and a Galapagos
Hawk and flycatcher and return to ship.
We land on San Cristóbal off Lobos
Island and pass where red-pouched frigates dip,
Sea lions, stingrays, larva gulls and yellow
Warblers. I sit on black larval rocks near
Sally Lightfoot crabs, a yellow wagtail,
Larval gulls. Paper-wasps dive at my ear.

At Puerto Baquerizo Moreno
Seals leap in splashing sea, boobies dive, inch-   130
Perfect. We bus to the highlands and see
On bushes a black vegetarian finch
And a woodpecker finch. I have now seen
Eleven of Darwin's thirteen finch species.
We sail to North Seymour where frigates fly
And back to Baltra to fly home, and tease.

Nine islands on the Equator, where like
Darwin I've mused on evolution's bent,
On species of tortoises and finches,
And feel its system's not an accident.   140
An order – purpose – drives turtles' instincts,
Improves and organises their advance.
In the Galapagos evolution
Thrusts forward with purpose, not random chance.
2–3 February, 4–5 April 2015

Nicholas Hagger travelled in the Galapagos Islands from 23 July to 11 August
2007.
136. 'Tease', 'pick (wool, hair, etc.) into separate fibres or threads'. (*Concise
Oxford Dictionary*.) Here used of experience.
138. 'Bent', 'inclination or bias'. (*Concise Oxford Dictionary*.)

In Peru: The Sun of the Incas

I

In Lima I see how Spanish building
Obliterated the Inca ruins: see
The cathedral and monastery and church
Of Santo Domingo, deliberately
Built by *conquistadors* on a brick temple –
Pizarro's palace on the Incas' seat.
A scant few Catholics erased the shrines

To the Inca sun-god Inti they beat.

In Cusco, surrounded by mountains at
Ten thousand feet, I stand by the base past   10
Of Pachacuti's Inca palace. I
Think how the Incas were wiped out. The last
Inca ruler was decapitated
In the plaza. Cusco was 'navel' in
The vast Inca Empire of 'Four Quarters'
Which stretched to Ecuador and Chile's shin.

We go to Qurikancha, the Incas' most
Important temple, whose traces – corbels –
Survived obliteration by the church
Of Santo Domingo; the five temples   20
Of the Rainbow; Three Worlds; Venus and Stars;
Lightning; the Moon. I see the altar head
On which hung the 'sun of Inti' that went
Missing soon after the Spanish landed.

We go to Saksaywaman, a Temple
Of the Sun on three levels – upper world,
This world and the underworld – and then on
To Puka Pukara, 'red fortress', curled
Above a view of four valleys which show
The 'navel' between two legs and two arms,   30
The 'Four Quarters' of the Inca Empire.
Below snow-clad Andes ranges: old farms.

We go on to Qenqo, a rocky cleft
And pass that leads to the Underworld where
In the middle there is a granite slab
On which animals and humans, hearts bare,
Were sacrificed to the god of earthquakes
And the Underworld, and were mummified.
Common people lived in the Underworld,

Nobles in the upper world, when they died.   40

I visit an Indian community
Twelve thousand feet up in the sheer Andes.
We bus through mud to high Ccaccaccollo
Where Indian ladies weave in a strong breeze.
Rufino, a hundred, sits between sticks,
Tells me to avoid alcohol, liqueurs
And food containing chemicals. We go
To a farm for llamas and alpacas.

II

We pass the Urubamba, the Sacred
River that winds through a green valley where   50
The Incas came for fruit, and reach Pisac
Eleven thousand feet up. Cliff-face holes bear
An Inca cemetery that's reached by rope.
I see abandoned Inca houses, see
A Temple of the Sun, and, perched above
Tiers of terraces, an observatory.

We go to Ollantaytambo, see high
On tiers a Temple of the Moon ruin
With windows and a Temple of the Sun.
Across the valley high on a mountain   60
Tunupa, Inca-carved god of harvest,
Looks down with massive mouth and each vast eye
On the valley harvests that he protects,
A daunting face hewn from rock that's so high.

At 9 a.m. on the winter solstice,
June the twenty-first, sun moves from the blond
Temple of the Sun to Tunupa's eyes,
While on December the twenty-second,
The summer solstice, at twelve a shadow
Fills a hole in the rock-face, and one's still   70

On a table used for sacrifice on
A mountain carved with a condor and bill.

We trundle in a glass-topped train through crags
And reach a town beneath plunging gorges,
Then bus up zigzag bends to a crag's top
And stand by Machu Picchu's terraces
With mountains, wooded slopes and chasms round.
I climb to the top and watch the dawn stir.
Inti the sun shines rayed above the range.
Swifts dart. Lost in steepling rocks I quiver.   80

We walk to buildings on the plateau that
Were abandoned in 1542
And covered in jungle till discovered
In 1911. Now I construe
The Temple of the Sun had two windows.
When winter/summer solstices occur
The sun strikes the same point in the Temple.
The angle between June and December

Sun lines is 46.9 degrees.
A line bisecting the sun angle at   90
23.45 degrees connects
The sun to earth's axis, suggesting that
Inca astronomers and engineers
Knew how the universe worked, how it ran.
Do these angles show they knew the earth moves
Round the sun before Copernicus span?

III

The Incas knew about the solstices
And equinoxes and could predict when
Crops should be sown and calendars be changed.
Pachacuti's Cusco court was near (then)   100
The Temple of the Sun so he could claim

Mastery of the universe at feast.
Though Greeks showed Atlas holding a round earth
And Columbus sailed west to reach the east

The Spanish Catholic *conquistadors* still
Believed the sun revolved around the earth
And that Jerusalem was the centre
Of the universe, and looked down with mirth
On native Incas who were ignorant
Of how Christianity saw the One.   110
Did the Incas worship the sun because
They had worked out the earth moves round the sun?

Probably not. They had mastered the sun,
Controlled it, worked out its angles. We go
To Intihuatana, a tethering point
Where the sun was tethered to the earth so
It could not float off, guaranteed daylight.
I find the palace Pachacuti's guests
Stayed in and studied the power of Inti
Which ripened crops and multiplied harvests.   120

Back in Cusco's market I'm offered, buy
A wooden cup. A yellow-plant dye guides:
It represents the sun on a lake or,
As the sun's shown with rays on all four sides,
Inti rising, setting and 'Four Quarters',
Used for corn drinks or sacrifices, some
To Mother Earth, from Pachacuti's time.
There's such a cup in Lima's museum.

So the Incas did not think they lived in
A heliocentric universe, that blur –   130
They claimed the sun, tethered to their Empire,
Shone each day for them and for their ruler
Who acted as a priest of the sun in

Rituals and blurring that strengthened his grip.
Pachacuti controlled the sun and crops
To bolster his rule and dictatorship.

The Incas never knew what Christians know,
That an inner sun rises in the soul
And bathes it in rayed Light, that their Inti's
A powerful force within, like a warm coal.   140
Earth-centred Spanish knew their Church's truth
Was superior to sun-worship, more right,
So obliterated Inca temples
Beneath the churches of their inner Light.
4–5 February, 6 April 2015

Nicholas Hagger travelled in Peru from 1 to 10 August 2007.
96. 'Span', from 'spin', 'tell or write (a story, essay, article, etc.) (spins a good tale)'. (*Concise Oxford Dictionary*.)

In Antarctica: In the Southern Ocean and our Ice Age

I

I read 'Ushaia, the end of the world'
On a notice and board *Explorer II*
And head for Drake's Passage, the roughest sea,
Gulls screaming in our wake as a wind blew.
I have embarked for the Southern Ocean
To absorb its ecology and wring
The truth about our Ice Age and climate,
The ozone layer's hole, global warming.

Next day I see two fin whales. We land on
West Falklands New Island and climb a hill   10
To where rockhopper penguins stand on cliffs.
I see black-browed albatrosses and still
Penguin cormorants. We return in rain.

Here Argentinians in the Falklands War
Landed and daubed 'Viva Argentina'.
Two headless Argies lay near a street door.

We land on Carcass Island in a swell
And walk up from the sandy cove to choose
Tea and cakes at the McGills' remote house.
We return past gorse and distant gentoos   20
And take the Zodiac back to the ship.
It rises and plunges near steps at rest
And I am grabbed and dumped on the platform
To climb aboard as huge waves dip and crest.

We reach Stanley and tour the battlefields,
Beside minefields we drive through craggy calm.
We pass Wireless Range and Mount Tumbledown,
We pass Bluff Cove and stop at Fitzroy Farm
Which the British captured. In Port Pleasant
The *Sir Galahad*'s resunk as planes dive.   30
We return to the Governor's House, I stand
In a snowstorm in Margaret Thatcher Drive.

I lunch with a geologist, who shows
Me laptop data: our cyclic Ice Age.
We are within an Ice Age, and global
Warming's within a glacial period's stage.
We are in global cooling. We watch birds
In our wake, royal, wandering and black-browed
Albatrosses, giant and cape petrels, prions.
Icebergs loom towards us. We slow, all crowd.   40

We wet-land on South Georgia's Salisbury Plain.
Seventy thousand king penguins stand and reach
A mile as skuas fly low to snatch chicks.
Fur and elephant seals flop on the beach
And chase off rivals. We see grey-headed

And sooty albatrosses from 'transfers'
And gentoo and macaroni penguins.
I remove gloves. The cold numbs my fingers.

II

We moor at Grytviken under snow-white
Mountains and wet-land near the lonely grave   50
Of Shackleton, who rescued all his men
By rowing eight hundred miles and, so brave,
Reaching this island's far side, staggering
Starved through snow to this settlement; who died
Of a heart attack on *Quest* in this bay.
We toast "the boss" with white wine as our guide.

We follow the last two miles of his trek.
We land in Stromness Bay near about ten
Fur and elephant seals and then route-march
To the waterfall he and his two men   60
Lowered themselves down by rope at the end
Of their crossing of South Georgia. We hike
Through sloping scree and streams, dive-bombed by terns,
To the ruined whaling-station, ghostlike.

Next day we land on Gold Harbour's long beach
Under the Bertrab Glacier, see – split –
King and gentoo penguins. Skuas eat chicks.
We sail to Drygalski fjord, see a bit
Of Gondwanaland that separated
From Laurasia two hundred million years   70
Ago when rocks speared up from the earth's crust
By the Scotia plate – a continent's shears.

We leave the crust and Cape Disappointment.
I ponder how our continents, now slit,
Were formed from moving plates beneath the sea,
How all lands were one land mass till they split.

I ponder plate tectonics, plate movements
And continental drift, then from the ship
Watch a pod of orcas, of killer whales,
Attack a minke whale. Birds flap and dip.   80

We reach the South Shetland Islands and land
On Penguin Island, trudge up to our shins
In snow past Adélie penguins and reach
A large colony of chinstrap penguins
That have returned to their old breeding-ground.
We go to the British King George Island
And tramp through thick snow to a lone Polish
Antarctic station that is now still manned.

Next day we reach Deception Island through
A gap in the caldera and wade in   90
Knee-deep snow to the old British base hut
Abandoned after a volcanic din.
The beach is black volcanic ash, the pools
Steam and smell of sulphur. Cape penguins doze.
I see Neptune's Window high on a ridge
And gaze out at the gap, Neptune's Bellows.

III

In the Gerlache Strait the sun does not set.
We shelter from the wind, icebergs float past.
We ride at anchor near Brabant Island,
Magical sun and moon on ice that's vast.   100
At 3 a.m., all shimmers with white light.
We enter Paradise Bay, a 'lagoon'
Ringed by still white mountains and glaciers,
The Antarctic Peninsula at noon.

On the black water under the white peaks
Pack ice. A glacier's just calved – shed a slice.
Gentoos and blue-eyed shags, eerie stillness.

We go by Zodiac through clumps of ice
And wet-land on a tiny stone shelf. I
Climb ten feet onto a rock and stand still   110
Out of sight of humans, briefly alone,
In Antarctica's white silence, and thrill.

We lunch in the open air on Bridge Deck,
The sun warm on cheeks through the round hole made
In the ozone layer by our global
Warming within our Ice Age. Its rays raid
Unfiltered, and bear more radiation
Than when layered ozone protects our bones.
On the bridge the captain says an iceberg
Calved while we stood on the Antarctic's stones.   120

We reach Port Lockroy on Wiencke Island
And tread through thick snow to British Base A,
A hut surrounded by gentoo penguins.
We see from the Zodiac along the bay
Weddell seals and Dominican gulls. We
Proceed along the Neumayer Channel
To Dallmann Bay. I am all sparkling ice
In solitude behind my social shell.

We enter the notorious Drake's Passage.
The tannoy wakes us. Our sister ship's sunk   130
In the Antarctic Sound, *Explorer I*.
It may have hit an iceberg or ice chunk.
All aboard are safe, their luggage has gone.
BBC News reports that "the Explor-
-er" has sunk, shows a picture of *our* ship.
We send ship faxes home to reassure.

Back at Ushaia our passports are stamped
'The End of the World'. Leaving the world we
Have been on a voyage towards everything.

By a lake where Yamanas lived I see   140
Beavers, dwell on wildlife in the Southern
Ocean, our Ice Age and the ozone rent,
And see that I have voyaged through solitude
To true knowledge of our environment.
6–7 February, 4 April 2015

Nicholas Hagger travelled to Antarctica from 8 to 26 November 2007.

In North Norway: Arctic Circle and Northern Lights, Among Vikings and Altaics

I

We land in Tromsø on an iced runway,
Wheel luggage and at the port through thick snow
Board our ship in a freezing wind, and dine
In warm, black sea's white crests through glass, below.
'*Hagr*' means 'fit' or 'ready' in Old Norse,
My family may have come from Viking times
And my homing instinct may have brought me.
My ice-chilled forebears yearned for warmer climes.

We berth at Havøysund in cold daylight:
Dolls' houses under snow, church spire a speck,   10
Snow-clad mountains. We steam into blizzard.
I gaze at dark waves from the slippery deck,
See the lone Anglo-Saxon seafarer
On the bleak sea, dreaming of his lord's hearth
In the hardship of the northern winter
And of green lands and a more temperate path.

We alight in Honningsvåg, a small town,
And follow a fast snow-plough to North Cape,
Europe's northernmost point, in the Arctic
Circle. We pass tepees in the landscape: 20

The Sami, first Norwegians from Asia,
Came from 9000 BC, their offspring
Still have slit eyes. Much later immigrants
Were Kurgans whose descendants were Viking.

We're driven to a wooden jetty where
Giant king crabs are lifted from the sea
In a net, some with limpets on their shells.
Each is stabbed with a twisting knife for tea.
As their legs, moving from nerves, are cut off
They squirt poison, which drips. Legs and claws then   30
Are boiled on a birchwood stove and are served
On pine platters by Viking fishermen.

II

We breakfast by Honningsvåg harbour's calm,
Then coach by a fjord, through birch trees and snow,
To Alta, seat of Altaic culture's
Pre-7000-BC rock carvings' flow.
We stop at the Alta Igloo Hotel,
Eat reindeer burgers. I steer a dog sleigh
Six miles by a frozen river, braking
By standing on the footbrake to snow spray.   40

We reach a Sami tepee constructed
On twenty-two poles that meet at the top
In a hole for smoke from a birchwood fire
Designed from rock carvings, ancient-style shop.
We drink hot currant juice and get to know
How Altaians of 7000 BC
Lived, how spirits come and go through the hole.
We're shamans in Yggdrasil, the World Tree.

From the igloo we drive in a horse sleigh
Along a track between pines to a field   50
Where I gasp at the night sky of bright stars.

Our wizened old driver in skins, our shield,
Says "Listen to the silence" and: "It is
Beautiful." We drive back, I think – no cars –
On the cloudless, pollution-free night sky.
This was how Altaic man saw the stars.

The Northern Lights are gathering as we sup.
Minus 20, glimmers intensify.
We peer outside at a horizontal
Green band and vertical drapes in the sky,   60
A curtain with a rippling hem moving
Green with pale blue bits and brightest above
Woods, Aurora Borealis, the veil
Between Being's and Existence's love.

III

The hem fades back to glimmerings. I go
To the igloo and an ice room with drawn
Curtain, in minus 7, remove my boots
On ice bed and reindeer skins, get in – yawn –
My sleeping-bag, wearing my hat, and fall
Asleep at once, Northern Lights in each cell.   70
We wake at dawn and vacate our igloo
For the warmth of the neighbouring hotel.

We leave under a clear blue sky and drive
Through spruce on white snow to Lake Alta's blue
And in the tiny airport wait to fly
To Oslo. I have confronted anew
My Viking roots, the Altaic tepee,
Shamanistic Altaic culture's stand,
Cold Northern Lights; and have glimpsed the Vikings'
Dream of green pastures in southern England.   80
10 February, 4 April 2015

Nicholas Hagger travelled in North Norway from 26 February to 1 March 2009.

The Way to Rome

I. Grand Tour

The Grand Tour of the eighteenth century:
A choppy Channel, carriage to Paris,
A *trek* through the Swiss Alps to Turin, then
On to Rome, Naples and Pompeii – bliss –
To view the glories of imperial Rome,
Then back across the southern Alps to see
Germany and Holland, and nine months on
Return to England wiser for the spree.

The tour began on England's southern coast
For the young sent off to travel, in hope   10
Of gaining knowledge from imperial Rome
By fathers well versed in Dryden and Pope
Who had adopted an Augustan bent.
Soon literary fad yielded guidebook,
Nugent's *The Grand Tour*, 1749,
Baedeker for Rome's finishing-school look.

Journeys and quests transform the seeking soul,
And tourists sometimes find they are pilgrims.
Roads that lead to sites of antiquity
Open self's scallop shell so the One brims   20
Pervasively like this surrounding sea.
Ruins and much-seen holy bones and creeds
Bring seekers knowledge of what past men did.
Pilgrimages connect souls to past deeds.

The white cliffs of Dover slide by our stern.
Winds lash with rain and gust across the waves
As our *Minerva* turns and steams beyond
Shallow choppy waters, sways, rolls and staves
On a sea swell till stabilisers work
And steady our progress across the deep.   30

We dip and rise and throb all through the night
Until Neptune-Poseidon calms to sleep.

The Western Approaches have seen three wars.
In each the UK was threatened from France –
In 1759, 1805
And 1942, when at each chance
U-boats sank convoy ships in the Battle
Of the Atlantic – and in each, like forts,
The English Navy bottled up the French,
And Germans trapped them in their distant ports.   40

St Peter's Port on Guernsey's "green island",
Ancient castle and fort. I pass stone blocks
Along an Atlantic wall of bunkers
The Germans built to fortify these rocks,
Pass sandy bays, sparse bungalows and walls
Of blue, red, grey granite and dolmens, view
Ten parishes and a parochial life
Warmed by the Gulf Stream, quaint, welcoming blue.

II. Pilgrimage

La Coruna, whence the Armada sailed;
Now Santiago de Compostela where   50
St James's bones were interred seven hundred
And fifty years after they landed there
In a crewless, sailless boat, and were revealed
By miraculous lights, a "field of stars"
(*Campus stellae*), or in a "burial ground"
(*Composita tella*), Latin that jars.

A place of medieval pilgrimage,
Mass tourism during the First Crusade,
For James, the brother of John, had become
Christ's disciple when St Peter first prayed.   60
One visit here guaranteed remission

Of half a sinner's time in purgatory
And full indulgence in a holy year
When James' Feast falls (as now) on a Sunday.

Four routes brought pilgrims via Canterbury –
Chaucer's pilgrims stopped where merged routes begin –
And passed through La Rochelle, Le Puy, Limoges
And Arles to converge at Pamplona in
El Camino – where pilgrims of the long
Sacred Way bought, nothing to do with diet,   70
A scallop from fishermen who had come
From La Coruna, as a badge of quiet.

I stand in the "hostal" the Catholic kings
Founded in the late fifteenth century
To act as pilgrims' accommodation
When they arrived in town, and drink coffee
And speak to a Canon who walked here, two
Thousand kilometres in eighty days,
And says, "Drop into Westminster Abbey,
I'll roll back the carpet above the 'maze'."   80

I stand in the twelfth-century Cathedral
Near pews packed with tranced worshippers and view
The back of the old Romanesque *façade*,
St James as pilgrim and serene Matthew,
Look up at early Gothic carved faces,
Step over knelt confessors' heels and stains,
Head past the high altar which stands above
A chest in the crypt that holds James' remains.

III. The Way: Life Path

This Grand Tour has become a pilgrimage
And its destination's imperial Rome   90
That calls us back to our original search
Among classics for a spiritual home.

A lecture on Nelson. Peter O'Toole
Totters in with his nurse. I say in gloom
"Hello from sixty years ago. You brought
Your vodka and chauffeur back to my room.

"You had been playing Shylock at Stratford.
We talked till midnight on what the lines meant.
You had to climb out over the nine-foot-
High gate. The history tutor climbed up, bent,   100
And you roared at him, 'I hate thee for thou
Art a Christian.' He ran off terrified.
I lifted you, pushed you over the top.
At the start of your career you had side."

He roars with laughter and shakes my hand twice,
Says, "Thank you for telling me all these things."
But he's in drink, a shell of his old self.
I say, smiling, to this player of kings:
"While you were filming *Lawrence* I was in
Iraq with Arabs. I told you I'd write.   110
Our ways have opened up since they last crossed,
Mine through books, yours through films." Truth sets alight.

I see him sitting in the dining-room
Wearing a pink jacket, as if to say
"I'm here, look at *me*", his actor's ego.
I learn he's being a recluse, in play;
Does not go ashore or appear, but writes
"A work of writing" with his 'PA', who's
Dressed like a nurse and keeps him from his flask.
He's booked for six weeks on a working cruise.   120

I look at the golden boy of *Lawrence*,
A grey-haired fop with vacant eyes and smile
Who rises from his table, grasps the arm
Of his nurse to walk with unsteady style.

The legs that stood on top of carriages
To cheers from Arabs who'd blown up the train
Are frail now and fuelled by his flask. Age
That slows down golden boys will slow my brain.

Communion on the ship with the Canon
Who says in his address, "In India   130
I was with Mother Teresa, watching
A young girl feed a destitute pauper,
And she said, 'This is the body of Christ.'
It opened my eyes: crucifixion now."
I receive the host, sip wine as ship rolls,
Called back to a way I left for a vow.

Oporto. We dock at Roman Portus
And drive to the twelfth-century Cathedral,
The Stock Exchange, then a port wine cellar
On the Douro's far side, Cale (locale   140
Now joined as Portucale, Portugal),
Drink a glass of white port, leave the red. Yes,
My path is to be moderate in all things,
Not to pursue the golden boy's excess.

The images are calls to a lone path.
I stand at Cadiz, La Caleta strand
Where Drake landed in 1587,
'Singed the King of Spain's beard' – burned his ships – and
Delayed the armed Armada's departure.
Essex sacked the port six years on. Today   150
Turnstones peck at the sand between two moles.
I pick at my Elizabethan way.

I wander past the Roman theatre, hear
Our guide, who has Arab-Moorish blood, say
Proudly of his home town's history, "Julius
Caesar visited Gades, in his day

The Roman town, twice in the first century
BC, and must have sat there in his prime."
I think of how at school I dreamt of Rome
And of my path into the Roman time.   160

I toss with Nelson off Cape Trafalgar
Between Cadiz and Europa Point, lead on
The *Victory* through Villeneuve's larger fleet.
Having bottled the French up in Toulon,
Made a base on Corsica and then seen
French troops occupying Naples, a defeat,
Nelson turned the war round before he fell.
I think of my way of not 'getting beat'.

Where Atlantic joins Med I dip and roll
Between the Pillars of Hercules, who   170
Placed two columns inscribed '*Non Plus Ultra*'
To mark land's end and ocean's start and view,
One on Gibraltar, one on Morocco's
Monte Hacho, limits of discovery
To west for that Mediterranean world,
And reconnect with Homer's "wine-dark sea".

I pass through the Alhambra gardens that
Shimmer Paradise in water. My path
Was to find Paradise. I make my way
To the Ambassadors' Hall, by whose hearth   180
Near still water and myrtles the Sultan
Sat under a ceiling that showed seven
Heavens as seven stars, and hid his face
For his power mirrored Allah's, which was hidden.

I hide my face and ego and reflect
That in this dark Hall bold Columbus sat
Before Isabella and Ferdinand
And won support for his New World voyage that

Turned 'Non Plus Ultra' to the 'Plus Ultra'
Ribbon on the Pillars of Hercules   190
That under Franklin formed the dollar sign.
There's an American way from my seas.

I stand in Siena's Basilica
And see St Catherine's waxed head, deathly pale,
Eyes closed and wimpled round, and her right thumb
Delicate, shrivelled, and manicured nail.
I look up at the Duomo, at statues
Of Plato and Aristotle that – hey!
Date to 1290, long before Plethon.
I took the mystic philosopher's way.   200

I think how Gemistos Plethon conveyed
Plato to Florence, where Ficino taught,
And texts followed when Byzantium fell.
But here the Fourth Crusade's Crusaders brought
Plato and Greek philosophy over
Two hundred years earlier. The Town Hall shows
Thirteen-thirties' paintings, *The Allegory
Of Good and Evil – The Republic*'s foes.

Now in the Duomo I see the Pavement
Hewn in marble, from 1369,   210
Take in Hermes Trismegistus, Sibyls
And the Greek philosophers' seeking line;
Old Testament themes towards the altar,
Each figure suggesting the mystical,
And ponder an early Renaissance work.
I took the path of traditional symbol.

And now in San Gimignano I stand
Where Dante stood in May 1299
When an Ambassador for the White Guelfs
As a fresco in the Town Hall shows sign: 220

He stood where I stand on this red tiled floor,
Wore red and addressed the men sitting – look! –
On these wall settles under these same shields.
I have taken the path that Dante took.

I stand by Our Lady of the Hillside,
Above Calvi and look down at past fights,
At the hill where the French fired at Nelson,
Whose guns had been dragged up to rocky heights,
Where a cannon-ball hit the large grey slab
I passed, whose splinters blinded his right eye.   230
The 1794 siege of Calvi
Reflects my way of war for my country.

IV. Rome

The Canon speaks on the first Popes and says
The Latin words round St Peter's Dome claim
Peter founded Rome's church. In 180
Irenaeus virtually said the same:
Peter and Paul were in fact joint founders.
But first were churches in a house or tent.
Rome's claim to Church supremacy is flawed.
I think of my way of English dissent.   240

I gaze at the Colosseum and see
Rome's order upheld by violence on slum
Bandits, robbers, criminals, runaway
Slaves and Christians, who sought their martyrdom
To die challenging the order of Rome,
Innards torn out by starved lions, not their soul.
Panis et circenses, the Emperors' gift,
Kept the masses under their State control.

I stand on Rome's Palatine Hill and see
Where the House of Augustus stood beside   250
The Temple of Apollo (part of it

Once struck by lightning), and now, lured in, stride
And close to frescos of yellows and reds,
Of masks and satyrs by Egyptian hands
Just after Actium, stand where Virgil stood.
I think of my path through classical lands.

And now I survey from Tarquinia,
Etruscan capital, port, iron mines, blooms
And paths to eleven subcapitals
And descend steps to view a dozen tombs   260
With frescos of everyday banquet scenes
And outdoor games, in red and yellow loam
And reflect on the first Roman builders.
I reflect on my path to early Rome.

Rome was my lodestar in those early days:
Augustus's deeds, Virgil's *Aeneid*,
Horace's *Odes* and Greek mythology,
The ruins of imperial Rome amid
Augustan classical virtues I learned.
Now I'm back to my original way,   270
My pilgrimage has been to truth through Light
Which counters all the vices with each ray.

I stand in Pompeii and look beyond
The Temple of Zeus to Vesuvius
From which, as Pliny the Younger described
In a graphic letter to Tacitus,
An ash-cloud rained a pyroclastic surge
That choked this Roman colony's last breath
And buried its streets for hundreds of years.
I think how my path led through captured death.   280

I recall how I climbed Vesuvius
When seventeen, looked into the crater, sat,
Then took great strides back down the mountain slope,

Skidded on soft grey ash, uplifted at
My plunge from cloudy height to distant ground,
God-like till I hit a buried rock, chin
Up, flew through air, slithered face down, grit – ash –
In my grazed arms and knees, under my skin.

I sit in the ship's library and wait
To disembark. The Canon leans, I lurch. 290
He says, "Thank you for listening," and I
Stand and discuss the future of the Church:
"You can be Archbishop of Canterbury.
You need to see him and discuss his heir.
The visit of the Pope's a catalyst,
A call to the decaying Church to share."

He says, "If I were Archbishop I would
Break free from Rome and open it all up
To all who've been excluded far too long."
I say, "It's a new order's loving-cup, 300
A Universalism of all faiths."
He, "Yes, Christians, Jews and Muslims are one.
All humans have an equal way to God.
It's not in the Pope's gift." Nor is the sun.

And I realise that my time has now come.
I have seen the way forward for our time.
In mysticism and philosophy,
Literature, history, world government's prime,
Culture and the essence of religions:
Seven disciplines like bands of one rainbow, 310
The oneness in all things, beyond Rome's sway.
I think of my path to the One's bright glow.

My Grand Tour is over now I have reached
Naples and Pompeii. In Nugent's day
Britain broke out of island consciousness

To join with the Continent. In the grey
Next century travel was more Romantic.
Shelley wrote of the One's mystic order
In 'Ode to Naples', of the earth's "deep heart".
The Grand Tourist was now Grand Traveller.   320

We each in our self-interested worlds
Pursue our imaginative desires
As Grand Travellers. Not above the news,
I busy myself with Augustan squires
And stand where Virgil stood before Actium
And let my imagination when whole
Resolve silent atmospheric places
That shock the mind and nourish the starved soul.

And now we are no longer Grand Tourists
But travellers – who as if by magic weave   330
Seven cultures into bands of a rainbow
That's both one spectrum and various – I cleave
My soul, admire the imagination
That's peopled with faces all lifeless stones,
See the way to Rome opens Rome to all
Who've shone into the dark from Light-filled bones.
26 August–9 September 2010; 9, 25 May–6, 10 June 2015

Nicholas Hagger journeyed to Rome from 26 August to 9 September 2010.
28. 'Staves', 'crushes'.
33. 'Western Approaches', a rectangular area of the Atlantic Ocean lying off the western coast of the UK.
71. Sir Walter Raleigh, 'The Passionate Man's Pilgrimage, supposed to be written by one at the point of death', "Give me my Scallop shell of quiet."
80. The 13th-century Cosmati Pavement covered by carpet but revealed during the Coronation Service and one day a year.
104. 'Side', 'boastfulness', 'swagger'.
193. Basilica. The Basilica San Domenico.
218. '1299', pronounced 'twelve-ninety-nine'.

248. State, i.e. imperial.

276. Pliny the Younger's letter to Tacitus was written on 24 August 79, the date of Vesuvius's eruption.

300. 'Loving-cup', 'a cup with two handles passed round at a banquet'.

327. 'Resolve', 'convert into concord'.

On Hadrian's Wall

Proem

All empires expand till
They stop, consolidate
And defend what they've gained
With a new frontier.
From North Sea to Black Sea,
Red Sea to Atlantic,
North Sea to Irish Sea,
A mighty ring of steel
Fort–ified Rome's empire,
Now gone under the earth.   10

I. Birdoswald

Green fields are splashed blood-red
Round Birdoswald's grey fort,
Rome's northern frontier
That kept Britannia safe,
Built of turf and timber
With earthwork or *vallum*
To the south of the Wall
Built by centurions' men
Who slept eight to a room
Next to their war horses.   20
Here, when Rome fell, Romans
Stayed on in the ruins
And built a Dark Age hall
Like Hrothgar's in *Beowulf*

For rings, treasure and feast,
Guarded locals for pay,
Living with local girls,
Cherished grown-up children,
Kept local families
And maintained the *limes*.   30
Here under turf and sheep
So many lived and died,
Their names carved on altars
To the god Silvanus
Or scattered to the wind.

II. Vindolanda

A quarry in the hills.
Below on the first frontier,
The pre-wall Stanegate Road,
To Vindolanda's fort
Came to this great palace   40
The Emperor Hadrian
Who gave his instructions
For no more expansion
But a defensive wall
Round the entire Empire,
For a wall like China's
To keep barbarians out.
Here letters on birch bark
Written by a hired scribe,
One signed by a lady,   50
Are the oldest written
Records in Britannia.
Here a father laments
His wife and children died
From an epidemic.
He laid them under earth
And now has been posted
To a new province, so

He can't honour his dead.
Here in the HQ hall   60
A statue of the Emperor,
A strong room and pay chest
To pay the legionaries
And foreign auxiliaries
Who built the Wall of blocks
To make a peaceful life
Behind the frontier.

III. Housesteads

High up this Housesteads slope
Look out for these barracks
At a long snaking wall,   70
Ditch, *vallum* and earthwork.
Here high up near the clouds
The commander had his
Bathhouse and own warm room.
In frost his men shivered.

IV. Carrawburgh

Grass slopes to a ruin:
Carrawburgh's Mithraeum,
Stone cave-like enclosure
Where initiate soldiers
From eastern provinces   80
Were buried to arise,
Be reborn to Mithras,
God of Light and fortune,
Who, in a stone statue
That wears a Phrygian cap
Pierced by four holes, behind
Which a lamp's light shines through,
When eastern soldiers asked,
Gave them their promotions.

V. Segedunum

The bathhouse changing-room   90
Rings with soldiers' dice games
In Segedunum, steam
Opens their pores to sweat
Out grime near Fortuna
Who holds horn of plenty.
Here at Wallsend all peer
For movements beyond these
Crenellations: a grey
Wall twenty foot high when
Seen by raiders below,   100
Just fifteen feet above
The strolling troops inside,
And a monotonous watch
With nothing happening.
We watchers on the Wall
Rub eyes and stay alert.
Cattle graze round the Wall.
The *limes* has shattered,
Green grows the grass on stones,
Poppies redden the fields   110
Where Roman soldiers lolled
In towns now under turf.

VI. Arbeia

In these soldiers' barracks
At Arbeia, eight men
Crowd into tiny rooms,
Four sleep on each plank bed
In squalor and vile filth
While on the other side,
The centurion has two
Bedrooms, one for himself   120
And one for his children.
Commanding officer,

He has a large villa
With passage and garden,
Dining-room with couches
And bedrooms with murals.
A wife on a tombstone:
Barates' freedwoman,
A Catuvellaunian,
Dead at thirty, alas. 130

VII. Chesters

Sunlight glints on green Tyne
Near where the Roman bridge
Was crossed from wall to wall
Under the sloping grass
Above Chesters bathhouse
For soldiers and the view
From the CO's grey walls
And phallus of good luck
Carved on a flagstone near
The ceremonial well. 140
And in the café trees
A chiffchaff twitters where
A carpet of clover
Beams in the July sun.

Envoi

Rome's frontier protects
All who have chosen Rome,
Who guard its grey stone walls
In a necklace of forts
And replicate the life
Of Roman citizens 150
In public buildings, baths
That fill the world with awe –
And now lies under turf.
4–5 July 2011; 17 December 2014

Nicholas Hagger visited Hadrian's Wall on 4–5 July 2011. He writes: "I was struck by the ruined forts and barracks and the lost grandeur of Rome's frontier."

India: Revisiting the British Raj

1. Delhi: Empire

I brood on empires and on Old Delhi.
I am welcomed: red dot on my forehead,
A garland of white flowers hung round my neck.
The British Prime Minister has just left.
I view the cremation site of Gandhi,
Drive past the Red Fort to the Friday mosque,
Climb steps, remove shoes, and in the courtyard
Open to the winds and the burning sun,
Take in the red sandstone and white marble
Laid for Shah Jahan; now take a rickshaw   10
Into the narrow streets of Old Delhi's
Seventeenth-century market: tiny bazaars,
Goods spilling out onto dusty gutters,
Selling spices, silver, lace, shawls, gems, books,
Tunnels of electricity wires slung
Across the upper windows near my head.
My boy pedals and points out all the wares,
Hoping for a tip, while hawkers we pass
Hold out their trinkets, urging me to buy.
I am a white man, thus a purchaser.   20

I drive round New Delhi, the capital
In place of Calcutta from 1911.
For twenty years the British poured in funds
To build a fitting showpiece of empire.
I pass Connaught Place, named after Arthur,
Duke of Connaught, one of Victoria's sons,
And reach the Government quarter, the curved

Parliament and now the Presidential
Palace, formerly the Viceroy's, and down
South Avenue, almost within full view,   30
The house of Nehru when Prime Minister.
From his balcony Nehru could have waved
To Edwina Mountbatten, the Viceroy's
Wife with whom, smitten, he was dallying,
Some said with her husband's consent so she
Could wring concessions from him as to how
The Raj would end. The British left quickly
And a million died. At India Gate
I see the sandstone canopy where King
George the Fifth's statue was grandly installed   40
In 1936, long since removed.
Gaze at the empty canopy and sense
The absence of the British Raj today,
Gone like the statue of its ruling King.

The turning-point was in Amritsar in
1919 when Gandhi called for strikes
And demonstrations in the Sikh city
Against the Rowlatt Act that allowed troops
To imprison all Indians accused
Of sedition. Without warning General   50
Dyer, who had proclaimed martial law in
The town and said gatherings would be fired on,
At Jallianwala Bagh faced with a mob
Of twenty-five thousand armed with lathis
(Metal-tipped sticks), billhooks, kerosene, swords,
A mob that had rampaged three days before
And lynched three officials and killed two more,
Beaten a missionary, left her for dead;
Outnumbered two hundred and seventy-five
To one, with only ninety men, fifty   60
Armed with rifles and sixteen hundred rounds
Out of nine thousand on an armoured car

Parked nearby with a machine-gun, showing
His action was not premeditated,
Panicked and ordered his armed troops to fire
As crowd control (an English eyewitness
Seconded from the British Royal Sussex
Regiment to the 14th Murray's Jat
Lancers told me some fifty years ago).
The firing lasted ten minutes, and they   70
Slaughtered three hundred and seventy-nine
And wounded twelve hundred, quelling Punjab,
Saving thousands of lives, shocking Indians,
Turning them into nationalists against
Forceful imperialism. Now the Raj
As a benevolent and caring rule
Was a scorned myth. This morning Cameron
Left my hotel for Amritsar to say –
Short of apologising, he would hold –
That he was sorry for what had happened   80
Long before he was born, in turbulent
Times, as he begged that the British should build
New roads, hospitals and schools in India
And participate in its coming growth.

Brooding on Amritsar and New Delhi
And on impregnable empires that fade,
I visit the domed tomb of Humayun,
A Persian paradise with four rivers:
The second Mughal emperor fell down stairs
On his way to pray, toe caught in his robe,   90
And so moved into his mausoleum.
I go on to the Qutab tower, a twelfth-
Century minaret for a ruined mosque,
A pre-Mughal ruin of empire gone.
Imperialism (running an empire
And conquered people bowed under its yoke
From a dominant territory) asserts

Itself in buildings that survive its leap,
Outlives the energy that thrust them up.
The confidence of the British in so 100
Certainly investing in New Delhi,
Despite the independence rioters,
Is breathtaking as was their conviction
The Empire would triumph over Gandhi
And civilise and improve the backward
In benevolence, not exploitation,
A noble aspiration that deserves
Praise even though it was an illusion
To believe that all the recipients
Would be grateful for being led forward 110
And would appreciate such vast outlay
And sacrifice of lives in their service.
In the end the British Indian Empire
Was unsustainable due to the war:
Churchill announced in 1942
That Britain would withdraw from India.
He could not afford India *and* the war.

A vast subcontinent held together
By English and the relics of the Raj.
The building of New Delhi was for us. 120
So much investment, so little return.
Indians have mixed feelings about the Raj,
And see both good and bad, admire its best.
The population has quadrupled since
The British left. I see the litter strewn
About the streets, the chaotic drivers,
Hawkers desperately holding out baubles,
Bare-footed beggars clutching children, flies
And shake my head at the sixty-six years
Since the Raj that left hundreds of millions 130
Struggling with poverty, bereft of hope.

2. Agra: Paradise

I ride by rickshaw to the Taj Mahal,
Go through the 'gateway to heaven' and see
The stream of Paradise in four gardens
(*Charbagh*) as in the Koranic account
And shown in the grounds of Humayun's tomb,
And four quarters with giant cypress trees
With rivers of water, milk, wine, honey
And at the north end, by the Yamuna,
Perfect symmetry of the Taj Mahal   140
('*Taj*' meaning 'crown' or 'very beautiful'):
Three domes, pointed arches, four minarets.
To distant thunder I walk to a white
Reflection – built by Mughal Shah Jahan
In twenty-two, some say eleven, years –
Of the order within the universe:
The tombs for his wife Mumtaz Mahal who
Died during the birth of their fourteenth child
Aged thirty-nine after seventeen years
Of marriage during which he selected   150
The five thousand women in his *hareem*;
And for himself. He built the Taj wanting
To leave behind an architectural
Work of perfection, a great monument.
I file into the chamber where two 'tombs' –
Cenotaphs of Mumtaz and Shah Jahan
With ninety-nine names of Allah and with
Pen-box (the symbol of a male ruler) –
Reflect the two tombs in the crypt below.
I am pushed round in gloom by a large throng,   160
Am jostled in a hubbub past the guards
Who blow whistles non-stop. No silence here
Among floral patterns of precious stones
And Arabic verses on Paradise
Which fringe the archways, finely proportioned.
I emerge the far side and overlook

The river and the back of the Red Fort.
I recross the gardens of Paradise
(Past the marble seat where Diana sat)
To where a film is being made, the Shah   170
Resplendent in bright clothes, raising a sword,
Bowed to by six attendants in white dress.
O Shah Jahan, how romantic to build
A mausoleum for wife died in childbirth.

Now at Agra's Red Fort – built by Akbar
In the sixteenth century – I climb a slope
To the courtyard and Hall of Audience
Where Shah Jahan issued proclamations
To the assembled throng, that were read out
By the Prime Minister who stood below   180
On a marble platform. I pass the Shah's
Royal palace and *hareem*, and the Hall
Of Copulation where girls danced, and grilles
Where five thousand women lived with their maids.
Any suspected of disloyalty
Were thrown to crocodiles in the river.
Here lived the builder of the Taj Mahal
Among his *hareem* of five thousand girls.

Back in Delhi I visit the Red Fort
Shah Jahan built from 1639   190
For nine years while he built the Taj Mahal.
I came here forty-five years back and know
What I am seeking and would revisit.
I pass the Hall of Public Audience
And see Shah Jahan's throne and canopy,
Go to the women's chambers and royal
Apartments through both of which run 'the stream
Of Paradise', see Shah Jahan's prayer-room,
Bedroom and sitting-room, and balcony
On which he appeared to all at sunrise,   200

Both white buildings, and pass on to the white
Hall of Private Audience, six columns by
Six, four by four inside where the Peacock
Throne stood, one of Shah Jahan's seven jewelled thrones.
The walls and pillars were inlaid with gems,
The ceiling with precious stones, all stolen
By Nadir Shah in 1739.
Over corner arches to north and south
Is inscribed a verse in Persian written
By Amir Khusrow, the Sufi poet: 210
"If there is Paradise on the earth, it
Is here, it is here, it is here." 'Here' was Delhi;
Not Agra, its Red Fort and Taj Mahal.
I chat with a soldier and cross the rope
And photograph the two verses and note
The opposite reliefs are blank. The verse
Has haunted me for forty-five years, for
Shah Jahan turned his back on his Mumtaz.
Paradise was not Agra's Taj Mahal
But here in Delhi at the new Red Fort.   220
Shah Jahan had moved on to *this hareem*.

In Agra's Red Fort I look at the rooms
Where Shah Jahan's son Aurangzeb brought him
To be imprisoned for his last eight years
While he seized the throne and ruled as Emperor.
From here he could look across the river
At the finished Taj Mahal. Shah Jahan
Had imprisoned two brothers, a cousin
And a nephew to secure the throne. Now
His son imprisoned his two brothers and   230
His father, and many times every day
Shah Jahan saw the finished Taj Mahal
And thought of Mumtaz, mother of his son,
Here in Agra's Red Fort, which he had left
To relocate to Delhi and announce

His new place Paradise. And it was just
He should return to where he and Mumtaz
Had lived and renew his attachment to
Her tomb, which would also be his tomb when
In 1665 he died beside   240
The balcony where as Emperor he'd waved
To crowds gathering beneath and cheering.

Empires rise like a flower and then wither.
They bloom in the morning and fade at dusk.
The British conquered both Red Forts and built
Military barracks to defend the Raj.
The Mughals shrivelled as the British rose.

3. Fatehpur Sikri: Tolerance

I stand within Akbar's red sandstone fort,
His capital for fourteen years, built in
1569 near Sheikh Chishti, whose   250
Advice had given him, at last, an heir.
I pass the Hall of Public Audience
And stand beneath the seat of power, a high
Balcony in the Private Audience Hall –
Near Paradise as at Humayun's tomb –
Where Akbar stood invisible and spoke
To all below, Jain masonry all round.
I pass the seat where Akbar played choppers
Like chess; the musicians' pool; and the house
Of the Sultana, his Turkish queen; then   260
In a new courtyard the larger quarters
Of his Christian queen; and the vast palace
Of his Hindu queen, who had two kitchens
And a dining-room (or *vice versa*).
Three queens, each one served by maids and eunuchs,
Each espousing a different religion –
Akbar tolerated non-Hindu creeds.
His *hareem* was elsewhere in the walled town.

He lived among maids and eunuchs till wars
Called him away. The water supply dried.   270
This fort was abandoned, and now it looks
As if it was lived in till yesterday;
A ghost town from a time of tolerance
When Muslim and Hindu co-existed
Without our riots and our partition.

In the wild-life sanctuary, formerly
A Maharaja's hunting-ground, I cross
Marshes in a battered rickshaw pedalled
By a wizened, turbaned man who points out
A green bee-eater near rhesus monkeys,   280
A snake bird, rufous treepie, black-headed
Ibis, purple heron, jungle babbler
Near an antelope drinking at a swamp,
And takes us to painted storks' breeding-ground
And says, "I am happy for I have got
The Maharaja and Maharanee
In the back and I will get good *bucksheesh*."
I ride like a Maharaja on hunt.

All birds in this sanctuary are protected
As were all creeds by tolerant Akbar   290
In his Universalist Paradise.

4. Jaipur: Horoscopes

I drive through Jaipur's terracotta 'pink'
In honour of Prince Albert, who came here
For Victoria in 1883,
Pass the Palace of Winds where royal ladies
Peeped through slanting slats down at processions;
At Amber Fort queue for an elephant,
Sit back into a railed box, roll and sway,
Legs hanging down, up a steep ramp, long slope
Like Albert or Victoria's Viceroy,   300

Through a gate towards a courtyard, dismount
And walk up towards the elephant gate's
Magnificent seventeenth-century colours,
See the window where Maharanees showered
Victorious Maharajas with fresh flowers,
Go through to halls of audience and pleasure,
Walk down the long slope to the *hareem* where
The Maharaja of Jaipur was wheeled
On a palanquin to his favourite,
And see the women's rooms and where the queens   310
Lived in the sweltering shade, overlooked by
A long balcony where Maharajas
Walked and see how Jai Singh lived, just before
His astrologer told him to remove
His capital to Jaipur on the eighteenth
Of November 1727:
The favourable day in horoscopes.

In the Maharaja's Observatory
Built in 1716 down in Jaipur
(One of five he built in different places)   320
I see 'instruments of calculation'
('Jantar Mantar'), fifteen stone measurers,
Some like parked aircraft steps that lead nowhere,
Some like rocket launchers, that measure time
(One accurate to within two seconds),
The movement of the sun and of the stars
And one (a concave pit) constellations:
A solar calendar worked by shadows
That show a birth date in the zodiac.
Here Jai Singh used astronomical stones   330
For the purposes of astrology:
To give horoscopes for daily life;
A medieval Stonehenge to tell him
When to take decisions, favourable times.
He researched all the known astronomy,

Studied both Kepler and Copernicus,
And created – all measurers would say –
One of the Seven Wonders of the World.

Now in the city palace, the fourth fort
Built by Jai at the astrologer's urgings,   340
I wander past the Hall of Audience
And two inner courtyards and marvel at
The exquisite peacock gate and *hareem*
And, peeping over the rooftop, the flag
And balcony of the small palace where
The present Maharaja lives and preens.
Jaipur, 'city of Jai', and its two forts
Were soon absorbed into the British Raj
And turned terracotta pink to express
Its loyalty to Queen Victoria –   350
Events that had not been foreseen and were
Not in Jai's astrologer's horoscopes.

5. Ceylon: Road

Slogging on up the British road built by
Teams under Captain Dawson, engineer
Who oversaw the progress of the road
Through rain forests up hills, coped with tunnels
And plunging waterfalls and gave his life
As did the many British troops who worked
In the malarial hills up to Kandy
And on the railway he too supervised,   360
I pass the tower that honours his great feat,
And in hill country reflect on the work
That after 1815 beautified,
Transformed old kings' Ceylon: recreating
Distant England in houses, gardens, golf-
And race-courses, fishing for rainbow trout,
Introducing tea plants, planting oak-trees,
Lawns and petunias, dressing for dinner,

To make a hill station where all could live
In a replica of a lord's England.   370

And standing in Mountbatten's Viceregal
Residence in Ceylon (now a hotel)
While drummers beat and Sufi dervish whirls
(Arms by his side and spinning like a top),
I saunter to room 204 and peep
Into the Viceroy's bedroom and the room
With four chairs where he negotiated,
And ponder the too-hasty withdrawal
Forced on him by Atlee via the King
Which killed a million in disturbances   380
As Hindus and Muslims were partitioned
And had to flee their villages in fear.
Trains arrived with many slaughtered bodies
And I am sad that the British Empire
Whose showpiece was New Delhi, just finished,
Should have been undermined by a loinclothed
'Pest' and the folly of an out-of-touch
General bent on spreading terror throughout
The Punjab, leaving the Viceroy no choice
But to leave and fragment the massive state.   390

And lurking in the gateway of the old
Temple of the Tooth near where a truck bomb
Killed twenty Kandians not long ago
I recall offerings near the golden door
(Lotus, water lilies, frangipani)
Which hides the Buddha's tooth saved from the fire
Of his cremation and locked in seven urns
Like *stupa*s (or Horse Guards' helmets), and think
Few have seen it for it is locked away
When it rides on an elephant each year,   400
Shown in casing before a trusting throng.
And I see why the Viceroy ruled from here,

Across the lake from this so sacred place
That's honoured by Ceylon's entire people,
Deriving honour from proximity,
As I lament the passing of the Raj.

On the way back along the British road
I stop at a spice grove, am shown herb plants –
Pepper, ginger, cinnamon – and a room
Of bottles and a list of cures by each: 410
Ayurveda, a homeopathy.
Two men fall on me and massage my neck
And tell me I need aloe vera,
Psychic diagnosis of what I lack.
I feel a burning from their hands and lo!
My neck has eased, I look behind both sides.
Medieval apothecarists knew
The cures in plants, and so do these young men
Who have left behind British rule and see
People with intuitive powers that heal.   420

The British road to Kandy that carried
A Viceroy to his Ceylon residence
And Buddhists to the Temple of the Tooth
Now brings customers to traders in herbs
Who have forgotten Dawson's sacrifice.

                6. Tirunelveli: Assassin
Lingering in the graveyard of Christ Church
Where British missionaries gave their lives
To convert Indians to the Lord's path,
I bow to the memory of brave Ashe
Who worked for the Indian Civil Service,   430
Assassinated in 1911,
The year that the decision was taken
To move the capital to New Delhi
And spend a fortune on the new city

Although pro-independence assassins
Were killing British servants such as Ashe
(A collector and district magistrate).
Should the decision have been taken then?
I ponder this inside the church as all
Are asked to stand and (captive) sing a hymn,   440
'Eternal Father'. As we cry "for those
In peril on the sea" I wonder if
We will be in peril during our cruise,
Not knowing pirate waters are ahead.

    O Vishnu with your disc and conch
    (The wheel of time, awakening blast),
    Nine incarnations, last to come,
    In your Krishnapuram temple;
    O sacred cow who will bear us
    When dead to Paradise's door,   450
    Mother who gives us milk to drink,
    Cow-pats to burn on cooking fires;
    Awaken us from time and feed
    Us all the milk of Paradise.

An assassin kills in the wheel of time.
Vishnu the preserver yields to Shiva
The destroyer who blows away the old
Like autumn leaves and brings in a new time,
A new spring as the wheel turns for new life.
Ashe had to fall so the wheel could turn on   460
And civil servants funding New Delhi
Were blind to turning disc, and deaf to conch.

7. Cochin: Spices

Somali pirates prowl the Arabian Sea
Near Cochi, we are told on the tannoy.
We must put razor wire near the lifeboats
To deter boarding, and we have armed guards.

"Pirates want cargo to sell back for cash,
They come from Somalia in fast launches
And may attack on the Indian side.
How can just five take over this vast ship   470
And cover all the stairways and exits?
If they take hostages, they're terrorists
And that brings in NATO and submarines.
I was a Russian marine. We have men,
Armed security marines who'll resist."
So spoke the Russian Maître D' at dinner.
But in Mumbai ten men took two hotels
And killed a hundred and seventy-two guests.
They had surprise whereas pirates would not.
Now the Russian captain, on the tannoy,   480
Calls a piracy alert drill. We all
Take life-jackets out to the corridor.
"If the order is given 'Get down', lie down
Away from windows, clear of flying glass."
But might not pirates storm the bridge and guard
Us in the corridors with machine-guns?
Once pirates sought spices, now containers.
We edge past dolphins into the harbour.

We moor on Willingdon island, built by
British engineer, Bristow, for thirteen   490
Years till 1935, in great heat
Drive to the Portuguese-built 'Dutch palace'.
I wander in the spice market that's near
The ancient synagogue and sniff the smell
Of fourteen spices: saffron, vanilla,
Cardamom and pepper (green, ripening
To red, dried to black or, husks shed, to white),
Of cinnamon, nutmeg, coriander,
Turmeric, cloves, cumin, ginger and mace.
I saunter past the Chinese nets first rigged –   500
With poles, ropes and pulleys, worked by four men –

By Mongolians from Kubla Khan's court
Who took spices to China, Arabia
And Europe by road, inspired Portuguese
To search for a sea route to Kerala.
I pass the stench of the small fish market,
Proceed past huge rain trees and banyan trees
And drive through Fort Kochi's exotic shrubs,
Pass golden shower, Kerala's national flower,
And enter St Francis churchyard and gaze 510
At the teak, sandalwood and rosewood trees.
I remove my shoes and stalk down the church
Past *punkahs*, cloth fans *punkah-wallahs* swung
On frames devised by British settlers,
To Vasco da Gama's floor-set tombstone.
(His body was removed after eleven
Years.) He rounded the Cape of Horn, seeking
Spices – black pepper that preserves food from
Bacteria – and connected Europe
To the Indian spice market, opened up 520
A maritime route to west-Indian spice.
Before the house he lived in as Viceroy
Six months before he died on Christmas Day
(Where St Francis Xavier also stayed
When a parish priest), I reflect on how
(If we do not doubt oral tradition)
Doubting Thomas, Didymus, landed in
Kerala (having sailed from Palestine
To Europe), and founded seven churches
After 52, fell to a Hindu 530
Assassin in 72; and on how
Vasco founded a Portuguese Empire.
Some Indians see him as a pirate who
Stole their pepper, waylaid a Muslim ship,
Burned seven hundred passengers and crew,
Bombarded Calicut and took prisoners
Whose hands, ears and noses he hacked off, then

Sent the pieces ashore in a small boat.
But to the Catholic Portuguese he brought
Keralan spices from Malabar's coast.   540

The worst empires took and gave nothing back.
In the ship's lounge, having applied make-up
A Kathakali demon, face in green,
In mesmerising costume and gold crown,
Moves hands to beating drum and loud chanting,
Cuts off the nose and breast of a 'woman'
With a sword he has tucked under his arm,
A Hindu tale from the *Ramayana*
Of how human's transformed into divine,
A dance in trance: spirit controls body.   550
The Hindus suffered from a green demon,
And now Muslim pirates are the demon.

Vasco da Gama improved mankind's lot.
And in the Alleppey backwaters I
Pass through green coconut and mango trees,
Pass white-throated kingfishers, bee-eaters,
A black drongo and red hibiscus flowers,
A woman thrashing clothes upon a stone,
And see vast paddy-fields of monsooned rice
Which the British once farmed in early days,   560
A gift to India from British skill;
Like Willingdon island, built by Bristow
And also given to the Indians.
The worst empires took, the best trained and gave.
Our ship has left Kerala's spicy air.
Our ship ploughs on into the pirates' sea
And razor wire loops over my window.
I think of what Vasco gave, what he took
As he brought spices to Western tables.
I think of what we give and what we take   570
As we sail in his wake, like our Bristow.

8. Goa: Missionaries

Alfonso de Albuquerque captured
The Panjim Goan fort in 1510,
Began a Portuguese occupation
Lasting four hundred and fifty-one years.
I drive through palms and bougainvillaea,
Past frangipani, water-buffalo,
To old Goa's Basilica and find
The tomb of the missionary St Francis
Xavier of Spain in marble and jasper,   580
And in a crystal casket on its top
I see his uncorrupted tousled head:
The founder of the Jesuit mission
In 1542 to convert all
From anti-Catholic worship. Soon after,
The Inquisitor banned all other faiths,
Destroyed Hindu temples and censored books.
I walk to the Cathedral and look at
The gilded altar: St Catherine's 'no'
To Emperor Maxim's marriage proposal,   590
Her torture on a wheel (a Catherine wheel),
Beheading and ascension to Heaven
Blessed by the Virgin Mary. And I gaze
At the Garden of Eden on an arch,
Naked Eve and Adam with flowers and birds,
Also seventeenth-century. Outside
The Inquisition held *auto da fé*s,
Tortured and burned heretics at the stake.
I ponder the missionaries who brought
Christianity to these scented shores.   600

Now up a creek of the green Mandovi
I wander in Panjim's Portuguese town,
All bright colours with hanging balconies.
The Portuguese who lived here early on
Were forceful Christians who burned heretics,

Believed in Xavier's undecayed body
And sided with Catherine against all lust,
Against Indians having more than one wife,
Living in a Paradise of pink flowers.
The missionaries asserted Christian faith   610
In communities of backward Hindus
Who could not progress till they changed their ways –
Their outlook, habits and their way of life.

9. Bombay: Confidence
Seven islands controlled by the Portuguese,
Malarial and useless, passed to Britain
With Catherine of Braganza's dowry, turned
Into a trading centre, sea filled in.
It grew when the Suez Canal opened,
Took trade from Calcutta on the east coast.
Bombay looks like London: its mint and banks.   620
I stand by the Gateway of India,
Memorial to the royal visit by
George the Fifth (and Mary) in December
1911: the only Emperor who
Visited his distant Indian Empire.
I wander to look at the Taj Hotel
Which terrorists took over for three days,
Then go to the domed Prince of Wales museum
And then pass the High Court and Victoria
Terminus, Indo-Gothic and massive,   630
Built with confidence that the Raj would last.
I see the skyscrapers at either end
Of reclaimed Marine Drive, Chowpatty beach:
A new Mumbai grown round British Bombay.

The house where Gandhi stayed when in Bombay.
I climb the stairs and take in on the walls
Photos of him, copies of his letters
To Tolstoy, Hitler, Roosevelt. Now his room:

Mosaic floor and spinning-wheel – spinning
Kept him in touch with the poor and with God –   640
And a mattress and pillow on a rug,
And wooden clogs. He lived very simply.
From here he called for strikes against the Act
That sanctioned imprisonment without trial,
Here he called for civil disobedience.
I go up to the rooftop balcony
Where he was arrested within his tent
For here he prayed and slept under the stars.
A holy man or sly politician?
Ahimsa, religious non-violence, or   650
Canny protest that stayed within the law?
I stand outside and think of his frail force,
With loincloth, a staff and bare feet that shook
The huge commercial boardrooms of Bombay.
But he was blamed for partition and fell,
Bowing to his assassin, hands in prayer,
For not preventing the separation
Of Muslim Pakistan and triggering
Events that killed a million in riots.
A failed politician with bloody hands,   660
Who wore the disguise of a holy man?

I look down at the open-air laundry
Beneath skyscrapers, where locals hire stalls,
Tread in water, thrash clothes, hang them on lines
To dry over shed roofs in the hot sun.
At a Hindu temple I remove shoes
And upstairs look at pictures of Krishna:
A Hare Krishna temple for chanting
That Gandhi often visited to pray.
A shaven-headed man tells me, "I've been   670
A monk seven years, I chant at 5 a.m.
And purify my consciousness and know
Money-making is an illusion. I

Am in bliss for I know Reality."
An Indian in the Hanging Gardens says,
"Indians retire at fifty-eight, there's no
Pension or unemployment benefit
For most Indians. Some say, 'It was better
Under the British Raj.'" My guide questions:
"Perhaps he has had no experience   680
Of the British Raj." But it ended just
Sixty-six years ago, he was eighty-
Three and experienced it till seventeen.

From Malabar Hill to Nariman Point
Mumbai's skyscrapers peep through sunny mist.
They make so much money that seventy-five
Per cent of India's taxes are raised here.
Mumbai shimmers in mist and affluently
Exudes a confidence despite those who
(Like Gandhi and my monk) see money as   690
An illusion from which men can be free.

Emperor George the Fifth's Gateway of India
And now these skyscrapers reach to the stars,
But the confidence Bombay and Mumbai
Have known may not be enough to transform
Third-World India to top economy.

10. Porbandar: Maze
Welcomed at the dockside with a red dot
(The point focused on in meditation
Between eyebrows) I pass pink flamingos
On a lake and pelicans. Now outside   700
The Temple of Sudama, Krishna's friend,
Where angelic children tap arms for food
Directed by a squatter by the gate,
I gaze at a maze with ankle-high walls
That shows the great cycle of births and deaths,

335

The wheel of time and the rebirth of souls.
A bell calls to focus (like conch and "*Om*").

In Gandhi's green-windowed birthplace I stand
Where he was born, marked by a swastika:
A three-hundred-year-old house with stone floors,   710
A storage room, steep steps to family rooms
And a guest room; up more steps to living
Quarters and reading-room where he read books.
From the balcony outside, where he slept
Sometimes, I see his wife's house next door. He
Knew her from childhood through the barred windows.
Alcoves for candles, water from a well –
He did well: rose from here to rule India.
But his deeds are like an ankle-high maze.
For his call to strike at Amritsar, though   730
He was not there, made him responsible
In part for Dyer's Gurkhas' massacre;
And his call for independence made him
Responsible in part for partition:
A million dead as he lost Pakistan.
Actions have unintended consequences
For which leaders are co-responsible.
Some say he was a political saint.
Some a saintly politician. Rather,
He was a flawed man who did not expect   730
His calls to result in massacres that
Could have been anticipated. He sank
The British Raj that had brought India on,
And left the poor no better off under
Corrupt leaders who pocketed fortunes.
I stand in his birth room and shake my head.
I track a leader's actions through a maze.

I ponder births and rebirths in a maze
And the birth of a leader in his maze.

I nearly understand and am amazed.   740

11. Calcutta: Rule

I think of my night forty-five years back
In Calcutta, capital of the Raj,
Greatest colonial city of the East
Until the Suez Canal opened in
1869; where Job Charnock set
Up the East India Company's HQ
On the east bank of the Hooghly back in
1690; I go to my hotel
In Dalhousie Square, stepping round dozens
Of homeless Bengalis; pass the Black Hole   750
Where Suraj ud-Daulah's men forced a tired
Hundred and forty-six English prisoners
Into a tiny small-windowed chamber
Where most suffocated during that night
In June 1756, triggering
The battle of Plassey and Clive's victory
Which made the British masters of Bengal.
I go to the churchyard that holds Charnock,
The founding father of the East India
Company and of Calcutta city.   760

The Company held India until
The Indian Mutiny. Then the British
Government took over the rule and sent
A Viceroy and began the British Raj
In 1857 in Calcutta.
The opening of the Suez Canal killed
Calcutta as an international port,
And four decades later the capital
Of India was transferred to New Delhi.
I wander along to Government House,   770
Residence of British governor-generals
And, later, of the Viceroys of India,

Where India was run till 1911.

But despite the building of New Delhi
A rule supposed to last a thousand years
Withered away in ninety years of strife
And now a complex and diverse nation,
Corrupt and with six hundred million poor,
Is striving to turn Third-World villages –
With unmade roads, cows living on the streets,   780
Muck and litter, men sitting in the shade –
Into a new America, China,
By training the unqualified *en masse*,
And turning rural into city men.
I smile regretfully and shake my head.
28 February–12, 16–17 March 2013

Nicholas Hagger travelled in India and Sri Lanka from 20 February to 8 March 2013.

Delhi's Red Fort Revisited: Paradise

Forty-five years on I breach the Red Fort's
Red sandstone walls, head for the white-stone skin
Of royal tents where Shah Jahan, Mughal
Emperor, slept, prayed, sat and met nobles in

His Private Audience Hall, six columns by
Six, four by four within, on two of which,
Below the cornice is the Persian verse
By Amir Khusrow, Indian Sufi's stitch:

'If there is Paradise on the earth it
Is here, it is here, it is here' – in Delhi.   10
Shah Jahan, who had built the Taj Mahal
In Agra, was haunted by this Sufi.

He moved his capital to Paradise,
To Delhi, and ignored his dead wife's tomb,
And swore this verse meant Paradise was here
And not back there round Agra's chambered room.

The stream of Paradise flows through the Shah's
Apartment and his *hareem*, cooling feet
From the nearby river. The gardens show
The *Koran*'s Paradise despite the heat.   20

Forty-five years have passed since I first found
These two Persian inscriptions on this wall
Where the jewelled Peacock Throne once proudly stood
Among the flashing gemstones in this hall.

How did I get myself here when so young?
I had my life ahead of me that day.
I was sincere and had not been assailed
By powerful men who cast me in their play.

That day these Persian verses haunted me.
I thought Paradise was here, 'now' – then, near.   30
And now my life is past they still haunt me
For Paradise is still now, not that year.

I have learned much since that young man stood here
And just as Shah Jahan had left behind
The Taj Mahal and Mumtaz I have moved
On from all tombs that fester in the mind.

And yet I stand in the same place and gaze
Through the same eyes at the same haunting text
That Paradise is now, and would not leave
My present life for yesteryear or next.   40
27 February 2013

Reflections in Arabia

I leave Fujairah and its piped-oil tanks.
I pass sand-dunes and oases with palms
And drive through the treeless Hajar mountains
And trundle into Dubai, where two tribes
Came in the 1820s and settled.
I pass the Fort and round tower where Dubai's
Early rulers lived, and traders' houses
That were once under British protection.
I drive through Old Dubai, reclaimed from sand,
Pass rulers' palaces: Sheikh Mohammed's   10
The Crown Prince's and other relations'.
The tribal family have built huge homes
And laid out lawns with thousands of flower-beds.
I pass to New Dubai and its high-rise
Buildings, and the Burj al-Arab, 'the Sail',
And, nearby, 'the Wave' and its water-park.
I cross fine sand to the sea's edge. Out there
Are two marine 'palm-tree' resorts. I head
For Burj Khalifa, the tallest building
In the world (eight hundred and twenty-eight   20
Metres) and named after Sheikh Khalifa,
President of the UAE who bailed
Out Dubai's debt. There are plans to build through
To Abu Dhabi seventy-five miles
Away. This ruler Sheikh Mohammed has
Thrown down a gauntlet to the world: the world's
Tallest building and biggest shopping mart,
A bold way of announcing his advent.

The Sheikh eschews democracy but gives
His oil wealth back to his people in free   30
Education and health; no taxes; jobs
Within the government; wedding funding.
The people seem content to let him rule

And he responds with enlightened measures
And displays his benevolence to all.
There are few portraits of Sheikh Mohammed.
He does not seem a vain man but meets all
And asks for criticisms, to improve.
I queue for entry into the tall building.
At ten metres per second, ears popping,   40
I rise to the hundred-and-twenty-fourth
Floor in a lift that does not seem to move.
Strolling round the observation platform
Four hundred and fifty-four metres up,
I look down on skyscrapers and vistas,
And see the projects that now fill the sand.
There are forty-two metro stations on
An overrail, each named after a large
Corporate brand that pays for maintenance.
The Sheikh seems an imaginative man.   50
It is a miracle, the dynasty
Has transformed the city, has dredged the creek,
Created a river for wooden *dhows*
And built apartments for foreign workers,
Frozen their rents for twenty years to build
New Dubai, and more palaces, quickly.
Like Kubla Khan he's built a Paradise
In what was just desert. (To some it is
Ugly concrete on sand.) The dynasty
Has "spent the oil wealth wisely for the good   60
Of its people before the oil runs out".
How different from Gaddafi who squandered
Libya's oil wealth on funding terrorists,
And, starting in 1970, could
Have emulated Dubai's skyscrapers
If he had cared more for his own people.

Dubai and the six other Emirates
Were once linked to Oman. I cross Muscat,

Past Portuguese forts, to the Grand Mosque built
By Sultan Qaboos, who, having mounted   70
A palace *coup* against his father, ruled
From 1970, a time that saw
The building of both Old and New Dubai,
Liberating an oil-rich Sultanate.
He changed the country's name, its currency,
Its flag. I walk through another courtyard
Beside 'the stream of Paradise' fed by
Fountains, enter the ladies' prayer-hall
And, beyond another courtyard, the vast
Men's prayer-hall with a huge chandelier,   80
Sumptuous carpet with a billion knots
(The largest handmade carpet in the world)
And intricate dome. Sixty engineers
Completed the work in six years, a gift
From the Sultan to his people. He owns
Seven palaces in Oman, one in
Germany, one in Pakistan, several
Houses in England. Now I stand before
His low white palace in Old Muscat, flag
Flying to show he is in residence   90
Between two forts: Mirani, Jalali.
I pass his hundred-million yacht, *Al Said*,
In the harbour. He owns a private port
And a private airport. I am assured
All are happy with how he runs Oman
As he has used oil wealth to provide free
Education and health, jobs and weddings
And no Omani pays income taxes.
In the museum I see his dynasty
Began in 1744, that he   100
Is the fourteenth Sultan to rule since then.
He trained at Sandhurst and is pro-British
But he has just twenty-five years' oil left
And has spent much of his oil income on

The palaces, mosque, yacht, port and airport.
His priority is his family
But he has developed Oman which had
Just three schools when he inaugurated
The Sultanate. In the gift shop I buy
Bags of frankincense, dried raisin-like fruit   110
With a pungent smell. It only grows in
Yemen, Somalia and Oman. I too
Think family while I champion the poor.

In Nakhl in the Hajar mountains I
Climb the seventeenth-century Omani fort
Of a tribal leader, a *wali* who
Lived above the *wadi* of date-palm trees
While loyal to the dynasty before
The Sultan's. And on a turret I think,
The mountains all around, that the Sultan   120
Is an anachronism, like the Sheikh,
And I wonder if their heirs will survive,
Or will they be violently overthrown
In an army *coup* like old King Idris,
Toppled by stern Gaddafi who I knew?
Or by terrorists creeping from Yemen?
But I would like to think that the two men
Are enlightened, benevolent rulers
Who after building family palaces
Are caring for their people and their poor   130
Who, like that Bedouin who leads three camels,
Scrape a living from the Arabian sands.
12–13, 17 March 2013

Nicholas Hagger travelled in Arabia (Dubai and Oman) from 11 to 13 March 2013.

Verses on the Death of Mr Nicholas Hagger

When we peer in the human mind
What faults we see, what follies find.
These are not flecks in our eye's vein
But specks in human nature's brain,
Which is to say, on its left side
Of logic and language, the pride
Of the rational, social ego;
Not the right side's creative flow
That's intuitive, non-verbal,
Where Light pours into its channel.   10
Some vices lurk – is it not true? –
In disguise within each virtue.
In his maxims La Rochefoucauld
Finds personal interest below
Generous feelings, tributes, festoons:
In news of our friends' misfortunes,
He says, we find something that does
Not displease us, but brings a buzz
Of faint enjoyment – *Schadenfreude*.
When we are quietly overjoyed   20
At others' adversity we
Can greet their demise with quiet glee,
A secret catch in sorrow's breath
As we hear news of a sad death.

It is natural to envy each
Who's raised himself beyond our reach
And seems above us – our equal
Standing in a crown of laurel
So our view is now obstructed.
Who has not wished such a 'friend' dead?   30
Humankind's vain, full of self-love;
Pride, ambition and envy shove
And jostle to the fore, then mask

Themselves as smiling virtue, ask
"Has there ever been a quester
For the One like Larkin" (who never
Quested), or "Isn't she good on
Achilles" (that is, his tendon)
Or "How well he writes of follies"
(When foolishness is what it is).   40
That human nature's full of pride
And selfishness can't be denied
But when it's transformed from ego
To universal being, lo!
Sympathy and goodness exist:
Virtue's seen through a lifting mist.

It must be said, though with a sigh,
That it is certain all will die:
The Queen, your Aunt May, Uncle Don
Will somehow manage to move on   50
With dignity and with some style,
And possibly a rueful smile.
It helps if we have known the Light
When we set off into that night,
As at a station take our leave
Waved off by relatives who'll grieve.
Alas! my final day has come.
I gaze out from my deathbed, dumb.
I look for sunshine, see the dark,
Familiar faces in an arc.   60
Wife, children and grandchildren mourn
Their protector's long end, and yawn:
"He founded the family business
And smiled a lot, often said yes
And played chess and table tennis."
My siblings text a distant kiss.
But beyond family warmth, what
Is being said out there? I've got

An inkling: "He's heading for tea
With William Shakespeare and Shelley."　　　　70
And: "His headstone will say 'No rhymes
Down here' – just restful, better times."
"His eyes have drooped, he'll soon be gone,
His breathing's laboured, cheeks look wan."
"Look, now he's slipped away. Listen.
A breath. Another breath." And then....
"It's over, he has passed away.
It's a blessing he could not stay.
It is a merciful release
Now his questing soul is at peace."　　　　80
Familiar faces drift for doors.
Work calls, and home. There's now a pause.

We like to pigeon-hole each friend
As "poet", "historian". A blend
Confuses, and: "Where do we start?
Poems and stories from the heart,
Verse plays and man-of-letters forms,
Histories, science – what are his norms?
Philosophy and religion,
Mysticism, education,　　　　90
Politics and statecraft, culture –
And so it goes on, it's simpler
To say he wrote poetry and prose
In seven bands like a rainbow's."
"But what was he? A this or that?
Can we define him by one hat?"
"Jack of all trades, master of none,
Wrote everything under the sun."
"All right during the Renaissance
But now leads us a merry dance."　　　　100
Intelligence men say, "He should
Be walled round with silence, not good."
And: "Shouldn't have been published for

The State is supreme, that's the law."
And: "Why turn against nation-state
To Universalist debate?"
And: "The World State's a hazy dream,
An everythingism regime."
There is bewilderment and lack
Of understanding, some hold back.   110

The public in bookshops aside,
Small groups receive the news I've died:
School and college contemporaries,
The few still alive then, that is;
Some staff at my four schools shed tears.
I sat with them for many years.
Some parents pay polite respect,
A remote figure has been wrecked.
Some past students and pupils frown,
A kindly soul has fallen down.   120
To some I am a named cipher:
Accountant and bank manager.
Writers who knew me exchange looks
And cross me off their address books.
My publishers express dismay
But now my backlist leads the way.
My readers all have favourite bits
As an audience sits and flits.
One year on my archive greets all
Who visit Colchester and scrawl   130
Their notes about my manuscripts
Better suited to dusty crypts.

Suppose associates discussed
What I wrote before I was dust,
How would they view my life's output?
"In verse he set out foot by foot
His quest through Nature for the One

Reality, bright as the sun,

That orders the universe and

Sets man in harmony with sand, 140

Earth, sea, hills, cliffs, mountains and sky

And the rest of society

And reconciles all opposites,

Vices and virtues, and transmits

A sense of purpose that seems sent

And transforms through self-improvement,

To bypass follies and then see

The secret hidden unity

And oneness of the universe

That all souls seek before their hearse. 150

His work in seven disciplines

Locates this theme in human skins

That frequent his Essex whose woods

He freely roamed in his boyhood's

Harmony with Nature, when he

Loved all creatures instinctively:

Grasshoppers, birds and butterflies

That filled the heaths and brightened skies."

And some might say: "He had one foot

In local life, social input, 160

And one foot at his desk where he

Wrote books and, perspicaciously,

Foresaw an impending World State,

A world government that can't wait

If humankind's to live free from

War, famine, disease, nuclear bomb

And poverty. And though a scourge

To the vicious, like a grass verge

He was kindly, he cared for souls

Whose vices burned like red-hot coals. 170

He was a caring man who saw

Mankind's best plan was to ban war

And bring in paradisal peace

And his works sought this Golden Fleece."
And some might say, stifling their glee:
"His quest was strange, and all can see
That normal living's not seeking
For some non-existent meaning.
No need for an adventurous life,
Just work, drink, telly and the wife.   180
All know life's pointless, that we just
Enjoy ourselves before we're dust."

And some, with mordant bite, might say,
"He swept man's illusions away.
He found darkness and bequeathed Light.
A shallow Age bestows its night."
27–30 December 2015

This poem follows Swift's 'Verses on the Death of Dr Swift' (1739) in dwelling on one of La Rochefoucauld's maxims, "In the adversity even of our best friends we always find something not wholly displeasing" (no.583 in La Rochefoucauld's *Maxims*, trans. by L.W. Tancock, Penguin, 1959); and in demonstrating it in humankind and in his friends; in applying it to his last illness and to public reaction to his death and to the reaction of his friends and associates; in applying it to the assessing of his works a year after his death; and in bringing it out in a final eulogy of his works. The references to Swift suggest the underlying ambivalence in most responses to a writer's death.

15. 'Festoon', 'a chain of flowers, leaves, ribbons etc. hung in a curve as a decoration'. (*Concise Oxford Dictionary*.)

186. 'Bestows its night', 'confers its gift of night', and also 'sees death as night'.

INDEXES

Chronological Order of Poems

Chronological order in which all poems in volumes 31–34 were
conceived and written

(Dates indicate when poems were written and revised. They reflect the dates
at the end of each poem but are listed here in the order in which the poems
were created. 'Idea' indicates when poem was conceived.)

Six-spot Burnets	23 July 2008;
	28 February 2015
House Martins	21 August 2008
House Martins in the Eaves	21 August 2008;
	28 February 2015
Undated Unused Fragments for	
Armageddon	2008–2009
Lisbon Treaty: The End of Great	
Britain, Demise of a Nation-State	5 November 2009;
	7–8 April 2015
Zeus's Emperor (A Mock-Heroic	
Poem)	23–27 November 2009;
	30 March,
	1, 9–11, 13–18 April,
	12–13 June 2015
A Breathless Calm	31 May 2010;
	16 December 2014
Gigs, Insects	31 May 2010;
	16 December 2014
Daisies, Mower	3 June 2010
At Great Milton Manor House: On	
Life and Death	18–19 July 2010
The Way to Rome	26 August–9 September 2010;
	9, 25 May–6, 10 June 2015
Storm	30 October 2010;
	revised 17 December 2014
Dripping Stars at Midnight	31 October 2010;
	16 December 2014
Leaves Falling 1	4 November 2010
Skimming Stones	12 November 2010;
	17 December 2014
Concorde	24 November 2010
Oak	11 December 2010;
	17 December 2014
A Wish for my Granddaughter	10 February 2011;
	26, 28, 31 July 2015

A Family Like Vases	4 July 2014; 4 March 2015
Song Thrush	15 July, 16 December 2014
Life Cycle	30 August–2 September,
	27–28 October,
	14–15 December 2014;
	31 July, 17 August 2015; 13–14
	February, 23 March 2016
The Lion and the Unicorn: Plebiscite	
in Scotland	20–21 September,
	18–20 October 2014
Caliphate	27 September–18 October,
	9, 10, 14, 16 November 2014
Mouse	1 October 2014; 3 March 2015
Time, in Tiers	27 October 2014;
	3 March 2015
Green Woodpecker	November, 16 December 2014
Parakeets	?7 November,
	16 December 2014
Poppies	19–20 November,
	16 December 2014
Brilliant Stars, Snapped Gravity	15–16 December 2014
Founder's Song	16 December 2014
Churchill 50 Years On: Great Briton	31 January,
	1 February, 3 April 2015
In the Galapagos Islands: The Purpose	
of Evolution	2–3 February, 4–5 April 2015
In Peru: the Sun of the Incas	4–5 February, 6 April 2015
In Antarctica: In the Southern Ocean	
and our Ice Age	6–7 February, 4 April 2015
In Iran: Persian and Shiite Empires	9 February, 6–7 April 2015
Blue Tit Chirping	10 February, 19 March 2015
In North Norway: Arctic Circle and	
Northern Lights, Among Vikings	
and Altaics	10 February, 4 April 2015
In Harmony with the Universe	13–14, 16 February,
	3 April 2015

Chronological Order within Volumes

Chronological Order in which poems in each of volumes 31–34 were written, listed under each volume

(Dates indicate when poems were written and revised. They reflect the dates at the end of each poem but are listed here in the order in which the poems within each volume were created. 'Idea' indicates when poem was conceived.)

Date

Volume 31: *Life Cycle*

Life Cycle	30 August–2 September, 27–28 October, 14–15 December 2014; 31 July, 17 August 2015; 13–14 February, 23 March 2016

Volume 32: *In Harmony with the Universe*

The Ghadames Spring: Bubbles	1970; revised 9 January 2016
Daisies	12 April 1975
Crystals	9 April 1990
Nightingale	27 May 1990
Fragment: Question	2 February 1992; 16 December 2014
Further Undated Unused Fragments for *Overlord*	1994–1996
Unused Draft for *Overlord*	1994
Quarry	19 July 2000; revised 16 December 2014
Terrorist	15 September 2007
Two in One	10 July 2008
Six-spot Burnets	23 July 2008; 28 February 2015
House Martins	21 August 2008

House Martins in the Eaves	21 August 2008;
	28 February 2015
Undated Unused Fragments for	
Armageddon	2008–2009
A Breathless Calm	31 May 2010;
	16 December 2014
Gigs, Insects	31 May 2010;
	16 December 2014
Daisies, Mower	3 June 2010
At Great Milton Manor House: On	
Life and Death	18–19 July 2010
Storm	30 October 2010;
	revised 17 December 2014
Dripping Stars at Midnight	31 October 2010;
	16 December 2014
Leaves Falling 1	4 November 2010
Skimming Stones	12 November 2010;
	17 December 2014
Concorde	24 November 2010
Oak	11 December 2010;
	17 December 2014
A Wish for my Granddaughter	10 February 2011;
	26, 28, 31 July 2015
Snails	28 May 2011;
	17 December 2014
Grace	27 June 2011
Bone	21 July 2011
Near Teignmouth	5 August 2011;
	17 December 2014
Splashes of Light	8 August 2011;
	17 December 2014
Bronze Age	20 August 2011;
	17 December 2014
River, Headlong	20 August 2011;
	17 December 2014
Sky	20 August 2011;

	17 December 2014
Fragment: Rain	2 September 2011;
	17 December 2014
The Wheel of Creation	2–4 September 2011
Fragment: Gold	18 September 2011;
	17 December 2014
Sunlight	19 September 2011;
	17 December 2014
Robin	20 November 2011;
	17 December 2014
Fragment, Where are my Friends	Undated, ?2012
Magpie in Snow	5 February 2012;
	7 May 2012
Song Thrush Piping	29 March, 27 April,
	7 May 2012;
	28 February 2015
Ladybird	29 March 2012;
	17 December 2014
Owl	29 March 2012;
	17 December 2014
Honey-bees	29 March 2012;
	17 December 2014
Spruce Cone	1 April 2012;
	28 February 2015
Song Thrush Dead	1 April, 7 May 2012;
	28 February 2015
Skull	5 April 2012;
	28 February 2015
Gulls	27 April 2012;
	1 March 2015
Smile	6 May 2012;
	1 March 2015
Sun and Snow	6 May 2012;
	1 March 2015
Time 1	6 May 2012
Time 2	7 May 2012;

	1 March 2015
Smiling Buttercups	6 June 2012
Wind: Change	7, 10 June 2012
Buddleia: From Nothing to Form	7 August 2012;
	14 December 2015
Olympian	7 August 2012;
	15 December 2015
Sea, Sky: Whole View	7 August 2012;
	15 December 2015
Mist over the Sea	17 August 2012
Downpour	22 August 2012;
	1 March 2015
Storm II	24 August 2012
Squirrel	22 September 2012
Squirrel's Reply	26 September 2012
Drowned	23 December 2012;
	3 March 2015
At Beverley Minster	24 December 2012
Marble	27 February 2013
Pirates: Question Mark	8 March 2013
Looking Down: Not Bestriding	13 March 2013
The Seven Hills of Loughton	3 April 2013
Savage	3 April 2013
Sun	Idea: 2 May 2013.
	Written: 15 December 2015
Taking Wing	25 May 2013
One's Reflection	7 August 2013
Unaware	8 August 2013
Moonlight	23 October 2013
Rain Hisses	18 December 2013
Sea Bird	18 December 2013;
	1 March 2015
The Old in the Cold	24 December 2013;
	3 March 2015
Ruby	2 March 2014;
	7 March 2015

Discovery of Inflation: At One with the First Cause	18 March 2014; 5–7 March 2015
Spring	23 March 2014; 2 March 2015
Fading	30 March 2014; 2 March 2015
White Hawthorn Blossom	1 April 2014; 3 March 2015
The Wind's Whistling	7 April 2014
Discord: Humans who Drop	13 April 2014
The Mild Wind's Blow	17–18 April 2014; 3 March 2015
A Blackbird's Clear Piping	18 April 2014
A Family Like Vases	4 July 2014; 4 March 2015
Song Thrush	15 July, 16 December 2014
Mouse	1 October 2014; 3 March 2015
Time, in Tiers	27 October 2014; 3 March 2015
Parakeets	?7 November, 16 December 2014
Poppies	19–20 November, 16 December 2014
Green Woodpecker	November, 16 December 2014
Brilliant Stars, Snapped Gravity	15–16 December 2014
Founder's Song	16 December 2014
Blue Tit Chirping	10 February, 19 March 2015
In Harmony with the Universe	13–14, 16 February, 3 April 2015
Hooting Owl	8 March 2015
Daffodils, Sunlight	3 April 2015
Full Moon	3–4 April 2015
Sheep	5–6 April 2015
Horses	5–6 April 2015
Dancing Light	6 April 2015

Rainbow	7 April 2015
Blackbird	16 May 2015
Ridging Waves	26 May 2015
Blushing Sky	26 May 2015
Helsingor	27 May 2015
Crown Prince's Palace	27 May 2015
Vikings	28 May 2015
Ghost	7 June 2015
At the Van Gogh Museum: Obscurity	7, 11 June 2015
Long-legged Fly	26 June 2015
House Martins Darting	29 June 2015
House Martins and Carnival	30 July 2015
Storm, Surge	5 August 2015
Force	7 August 2015
Shooting Star	7 August 2015
Meteorite	12 August 2015
Heron	18 August 2015
Spider	21 August 2015
Bat	21 August 2015
Moth	21 August 2015
Stag	24 August, 19 September 2015
Carp, Goldfish	2 September 2015
Box-Leaf Caterpillars	2 September 2015
Red Moon	27–28 September 2015
Blue Tit	1 October 2015
Snowfields	4, 27 October 2015
Bay in Sun	7, 27 October 2015
Planetary Trio	25, 27 October 2015
Wind Whistles, Force	26–27 October 2015
Golden Rose	27 October 2015
Scudding Stars	27 October 2015
In Gerard's *Herball*: Snake's-Head Fritillary	28, 31 October, 1 November 2015
Sea Lights	28–29 October 2015

Mist	1 November 2015
At Connaught House: Weather-vane	2, 4, 10–11 November 2015
Leaves Falling 2	3 November 2015
Leaves Flutter	10–11 November 2015
Return to Suffolk	12, 14–15 November 2015
Birds and Beasts: The Lament of Orpheus	25 November, 12 December 2015
Ferris Wheel: Life Cycle	6, 12 December 2015
Muntjac	8, 12 December 2015
Snake (Orpheus to Eurydice and Hades)	Idea: 25 November. Written: 12, 15 December 2015
Stars, Waves	13–14 December 2015
Rain	14 December 2015
Sea Surges	14 December 2015
Vein	14–15 December 2015
Pied Wagtail	15 December 2015
Time like the Sea 1	31 December 2015
Time like the Sea 2	31 December 2015
Goldfinch	31 December 2015
Nuthatch	31 December 2015
Epistle to King Harold II of Waltham Abbey and Loughton	31 December 2015; 1, 28–29 January 2016
House Spider	28 January 2016
Fox	28 January 2016
Stag, Trapped	19 March 2016

Volume 33: *An Unsung Laureate*

Pastoral Ode: Landslide, The End of Great Britain	1–26 May 1997, revised 2 July 1997
Second Pastoral Ode: Landslide Unchanged, The End of England	8–15 June 2001
In Westminster: The Passing of an Era	10 April 2002,

	revised 14, 16 April 2002
The Conquest of England	12, 17 April, 27 May 2003,
	revised 9–12 August 2003
Lisbon Treaty: The End of Great	
Britain, Demise of a Nation-State	5 November 2009;
	7–8 April 2015
Zeus's Emperor (A Mock-Heroic	
Poem)	23–27 November 2009;
	30 March,
	1, 9–11, 13–18 April,
	12–13 June 2015
Royal Wedding	29 April 2011;
	5, 28, 29 August 2015
Enigma	30 September,
	1 October 2011;
	19–21, 24 April 2015
Changelessness like a Fanfare:	
Trumpeting a Jubilee	6, 10 June 2012
Ceremonial: On the End of a National	
Era, The Funeral of Margaret	
Thatcher	17–21 April 2013
Reflections by the *Mary Rose*	20 July 2013,
	revised 2–8 August 2013
The Lion and the Unicorn: Plebiscite	
in Scotland	20–21 September,
	18–20 October 2014
Caliphate	27 September–18 October,
	9, 10, 14, 16 November 2014
Churchill 50 Years On: Great Briton	31 January, 1 February,
	3 April 2015
On Richard III: The Last Plantagenet	22–23 March, 8–9 April 2015
On Thomas Cromwell's Ruthlessness	26 March, 8 April 2015
Stability: On an Unlikely	
Conservative Election Victory	7–8 May 2015
In St Petersburg: Thoughts in	
Hermitage	31 May–2, 10 June 2015

In Tallinn: Premonitions of War	3, 11, 29 June 2015
Chaos in Iraq	6–8, 11 June 2015
Watcher and Two Carts	25, 27 October 2015
Oxford Bait	25, 27 October 2015
Symposium: Averting a Nuclear Winter	9, 26–27 October 2015
The Sorrows of Allah, The Nameless One	25 November 2015
Thoughts on Syria: Rush to War	3–5, 12 December 2015
At Berlin's Kaiser Wilhelm Memorial Church	5, 11–12 December 2015
Isles of Wonder	Idea: 27 July 2012. Written: 13 December 2015
Collapse of the Old Order	15 December 2015
Epistle to Gaddafi	Idea: October 2011. Written: 16 December 2015
Epistle to the Chancellor of the Exchequer	25–26 January, 3 February 2016

Volume 34: *Adventures in Paradise*

The Way to Rome	26 August–9 September 2010; 9, 25 May–6, 10 June 2015
On Hadrian's Wall	4–5 July 2011; 17 December 2014
India: Revisiting the British Raj	28 February–12, 16–17 March 2013
Delhi's Red Fort Revisited: Paradise	27 February 2013
Reflections in Arabia	12–13, 17 March 2013
In the Galapagos Islands: The Purpose of Evolution	2–3 February, 4–5 April 2015
In Peru: The Sun of the Incas	4–5 February, 6 April 2015
In Antarctica: In the Southern Ocean and our Ice Age	6–7 February, 4 April 2015
In Iran: Persian and Shiite Empires	9 February, 6–7 April 2015
In North Norway: Arctic Circle and	

Index of Titles

(Poems in alphabetical order, volume titles in italics.)

BOOKS

O-BOOKS

SPIRITUALITY

O is a symbol of the world, of oneness and unity; this eye represents
knowledge and insight. We publish titles on general spirituality and
living a spiritual life. We aim to inform and help you on your own
journey in this life.
If you have enjoyed this book, why not tell other readers by posting
a review on your preferred book site?

Life Cycle
and Other New Poems
2006 – 2016

Collected Poems volumes 31–34

First published by O-Books, 2016
O-Books is an imprint of John Hunt Publishing Ltd., Laurel House, Station Approach,
Alresford, Hants, SO24 9JH, UK
office1@jhpbooks.net
www.johnhuntpublishing.com

For distributor details and how to order please visit the 'Ordering' section on our website.

ISBN: 978 1 84694 580 9
978 1 78099 727 8 (ebook)
Library of Congress Control Number: 2016946103

A CIP catalogue record for this book is available from the British Library.

Design: Stuart Davies

Printed in the USA by Edwards Brothers Malloy

We operate a distinctive and ethical publishing philosophy in all areas of
our business, from our global network of authors to production and
worldwide distribution.